self-healing is more desirable than healing by others; the former strengthens the will, the latter weakens it. ... the healer must first heal himself by the practice of the strictest morality from the lowest to the highest phase of his existence. He must purify himself by Iman, or faith. Then to be a healer.

D0622804

- controlling breath, eyes
- strengthen will
- absorbing electricity of the sphere
- still / purify the mind

THE SUFI MESSAGE
OF
HAZRAT INAYAT KHAN

Pir-o-Murshid
Hazrat Inayat Khan

THE SUFI MESSAGE
OF
HAZRAT INAYAT KHAN

HEALING AND THE MIND WORLD

Published for
International Headquarters of the Sufi Movement, Geneva

First published by Barrie and Rockliff 1961
Second Impression 1978
Third Impression (revised) 1982
Published by Servire BV, Secr. Varkevisserstraat 52,
2225 LE Katwijk aan Zee, Netherlands

© 1982 in its re-edited form by
International Headquarters Sufi Movement, Geneva
ISBN 90 6077 952 5
Series ISBN 90 6325 101 7
Library of Congress Catalog Card Number 79-67746

Set in 12 on 13 point Bembo
Printed and bound in the U.S.A.

The Sufi Message Series is distributed by

Servire BV, Netherlands

Momenta Publishing Ltd., U.K.

Hunter House Inc., Publishers, U.S.A.

CONTENTS

PREFACE

WHEN *Health*, the first book of this volume, was published in 1931 it met with great interest, for it is just as rare to find a book on spiritual healing in which the advance of modern medical science is appreciated, as to find acknowledgment of spiritual healing in a medical text-book. Hazrat Inayat Khan, the Sufi mystic, has set forth in the lectures and other papers included in *Health*, which were originally intended only for his pupils, the basic laws governing the divine healing power as well as several methods for its application. As with all mystical knowledge, the printed word alone can never confer the power and knowledge of healing upon anyone; a guide, a teacher is essential; but the reader will find in Inayat Khan's sober but profound words a wealth of material for further thought and meditation.

Mental Purification is a collection of Inayat Khan's hitherto unpublished lectures on the workings and hygiene of the mind and kindred subjects. This volume ends with *The Mind-world*, a book which was first published separately in 1935 and reprinted in 1955; its title speaks for itself.

While Volume III contains most of Hazrat Inayat Khan's books and lectures on human relationship, Volume IV may be considered as a continuation of Volume II, which deals principally with the metaphysical aspect of creation, tracing a line from its origin, sound, to the human mind.

THE BOOK OF HEALTH

CONTENTS

PART I

PART II

HEALTH

i

ILLNESS is an inharmony, either physical inharmony or mental inharmony, the one acts upon the other. What causes inharmony? The lack of tone and rhythm. How can it be interpreted in physical terminology? Prana, or life, or energy is the tone; circulation, regularity is the rhythm, regularity in the beatings of the head, of the pulse and the circulation of the blood through the veins. In physical terms the lack of circulation means congestion; and the lack of Prana, or life, or energy means weakness. These two conditions attract illness and are the cause of illness. In mental terms the rhythm is the action of the mind, whether the mind is active in harmonious thoughts or in inharmonious thoughts, whether the mind is strong, firm, and steady, or whether it is weak.

If one continues to think harmonious thoughts it is just like regular beating of the pulse and proper circulation of the blood; if the harmony of thought is broken, then the mind becomes congested. Then a person loses memory; depression comes as the result, and what one sees is nothing but darkness. Doubt, suspicion, distrust, and all manner of distress and despair come when the mind is congested in this way. The Prana of the mind is maintained when the mind can be steady in thoughts of harmony; then the mind can balance its thoughts, then it cannot be easily shaken, then doubt and confusion cannot easily overpower it. Whether it is nervous illness, whether it is mental disorder, whether it is physical illness, at the root of all these different aspects of illness there is one cause, and that cause is inharmony.

The body which has once become inharmonious turns into a receptacle of inharmonious influences, of inharmonious atoms; it partakes of them without knowing it; and so it is with the mind. The body which is already lacking in health is more susceptible to illness than the body which is perfectly healthy; and so the mind which already has a disorder in it is more susceptible to every suggestion of disorder, and in this way goes from bad to worse. Scientists of all ages have found that each element attracts the same element, and so it is natural that illness should attract illness; thus in plain words inharmony attracts inharmony, whereas harmony attracts harmony. We see in everyday life that a person who has nothing the matter with him and is only weak physically, or whose life is not regular, is always susceptible to illness. Then we see that a person who ponders often upon inharmonious thoughts is very easily offended, it does not take long for him to get offended; a little thing here and there makes him feel irritated, because irritation is already there, it wants just a little touch to make it a deeper irritation.

Besides this the harmony of the body and the mind depends upon one's external life, the food one eats, the way one lives, the people one meets, the work one does, the climate in which one lives. There is no doubt that under the same conditions one person may be ill and another may be well. The reason is that one is in harmony with the food he eats, with the weather he lives in, with the people whom he meets, with the conditions around him. Another person revolts against the food he eats, against the people he meets, against the conditions that surround him, against the weather he must live in. This is because he is not in harmony; and he perceives and experiences similar results in all things in his life; disorder and illness are the result.

This idea can be very well demonstrated by the method that present-day physicians have adopted, of inoculating a person with the same element which makes him ill. There is no better demonstration of this idea than the practice of inoculation. This puts a person in harmony with the thing that is opposed to his nature. If one understands this principle one can inoculate oneself with all that does not agree with one, and with that to which one is continually exposed and from which there is no means of getting away. Woodcutters do not as a rule get sunstroke: seamen do not catch cold easily. The reason is that the former have made themselves sunproof while the latter have made themselves waterproof. In short, the first lesson in health is the understanding of this principle, that illness is nothing but inharmony and that the secret of health lies in harmony.

ii

Disorder of the tone and irregularity in the rhythm are the principal causes of every illness. The explanation of this disorder of the tone is that there is a certain tone which the breath vibrates throughout the body, through every channel of the body; and this tone is a particular tone, continually vibrating, in every person. And when the mystics have said that every person has his note, it is not necessarily the note of the piano, it is the note which is going on as a tone, as a breath. Now, if a person does not take care of himself and allows himself to be influenced by every wind that blows, he, like the water in the sea, goes up and down disturbed by the air. The normal condition is to be able to stand firm through fear, joy, and anxiety; not to let every wind blow one hither and thither like a scrap of paper, but to endure it all and to stand firm and steady through all such influences.

One might say that even water is subject to influences if not the rock. Man is made to be neither rock nor water; he has all in him; he is the fruit of the whole creation, he ought to be able to show his evolution in his balance. A person who is likely to rejoice in a moment and to become depressed in a moment, and who changes his moods, cannot keep that tone which gives him equilibrium and which is the secret of health. How few know that it is not pleasure and merrymaking that give one good health! On the contrary, social life, as it is known today, is merrymaking for one day and afterwards one may be ill for ten days, for that kind of life does not take care of equilibrium. When a person becomes sensitive to every little thing that he comes across, it changes the note of the tone; it becomes a different note to which his body is not accustomed; and that causes an illness. Too much despair or too much joy, everything that is too much should be avoided, although there are natures who always seek extremes; they must have so much joy and amusement that they get tired of it, and then they have a collapse with sorrow and despair. It is among these people that you will find continual illness. If an instrument is not kept in proper tune, if it is knocked about by everyone who comes and handled by everyone, then it gets out of order. The body is an instrument, the most sacred instrument, an instrument which God Himself has made for His divine purpose. If it is kept in tune and the strings are not allowed to become loose, then this instrument becomes the means of that harmony for which God created man.

How must this instrument be kept in tune? In the first place strings of gut and wires of steel both require cleaning. The lungs and veins in the body also require cleaning; it is that which keeps them ready for their work. And how should we clean them? By carefulness in diet, by sobriety, and by breathing properly and correctly; because it is not only water and earth that are used for cleansing, the best means of cleansing is the air and the property that is in the air, the property that we breathe in; and if we knew how by the help of breathing to keep these channels clean, then we should know how to secure health. It is this which maintains the tone, the proper note of each person, without being disturbed. When a person is vibrating his own note which is according to his particular evolution, then he is himself, then he is tuned to the pitch for which he is made, the pitch in which he ought to be and in which he naturally feels comfortable.

And now we come to the rhythm: there is a rhythm of pulsation, the beating of the pulse in the head and in the heart; and whenever the rhythm of this beating is disturbed it causes illness because it disturbs the whole mechanism which is going on, the order of which depends upon the regularity of rhythm. If a person suddenly hears of something causing fear the rhythm is broken, the pulsation changes. Every shock given to a person breaks his rhythm. We very often notice that, however successful an operation, it leaves a mark, even for the rest of one's life. Once the rhythm is broken, it is most difficult to get it right.

If the rhythm has been lost, it must be brought back with great wisdom, because a sudden effort to regain the rhythm may make one lose it still more. If the rhythm has gone too slow or too fast, by trying to bring it to its regular speed one may break the rhythm, and by breaking the rhythm one may break oneself. This should be a gradual process; it must be wisely done.

If the rhythm has gone too fast, it must be brought gradually to its proper condition; if it is too slow, it must be gradually made quicker. It requires patience and strength to do it. For instance, someone who tunes the violin wisely does not at once move the peg and bring it to the proper tone, because in the first place it is impossible, and then he always risks breaking the string. However minute may be the difference in the tone, one can bring it to its proper place by gradual tuning; in this way effort is spared and the thing is accomplished.

Gentleness which is taught morally is a different thing, but even gentleness in action and movement is also necessary. In every movement one makes, in every step one takes there must be rhythm. For instance you will find many examples if you look for them of the awkward movements people make; they can never keep well because their rhythm is not right; and that is why illness continues. It may be that no illness can be traced in these people, and yet the very fact of their movements not being in rhythm will keep them out of order. Regularity in habits, in action, in repose, in eating, in drinking, in sitting, in walking, in everything, gives one that rhythm which is necessary and which completes the music of life.

When a child's rhythm and tone are disordered, the healing that a mother can give, often unconsciously, the physicians cannot give in a thousand years. The song she sings, however insignificant, comes from the profound depths of her being and brings with it the healing power. It cures the child in a moment. The caressing, the patting of the mother does more good to the child than any medicine when its rhythm is disturbed and its tone is not good. The mother, even without knowing it distinctly, feels like patting the child when it is out of rhythm, singing to the child when it is out of tune.

And when we come to the mental part of our being, that mechanism is still more delicate than our body. There is a tone also, and every being has a different tone according to his particular evolution, and everyone feels in good health when his own tone is vibrating; but if that tone does not come to its proper pitch, then a person feels lack of comfort, and any illness can arise from it. Every expression of passion, joy, anger, fear, which breaks the continuity of this tone interferes with one's health. Behind the thought there is feeling; and it is the feeling which sustains that tone; the thought is on the surface. In order to keep the continuity of that tone the mystics have special practices.

There used to be a custom in ancient times, that instead of using an organ in churches four or five persons with the lips closed used to keep one tone, humming that one tone together. I was most impressed by this, hearing it again in a church in Russia after coming from India. The secret of the continual ringing of the bell practised by the churches at all times and even up till now, is that it was not only a bell to call people; it was to tune them up to their tone, it was to suggest, 'There is a tone going on in you, get yourself tuned to it!' But if that tuning is not done, even if a person has recovered from his illness, weakness still remains. An external cure is no cure if a person is not cured mentally. If his spirit is not cured the mark of illness remains there and the rhythm of mind is broken.

When a person's mind is going at a speed which is faster or at a speed which is slower than it ought to be, or if a person jumps from one thought to another and so goes on thinking of a thousand things in five minutes, however intellectual he may be, he cannot be normal; or if a person holds one thought and broods on it instead of making progress, he will also cling to his depression, his fears, his disappointments, and that makes him ill. It is irregularity of the rhythm of mind which causes mental disorder.

I do not mean that the rhythm of the mind of one person must be like that of another person. No, each person's rhythm is peculiar to himself. Once a pupil who accompanied me on my walk, in spite of all his kindness and pleasure in accompanying me, felt a great discomfort at times because he could not walk as slowly as I did. Being simple and frank, he expressed this to me. And in answer I said, 'It is a majestic walk.'

The reason was that his rhythm was different. He could not feel comfortable in some other rhythm, he had to be galloping along in order to feel comfortable. And so one can feel what gives one comfort and what gives one discomfort in everything one does. If one does not feel it, that shows that one does not give attention to one's being. The wisdom is to understand oneself. If one can sustain the proper rhythm of one's mind, that is sufficient to keep one healthy.

Mental illnesses are subtler than physical illnesses, though up to now mental illnesses have not been thoroughly explored, but when this has been done we shall find that all physical illnesses have some connection with them. The mind and the body stand face to face. The body reflects its order and disorder upon the mind, the mind reflecting at the same time its harmony and disharmony on the body; and it is for this reason you will find that many who are ill outwardly also have some illness of the mind, and very seldom will one find a case where a person is mentally ill and physically perfectly well.

Once I happened to go to the asylum for the insane in New York, and the physicians very kindly laid before me a number of skulls showing the different cavities in the brain and the spots of decay which had caused insanity in the life of the patients. There is always a sign of it in the physical body. It may be apparent suffering or it may be some decay at the back of it, yet it is not known. I asked them, 'I would like to know whether the cavity brought about the insanity or the insanity brought about the cavity?' Their argument was that the cavity brought about the insanity. But it is not always so, the mental disorder is not always caused by a cavity in the brain; for the inner being has a greater influence on the physical being than the physical body has on the mental existence. Yet it is not always the mind that brings about the physical illness; very often it is so, but not always. Sometimes from the physical plane illness travels to the mental plane, and sometimes illness goes from the mental plane to the physical plane. There are many causes, but in short, if there is a general cause, it is the lack of that music which we call order. Does it not show that man is music, that life is music? In order to play our part best the only thing we can do is to keep our tone and rhythm in proper condition: in this is the fulfilment of our life's purpose.

iii

Movement is life and stillness is death; for in movement there is the significance of life and in stillness we see the sign of death. One might ask if looking at it from a metaphysical point of view there is a stillness. No, but there is what we call no movement, or at least no movement which is perceptible to us in some form, whether it is visible or audible or in the form of sensation or vibration. The movement which is not perceptible to us we name stillness; the word life we use only in connection with the perceptible existence, the movement of which we perceive. Therefore, with regard to our physical health, movement is the principal thing, regulation of movement, of its rhythm in pulsation and the circulation of the blood. The whole cause of death and decay is to be traced to the lack of movement; all different aspects of diseases are to be traced to congestion. Every decay is caused by congestion, and congestion is caused by lack of movement. There are parts of the body where the veins, the nerves, adhere to the skin and there is no free circulation. There arise all sorts of diseases. Outer diseases of that kind we call skin diseases; when it works inwardly it manifests in the form of a certain pain. A physician may show us a thousand different reasons as being the cause of different diseases, but the one and central cause of each disease and of all diseases is lack of movement, which is in fact lack of life. This mechanism of the body is made to work according to a certain rhythm, and is maintained by a perpetual rhythmic movement. The centre of that perpetual current of life is the breath. The different remedies that man has found in all ages often bring cure to sufferers for a time, but they are not always completely cured, for the cause of the disease remains unexplored. At the back of all illness the cause is some irregular, unnatural living in the way of food or drink or action or repose.

Death is a change that comes through the inability of the body to hold what we call the soul. The body has a certain amount of magnetism, which is the sign of its perfect running order. When, owing to illness, the body, either suddenly or gradually, loses that magnetism by the power of which it holds the soul, it so to speak helplessly loses its grip upon something that it was holding; and it is this losing of the grip that is known to us as death. Generally it is a gradual process. A little pain, a little illness, a little discomfort first manifest themselves. One does not take notice of it, but in time it grows into an illness.

Very often diseases are maintained by the patients' not knowing that they are maintaining them, just by their ignorance of their condition, by their neglect of themselves. There is a larger number of patients who leave their condition to be studied by the doctor. They do not know what is the matter with them, from the beginning to the end of the illness. As in ancient times simple believers trusted the priest to send them to heaven or to the other place, so today the patient gives himself into the hands of the doctor. Can anyone with keen observation imagine that anybody else is capable of knowing as much about oneself as one could know oneself if one wished to?

Is it a fault not to wish this? No, it is a habit. It is a kind of neglect of oneself that one does not think about one's condition oneself and wants the physician to tell one what is the matter. The pain is in oneself, one can be the best judge of one's life; one can find out the cause behind one's own illness, because one knows one's life best. Numberless souls today living this way, ignorant of their own condition, depend upon someone who has studied medical science outwardly. Even the physician cannot help one properly if one does not know one's condition clearly. It is one's own clear knowledge of one's complaint that enables one to give the physician a correct idea. When there is a little hole in the cloth, if one does not look to it it will tear easily and become a large hole. So it is with health. If there is something a little wrong with it, one neglects it, absorbed in life as it is, and so allows it to become worse every day, drawing closer thereby the death which otherwise could have been avoided.

The question is, if it is right that one should think of one's body and the condition of one's health. It is, so long as one is not obsessed by oneself. If one thinks about one's health so much that one becomes obsessed by it, it is working against oneself. It is certainly wrong, because it is not helping oneself. If one pities oneself and says, 'Oh, how ill I am, and how terrible it is!

And shall I ever be well?' then the impression becomes a kind of fuel to the fire, one is feeding one's illness by the thought of it. But if on the other hand one becomes so neglectful of oneself that one says, 'Oh, it does not matter; it is after all an illusion,' one will not be able to keep that thought when the pain increases. It is as necessary to take care of oneself as it is to forget about one's illness. For an illness comes to a person as a thief enters the house, quietly. He works without the knowledge of the dwellers in it and robs them of their best treasures. If one keeps guard against it, it is not wrong as long as one does not dwell all the time on one's illness.

One might ask, 'Is it worth while to be alive? Why must we not end this life? What is it, after all?' But this is an abnormal thought. A person with a normal body and mind will not think in this way. When this abnormal thought grows it culminates in insanity, which causes many people to commit suicide. The natural desire of every soul is to live, to have a life of perfect health, to make the best of one's coming into this world. Neither God nor the soul is pleased with the desire for death, for death does not belong to the soul. It is a kind of agitation, a revolt that arises in the mind of someone, who then says, 'I prefer death to life.' To have the desire to live, and yet to live a life of suffering is also not a wise thing. And if wisdom counts for anything, one must spare no effort to arrive at the proper condition of health.

iv

In ancient times people attributed the cause of every illness to spirits. There was a spirit of every kind of illness, and they believed that particular spirit brought that illness. The healers made attempts to cure every patient that came with that illness, and they were successful in making them well. Today that spirit of illness has caused a material manifestation, for the physicians now declare that at the root of every illness is a germ, a microbe. Every day a new invention brings a new microbe to their eyes. And if a new microbe is discovered every day till the end of the world numberless microbes will be discovered and there will be numberless diseases; in the end it will be difficult to find one man healthy, for there must always be some microbe; if it is not of an old disease, then of a newly discovered one. As this is a world of innumerable lives, it will always show innumerable lives; each life having its power, constructive or destructive, will show that power even in a microbe; and so this discovery of microbes of diseases will go on with the increase of diseases, for to prevent microbes from existing is not always in the power of man. Sometimes he will destroy them, but often he will find that each microbe destroyed will produce in return many more microbes. What is life? Every atom of it is living, call it ray or electron, germ or microbe.

The people of old thought that they were spirits, living beings, in the absence of science which today distinguishes these spirits in the form of microbes; and yet it seems that the ancient healers had a greater grip upon the illness, for the reason that they did not see the outer microbe only, but the microbe in its spirit. In destroying the microbe they did not only destroy the outer microbe, but the inner microbe in the form of the spirit, of the germ; and the most interesting thing is that in order to drive away that spirit which they thought had possessed the patient, they burned or they placed before him certain chemicals which are used even now, having been proved to be destructive to the germs of diseases.

With every measure that physicians may take to prevent the germs of diseases from coming, in spite of all the success that they will have there will be a greater failure; for even if the actual germ is destroyed, it exists, its family exists, somewhere. Besides, the body which has once become the abode of that particular germ has become a receptacle of the same germ. If the physician destroys the germ of disease from the body of an individual, that does not mean that he destroys it from the universe. This problem, therefore, must be looked at from another point of view: that everything that exists in the objective world has its living and more important part existing in the subjective world; and that part which is in the subjective is held by the belief of the patient. As long as the patient believes that he is ill he is giving sustenance to that part of the disease which is in the subjective world. Even if the germs of the disease were destroyed, not once but a thousand times in his body, they would be created there again; because the source from which the germs spring is in his belief, not in his body, as the source of the whole creation is within, not without.

The outer treatment of many such diseases is just like cutting the plant from its stem while the root remains in the ground. Since the root of the illness is in the subjective part of one's being, in order to drive away that illness one must dig out the root by taking away the belief of illness even before the outer germ is destroyed. The germ of illness cannot exist without the force, the breath, which it receives from the subjective part of one's being; and if the source of its sustenance is once destroyed, then the cure is certain.

Very few people can hold a thought, but many are held by a thought. If such a simple thing as holding a thought were mastered, the whole life would be mastered. When once a person gets into his head, 'I am ill', and when this is confirmed by a physician, then his belief becomes watered like a plant, then his continual reflection of it, falling upon his illness like the sun, makes the plant of illness grow; and therefore it would not be an exaggeration to say that, consciously or unconsciously, the patient is the gardener of his own illness.

One might ask, 'Is it, then, right not to trouble about microbes? If a physician finds them and shows them to us, should we not believe it?' You cannot help believing it if you have gone so far as to make the physician show it to you. You have helped the physician to believe it, and now you are wondering whether you should believe it yourself. You cannot help believing something which has been shown to you, which is before you. No doubt if you rise above this, then you have touched the truth; for when you rise above facts you touch reality. Is it not deluding oneself to deny facts? It is no more deluding than one is already deluded. Facts themselves are delusions; it is the rising above this delusion that enables one to touch reality. As long as the brain is muddled with facts, it will be increasingly absorbed every day in the puzzle of life, making life more confused than ever before. It is because of this that the Master taught, 'Seek ye first the Kingdom of God.' This means: 'Rise above facts first, and by the light that you gain from there, thrown upon facts, you will see the facts in a clear light.'

This does not mean at all that you should close your eyes to facts. It only means, 'Look up first and when your eyes are once charged with divine light, then when you cast your glance on the world of facts you will have a much clearer vision, the vision of reality.' There is no lack of honesty if you deny the fact of illness; it is no hypocrisy if you deny it to yourself first. It is only a help, for there are many things in life that exist because they are sustained by your acknowledging their existence. Deluded by outwardly appearing facts you hold them in your thought as a belief; but by denying them you root them out, for they cannot exist when starved of the sustenance for which they depend upon you.

v

This does not mean that the fact of germs should altogether be ignored, for it is not possible to ignore something which you see; besides it does not mean that the discovery of microbes has not been of use to the physicians, enabling them to attend better to the patient. Yet at the same time one can be too sensitive to germs, one can exaggerate the idea of germs, making the idea more than the reality. But one person will be susceptible to those germs and tend to be their victim; while another person assimilates those germs and thus destroys them. In other words, the one is destroyed by germs and the other destroys them. It is said that contagious diseases are contracted by the microbes going from one person to another, in the breath, in the air, in everything; but it is not always the microbes, it is very often the impression. When a person has seen that his friend has caught a cold and has thought, 'I fear I shall catch it,' he has certainly caught the disease; because he has been afraid and has been impressed by it, he has caught it. It is not always necessary that the germs of the cold should have gone from one person to another by way of the breath; the impression that a person has received can create them, for behind the whole of creation there is that power. We often see that the more a person is afraid of a thing, the more he is pursued by it, for unconsciously he concentrates upon it.

There are germs and impurities, but there are also elements to purify them. Those five elements, earth, water, fire, air, and ether, as spoken of by the mystics, do not only compose germs, but can also destroy them, if one only knew how one could make use of those five elements to purify one's body with them and also one's mind. As there is need of sun and water for plants to grow, so there is need of the five elements for a person to keep in perfect health. These five elements he breathes according to his capacity of breath. But by breath every person does not attract the same properties; for everyone attracts from the breath elements according to his particular constitution. One attracts more fire element in his breath, another more water element, and a third attracts more earth element. Sometimes one receives an element which one does not require. Besides, the sun currents have a greater healing power than anything else. A person who knows how to breathe perfectly, who is attracting sun currents into his body, can keep the body free from every kind of impurity. No microbes of destruction can exist if the sun currents can touch every part of the body which is within, and that is done by the breath. The places of the earth which are hidden from the sun, which are not touched by the air, become damp; several little lives are created there, germs of destruction are born, and the air in that place becomes dense. If this is true, then the body also needs the sun and air. The lungs, intestines, and veins and tubes of the body all need the sun and the air; and these are taken in by means of perfect breathing; and even the mind derives benefit from this. For the mind too is composed of five elements, the elements in their finer condition.

Rest and repose as well as action and movement must have a certain balance, a certain rhythm. If there is no balance between activity and repose, then the breath is not secure either. Our great mistake is that with every little complaint the first thing we think of is the doctor. We never stop to think, 'What has been the cause in myself? Have I been too active, too lazy? Have I not been careful about my diet, about my sleep? Have I not breathed in all the elements which are necessary to keep this mechanism of body and mind going?' Frightened by every illness, a man first runs to the doctor. As long as the illness has not appeared before him he does not mind if it is growing inwardly without his having noticed it. It may continue to grow for a long time; for years the man, absorbed in his outer activities, never thinks that he is giving a home to his worst enemy in his body. Thus very often illness is caused by negligence.

Then there are others who become too careful, they think of nothing else except their illness. The first question before them is, 'How shall I get well?' Pondering upon their illness they give a kind of fuel to that fire of illness from their thoughts, keeping it burning; they do not know that by their unconscious effort the illness is kept alive. In order to keep the health in perfect order one must keep a balance between body and mind, between activity and repose; and it is the psychological outlook on one's health which helps more than any medicines.

I remember going to see a patient who had been suffering from an illness for more than twenty years and had lost every hope of getting better. Several physicians had been consulted, many different treatments had been tried. I told her a simple thing to do; I did not teach any special practices, but just an ordinary little thing to do in the morning and in the evening; and to the great surprise of those at home, she began to move her hands and legs, which had been thought impossible; and this gave them great hope, that a patient who had been so long in bed could do this, and to her too it was a great surprise. I went to see them after a few days and asked them, 'How is the patient progressing?' They said, 'She is progressing very well. We could never have believed that she could move her hands and legs; it is the most wonderful thing. But we cannot make her believe that now after twenty years of suffering she can ever be well again. This illness has made such an impression upon her that she thinks that it is natural for her, and that to be well is a dream, an unreality.'

This gave me the idea that when a person lives in a certain condition for a long, long time, that condition becomes his friend unconsciously. He does not know it, he may think that he wants to get out of it, yet there is some part of his being that is holding his illness just the same.

One day, remembering this peculiarity of human nature, I asked someone who was brought to me to be cured of an obsession how long she had had this obsession. She explained to me how horrible the obsession was, how terrible life was for her. I listened to it for half an hour, everything that she said against the obsession; but recollecting this amusing aspect of human nature, I asked her, 'You do not really mean to say that you want to get rid of that spirit? If I had this spirit I would keep it. After all these years that you have had it, it seems unjust and very cruel to this spirit. If this spirit had not cared for you, it would not have stayed with you all these years. In this world, is it easy for a person to remain so long with one? This spirit is most faithful.' Then she said, 'I do not really want to get rid of it.' I was very much amused to see how this person wanted sympathy and help, but did not want to give up the spirit. It was not the spirit that was obsessing this person, but the person was obsessing the spirit!

Psychic natures are more liable to illness, as they are more susceptible to gross vibrations, and especially those inclined to spiritualistic seances. Their bodies become so susceptible to any kind of illness, also to obsessions, that in reality they prepare themselves to welcome in their own spirit any other spirit.

vi

As medical science has advanced in modern times the different diseases and complaints have become more classified. Each separate complaint has been given a certain name, and in this way even if a person has only a slight complaint, after the examination by a physician he is told its name. His complaint may be only as big as a molehill, but it is turned into a mountain. There is no greater misfortune than hearing from a doctor that one has contracted an illness which is dangerous, the name of which is frightening. What then happens? That name being impressed on the heart of the man, creates the same element and in the end the man sees the thing come true about which he was told by the physician. In the same way the impression that the words of a fortune-teller make upon one in many cases brings about the realization of his fortune-telling in the end. The fortune-teller is not always a saint, he is not always a clairvoyant who sees what he claims to see; he may be only an imaginative person. But he has said something and that impression has remained with the person; and in the end he realizes that it came true. Then what an impression a physician makes who is authorized by the medical authorities, in whom one immediately places one's trust, even if he was mistaken in finding the real disease; because among a hundred physicians there is hardly one who has insight into the real nature and character of a disease, and among a hundred patients the physician can perhaps only tell correctly the nature and character of one man's complaint. Thus there is great danger of a person being impressed at the beginning of his illness by a right or wrong remark made by a physician about that illness. Among ancient peoples only the physicians knew the names of diseases; but the physician was not allowed to tell the patient what complaint he had, because from a psychological point of view he would be doing wrong. This was not only a medical science, there was a psychological idea attached to it.

I have seen numberless cases come to me frightened by something that a physician had said to them. Perhaps there is nothing the matter with them, or only a little illness; perhaps they have not yet realized what it is, but they are frightened just the same. And if there is an imaginative patient, then he has a wide scope for his imagination. Everything that is wrong, he attaches to something he has heard from the physician, he relates every condition of his life to that particular remark. In life such as we live it in the world, with so many things to do, so many responsibilities resting upon us at home and in the outside world, and with the strife that is reflected upon us by our life in this world, we naturally have our ups and downs physically. Sometimes one is tired; sometimes one needs a rest; sometimes one must fast one day, one day there is no inclination for food. If one attributes all these little things to an illness that a physician has once told of, one is certainly making the illness strong; for the root of illness is in the mind, and if that root is watered all the time by thought and feeling, then illness is realized in the end.

When we look at the surgical world, no doubt wonderful operations are being done, and humanity has experienced great help through surgical operations; yet it is still experimental, and it will take perhaps a century longer for surgery to mature. It is in its infancy just now. The first impulse of a surgeon is to look at a case only from one point of view, and to think that this case can be cured by surgery. He has no other thought in his mind, he has no time to think that there is another possibility. If he is a wise surgeon, he gives a word of confidence; yet he knows that it is an experiment. It is a person he is dealing with, and not a piece of wood or a stone that can be carved and engraved upon. It is a person with feeling, it is a soul which is experiencing life through every atom that it has, a soul which is not made for a knife. Now this person has to go through this experience, fearing death, preferring life to death. Very often what happens is that what was considered wrong before the operation, is found to have been right afterwards. No doubt something wrong has to be produced because the operation has been performed. And an operation is not something that is finished; it is something which has its action upon the nerves and then upon the spirit of a man, and then its reaction upon life again. Do we not see that after an operation a person's whole life has become impressed with it? A certain strain on the nerves, a certain upset in the spirit has been caused. The care of the surgeon continues only until the patient is apparently well, outwardly well; but what about the after-effect of it on the spirit of the person, on his mind, its reaction on his life? The surgeon does not always realize this, he is not concerned with it.

Cure means absolute cure, within and without. By this it is not meant that surgery has no place in the scheme of life. It is a most important part of the medical world, but at the same time it must be avoided when it can be avoided; one must not lightly jump into it. A young person with strength and energy thinks, 'What is it? I can go through it.' But once done, there remains an impression for the whole life. Man has intuition as his heritage, and it is intuition which is the basis of every science. At this time when science is treated as a book study, it takes away the part that intuition must perform. If in the medical world an intuitive development were introduced, if many physicians were occupied in finding remedies by which to avoid operations, surely a very great work could be accomplished. It is amusing that at one time when the operation for appendicitis began to be known in the United States, it became a fashion among the rich people to have that operation done because a few days at home are quite pleasant. And then the physicians began to choose appendicitis patients among those who had the means to stay at home for some time and rest. Everybody asked, 'Did you have it?' 'Yes, I had it.' It was just like a game.

Another subject is the use of drugs. Any physician, after life-long experience, will find that often he has prescribed drugs for people, and although he may have seemed to cure them for the time being, yet he was not really successful. The after-effects of drugs are sometimes so depleting, and the confusion that they create in the brain and mind so great, that they can ruin a person's life. I have seen many people who, after medical treatment for their illness, once accustomed to drugs, have made their body a kind of receptacle for drugs. They live upon the drug and cannot live without it. In order to digest their food they must have something, in order to sleep they must have something, in order to feel cheerful they must have some drug. Now, when these natural things such as digesting one's food, being gay and cheerful, sleeping comfortably, which are natural blessings, depend upon outside, material things, how can that person be called healthy? In order to make the best of today they take a drug, and then tomorrow becomes worse.

When we consider that the human body is an instrument that God created for His own experience, then what a mistake it must be to allow this body, through drugs and medicines, to become unfit for the use of the divine Spirit. It is not meant by this that medicine is never necessary. Medicine has its place; even drugs, when there is that necessity. But when a drug is used for little things that can be cured by some other means, in the end the health gets out of hand and even drugs cannot give the person rest. The best medicine is a pure diet, nourishing food, fresh air, regularity in action and repose, clearness of thought, pureness of feeling, and confidence in the perfect Being, with whom we are linked and whose expression we are. That is the essence of health. The more we realize this, the more secure will be our health.

I knew a person whom a physician had examined and had told that he would die within three months, No doubt if that person had been imaginative he would have taken that impression. But he came to me and he said, 'What nonsense! Die in three months! I am not going to die even in three hundred years from now.' And to our great surprise within three months the doctor died and this man brought me the news! We must learn to respect the human being and realize that a human soul is beyond birth and death, that a human soul has a divine spirit in it, and that all illnesses and pains and sufferings are only his tests and trials. He is above them, and we must try to raise him above illnesses.

Behind everything there is movement, vibration. What causes a certain movement of particles of matter is vibration. Vibration is felt by us, it is realized by our senses as a certain movement of particles of matter, but vibration in itself is a movement. It is because of this that the power of the word is stronger than any medicine or any other treatment or operation, because the word causes certain vibrations in our body, in the atmosphere, in our environment, bringing about thereby a cure which nothing else can bring about. When we see a healthy person and a person suffering from some illness, and we think of the condition of their pulsation and of the circulation of their blood, we shall find that behind it all there is a movement, there is a vibration which is going on. In one person that vibration is in a proper condition, there is health; in the other person vibration is not in its right condition, therefore there is illness.

There was a physician in America who happened to think of this. Only, the difference is that when a scientist thinks of such a thing, even if it comes by intuition, he pursues it by going from the foot of the mountain towards the top. And it is very difficult to climb the mountain, and very often before he has climbed the mountain his life is ended. The physician is now dead. His was a very good idea. Although he had not come to the secret of it, yet as an idea it inspired many physicians in the United States and in the world, and it created great excitement in the medical world. But, as the mystics say, seek ye first the Kingdom of God . . . and all these things shall be added unto you. That is another way. That is not climbing from the bottom to the top, which is so difficult; it is climbing; it is first reaching the top, and then all is easy. It is easy for the one who is on the top of the mountain to move anywhere he likes from the top. It does not take so much energy, it does not weigh him down. Avicenna, the great physician of ancient times, on whose discoveries medieval science was based, was a Sufi who used to sit in meditation, and by intuition he used to write prescriptions. Just lately a physician has discovered the great treasure that this man had given to medical science and has written a book to interpret the ideas of Avicenna in modern language.

vii

Most of the cases of physical and mental illness come from exhaustion of the nerves. Not everybody knows to what extent to use nerve force in everyday life and to what extent to control it. Very often a good person, a kind, loving, affectionate person, gives out his energy at every call from every side, and so, continually giving energy, in the end finds his nerves troubled and weakened. In the end the same person who was once kind and nice and polite cannot keep this up, because when the funds of energy have expired, then there is no control, there is no power of endurance, there is no patience to take things easily. Then the person who once proved to be good and kind becomes irritable and troubled, and tired and disgusted with things. Very often it may be called abuse of goodness; for it is not always giving out that answers the demands of everyday life; it is the balanced condition of one's body and mind which answers the demands of life satisfactorily. And sometimes it becomes a passion with a person to waste his energy either in doing something or in speaking continually; and this passion can grow to such an extent that even when that person has lost a great deal of his energy, he will still find satisfaction in giving out even more.

In the presence of that person others will feel depleted, because he has no energy left, he is trying to give out what little he has, and the irritation and strain fall upon the others; it makes them nervous also.

Weakness of nerves is not only the cause of physical diseases, but it leads to insanity. There is one principal cause of physical diseases as well as of mental diseases: overstrained nerves, exhausted nerves; and that person whose nerves are exhausted, in spite of all virtue and goodness, goodwill and desire to do right, will prove to be doing wrong, to his own surprise, because he has lost self-discipline. His high ideals are of no use to him, for he has not got himself in hand. His qualifications, his knowledge, his attitude, his morals will all prove to be futile in the absence of that nervous force which keeps man fit and capable of doing all that it is proper for him to do in the world.

Lack of soberness also causes nervous exhaustion. Therefore all alcoholic and intoxicating things consume the energy of the nerves, eat the energy of the nerves. One might ask why a person takes delight in such things, and again the answer is that it is a passion; that anything that produces intoxication for the moment, that excites the nerves, makes one feel, so to speak, more cheerful for that moment. But one depends upon something outside, and the reaction comes when the effect of that intoxicant has worn off. Then one feels twice as weak and exhausted as before, and needs twice the amount of drug or alcohol in order to make one feel, for a few hours, as cheerful as one did. And so one goes on and on until one has no power over mind and body but becomes a slave to something one takes. That is the only time that such a person thinks he lives; at all other times he feels miserable. That becomes his world, his heaven, his paradise, his life. All manner of excess in passion and anger, all manner of sensual life and rejoicing in it robs one of the energy, the power and vitality of the nerves.

Besides, every effect that is created in voice, in word, in singing, is created by the nervous power; the whole secret of magnetism is in the nerves. The whole secret of success of a public man, a public person on the stage or in the concert-hall is his nervous power, the success of the lawyer, of the barrister in the court is his nervous power. It will always be found that a good barrister who has made a name has that power, and it is magnetism. Therefore the sign of a person with health, both physical and mental, is that he develops that influence which is expressed by nervous power, and it has its influence upon all things.

Strength gives one more power, weakness causes a greater weakness. The proper condition of the nerves enables one to impress. A person nervously depleted, even if he be in the right, cannot impress it upon another, because there is no strength behind it. And so even if he is in the right, he will be at a loss what to do. There is no power to go forward, to stand up for his own right.

The system that we know today of keeping patients shut up in hospitals, in asylums, is just like making them captives to the disease. The atmosphere of the place and the very thought of being in the hospital make them feel ill; and so it is with the life in asylums. However efficient the treatment may be, it gives a person the impression that he is out of his mind, there is something wrong with his mind; and the whole atmosphere suggests the same thing. Besides, it would be kinder on the part of society and of the family, if the patients could be taken in hand by friends or relations in their difficult times. They could be helped better than by putting them in places where they can think of nothing but their illness. I have myself seen many cases whom relations or friends have looked after, and they have been helped much more than by what they would have received in a hospital.

One might say that medical treatments require a special place for such things, and that there they have everything besides the physician to look after them, and that that is the only way in large cities that such cases can be looked after. Yes, it is true, and one cannot help it where the situation is difficult; still, where it can be helped one should try to help.

Nervous diseases are very often treated by giving medicines. There is no medicine in the world which can do good to nerves; for nerves are the most natural part of one's being. They are the part of one's being which is linked with the physical world and with the mental world, it is the central part of one's being; and there is no better remedy for nerves than nature, a life of rest and repose, quiet, proper breathing, proper nourishment, and someone to treat the patient with wisdom. By understanding the law of environment and climatic influences, by understanding what influences people have upon such a patient, one can cure him.

Nervous energy is a kind of battery for the whole mechanism of the mind and body. For the mechanism of mind, therefore, it is the clearness of the nervous mechanism and the good working of the nervous mechanism which enable us to make our thought clear to ourselves, or to hold our thought, or to imagine, or to think, or to memorize; and when the nervous system is not clear, then one cannot keep things in mind, conceive things in the mind, or keep to one thought, and various conditions of mental disorder begin to show. Within the body the nervous system is called centres by Yogis. The different centres are the points of the nervous system, the centres through which one experiences intuition, one feels, one observes keenly.

And now the question is where to get nervous energy, and how to get it. Our body and mind are a battery of that power, they are made of it, we are that power. The magnetism of a human being is much greater than anything else in the world. No jewel, no gem, no flower, no fruit, nothing in the world has such magic as a human being has if he knows how to retain it, how to keep himself in that condition. Because with all the scientific discoveries of radium and electrons and all the different atoms, there is no atom in the world which is more radiant than the atoms with which the human body is composed, atoms which are not only attractive to the human eye, but attract the whole of creation towards the human being. The horse serves man, the camel carries his load, the tiger surrenders to man, the elephants walk by his command. But when he loses his proper spirit, then it is just like losing salt: as it is said in the Bible, 'Ye are the salt of the earth, and when the salt hath lost its savour, wherewith shall it be salted?' When man's own body, his own spirit, are more radiant than anything else, then there is nothing else that can give him more spirit. He himself is the spirit.

viii

One often wonders to what extent the spirit has power over matter; and the answer is that, as matter is the outcome of spirit, spirit has all power over matter. One becomes pessimistic after having tried the power of thought to cure oneself or to cure others, and failed; and then one begins to think that it is not the spirit that can help, it is something outside. It is not meant for one moment that the things outside have no effect, but that the spirit has all power to cure a person of every malady. No doubt in order to cure every malady the spirit must reach a state so high that it is able to do so perfectly. In the present age a person thinks that spirit is born of matter. Through biological study one begins to realize that first there was matter, and then it evolved, until in man it developed and sprang up as an intelligence, as a human intelligence; but according to the mystic the whole thing is a play of the intelligence. In the rock, in the tree, in the plant, in the animal, and in man the intelligence has gone all along and developed itself, and through man it comes to its pure essence. And it is arriving at the pure essence that makes man become aware of his origin.

Christian Science teaches that matter does not exist. Even if it does not explain it fully, nevertheless there is one life; and what we call matter and spirit are simply different aspects of it. We must realize that there is one life and that it is all spirit; even matter is a passing state of spirit. And spirit is intelligent; it is intelligence itself, besides being powerful and free from death and decay. It is capable of giving its life even to the dense substance which has been made out of itself, and which is matter. Therefore it is beyond words to tell to what an extent the thought, the feeling, and the attitude help one to become cured.

The feeling that through the nerve-channels, through the veins and tubes, it is the divine blood that is circulating, which is perfect, which is complete, which is pure, helps one very much. In other words, what is illness? Illness is an inharmony. If inharmony causes illness and failure, so harmony brings the cure. If one can harmonize one's life in every way, in every form, certainly it must result in a perfect harmony, and that will manifest also as the cure of illness. No doubt sorrow can cause all illnesses, because it makes both mind and body inharmonious, and then one can easily catch an illness. To me a really brave person is he who says, 'What has happened has happened; what I am going through I shall rise above; and what will come I shall meet with courage.' If one wants to be sad, there are many things that can make one sad. One need not wait for causes to arise that make one shed tears; every moment one could shed tears if one had that inclination. One should not look for ill-luck. Ill-luck can easily be found everywhere if one will look for it; and many unconsciously do so. There are many illnesses, but hopelessness is the worst illness. When a person has lost hope his illness cannot be cured. Hope is part of intelligence, hope is the strength of intelligence. If intelligence works against all disorder, whether physical or mental or moral disorder, certainly a cure can be obtained.

The mystics have always known and practised in a most perfect way the idea which is generally talked about in its most elementary form—the idea that by repeating to oneself, 'I am well, I am better, I am better,' one becomes better. There are many who do not see any reason in it, but you will see that in time the most materialistic people will come to realize the truth that it is the attitude of mind, the willingness to be cured, the desire to get above one's illness, the inclination to fight against disorder, which help one to health.

There is a difference between belief and thought. One might say, 'I am thinking every day I shall get well, but that does not come to pass.' Yes, thought is one thing, belief is another. When you compare thought with belief, one is automatic, the other is more living. And when a person says, 'I am thinking, or, I am practising this every day, but I don't get any benefit', it only means that he is practising one thing and believing another. He is practising, 'I shall be well', and he is believing, 'I am ill'. It may be his unconscious belief, but there is a belief: 'This will not cure me, I shall continue to be ill'; and though he may be repeating a thousand times a day, 'I shall be well, I shall be well', yet he does not believe it.

When a child is ill it can be helped by helpful thought. Sometimes the mother's healing thought, the mother's sympathy, works with the child more successfully than any medicine that is given to the child; and in this is the proof of the power of healing. There are numberless cases that can be observed when consciously, or even unconsciously, the desire of the mother for the child to recover becomes a healing influence. If a mother is anxious and worries about a child, no doubt that has a contrary effect; because unconsciously the mother then holds an illness in her thought for the child.

The way that mystical healers have brought about wonderful cures is beyond comprehension. What thought-power can do is seen in their work. No doubt if a person is a hindrance to healing influences, then even a healer cannot do his work properly; but if a person's attitude is right, if one believes that spirit has all the power to cure, certainly one can be cured. The mystics have proved in their lives that not only their power can cure, but even death stands before them as their obedient servant. Death for them is not a constable who arrests and takes a person when the time has come, death for them is a porter that carries their baggage when travelling. But healing apart, even medicine will not do any good to a pessimistic person. If he does not believe in it, it has no power over him.

If belief makes even the power of medicine perfect, then how much more can it do if one believes in the power of the spirit over matter. What generally happens is that one does not know if there is a spirit. Often one wonders if there is any spirit, for what one knows is matter. Once, when travelling on a ship, a young Italian came to me and said, 'I only believe in eternal matter.' I said, 'Your belief is not very different from my belief.' He was very surprised to hear a priest (he thought that I was a priest) saying such a thing. He asked, 'What is your belief?' I said, 'What you call eternal matter, I call eternal spirit. You call matter what I call spirit. What does it signify? It is only a difference in words. It is one Eternal.' He became very interested from that time; before that he was very much afraid.

The secret of healing is to rise by the power of belief above the limitations of this world of variety, that one may touch by the power of intelligence the oneness of the whole Being. It is there that one becomes charged with the almighty power, and it is by the power of that attainment that one is able to help oneself and others in their pain and suffering. Verily, spirit has all the power there is.

ix

The idea of calling certain diseases incurable is the great mistake that man makes today. It is really that he has not got the remedy for curing those diseases, and so he calls them incurable. But by calling a certain disease incurable he makes that patient hopeless, not only regarding the help of man, but also regarding the help that he can get from above; therefore it cannot be a right idea to make a living being believe that there is no cure for him. If the source and goal are perfect, then the attainment of perfection is possible; and as health is a perfection, it can be attained. All the strength is in the spirit. Everyone has strength to the extent that he is close to the spirit, but everyone has a spark of that spirit in himself; and everyone should know that he has a responsibility for his own health as a healer to himself, and that he has a part to play for himself that is not only a physician's responsibility or a healer's. But at the same time he must be ready first to play his part as a physician, as a healer, himself; first to see what is his condition, what is lacking, what is the matter with him, how to heal. If he cannot do it well enough he may ask another to help him, but he must be the first to desire it.

Is healing by hypnotism a desirable method? Now surgeons make use of ether in order to perform operations. Although it is harmful to the patient, yet at the same time it is necessary; and so if this way is used to make a person better, if it is necessary, it may be allowed. Every person, however, should be able to care for himself by prayer, by meditation, by silence, and to cherish that belief in perfect health and root out the belief in illness.

Curing by magnetism is another thing. It is another form of

prescription. There is a prescription given by a physician, a certain medicine is given to act or to react against a certain condition. So the power which is the life-energy is given in a certain form in order to give the patient what he lacks. It is not exactly an objective remedy, but it is external just the same.

There is no illness which is incurable; and we commit a sin against the perfection of the divine Being when we give up hope of any person's cure, for in that perfection nothing is impossible; all is possible. We see it with our limited reason, and make the divine perfection small, as small as we are; but in reality the vastness, the greatness of the almighty power is beyond our comprehension, and limiting it would be nothing but an error. What generally happens in the case of what is called incurable disease is that the impression made upon the patient of knowing and feeling that his disease cannot be cured becomes the root of his illness, and so the illness becomes rooted in the belief of the patient. Then no remedy, no help can root it out. The best treatment that a healer, a physician, can give to a patient is to give him first the belief that he can be cured, then medicine or healing treatment, whatever method he may adopt to cure him.

We hear accounts of the physicians of ancient times, of the mystics and thinkers, that they used to find out a person's illness just by looking at him. This came by intuition; and if the people in past ages were proficient in it, it does not mean that the soul has lost this quality. Even today, if one develops that quality one can find out at the first glance all that is wrong with a person in body, mind, and spirit—all. For his outward expression tells of the inner condition; any disorder in the spirit, mind, or body is clearly manifested outwardly; and it is only a matter of developing that faculty in order to read it and to find it out. When this faculty is developed a little further it makes one know also what is the reason behind every illness that a person has, whether mental or physical; and when this faculty is developed still further, one can also find out what would be the best way, the best remedy to cure this person. Avicenna, the great mystic of Persia, was a physician and a healer at the same time. The mystic is a healer by nature, but the attainment of the outer knowledge enables him to use his faculty best in the work of healing.

What must one do in order to develop this faculty, to find out if one has this faculty in oneself? As a mechanism wants winding every day, or a musical instrument wants tuning, so every person, whatever be his life and occupation, wants tuning every day. And what is this tuning? This tuning is the harmonizing of every action of the mechanism of the body, the harmonizing of the pulsation, of the beating of the head and heart, of the circulation of the blood; and this can be done by the proper method of repose. When once this is done, then the next step is to harmonize the condition of the mind. The mind which is constantly wandering, which is not under the control of the will, which cannot be made to respond in a moment, which is restless, this mind should be harmonized; it can be harmonized first with the will. When there is harmony between the will and the mind, then the body and mind, thus controlled and harmonized, become one harmonious mechanism working automatically. Merely bringing the mind and body into order allows one's every faculty to show itself in its fullness, to manifest. A person begins to observe life more keenly, to comprehend life more fully; and so perception becomes keener and the faculty of knowing develops.

No doubt the more a person evolves, the more he gains insight into the lives of things and beings. The first thing is to understand the condition of one's own body, the physical health, the mental condition; and when one can understand one's own condition better, then to begin to see the condition of another person. Then intuition is born and becomes active. As a man develops intuitively he begins to see the pains and sufferings of people; and if this sympathy grows and becomes vaster, his sight becomes more keen and he begins to observe the reason behind the complaint; and if he goes still further in the path of intuition, he begins also to see what remedy would be the best one for the person who suffers.

Furthermore, there are some signs a seer sees, outward signs which explain the fundamental principles of health. Every person represents the sun, his heart, his spirit, his body, all of him; and there is, as in the case of the sun, the sunrise and the sunset. There is a tendency of the body which draws it towards the

earth, which shows the sunset, because the soul is drawing itself
towards the goal. And there is another tendency which is like
the sunrise, and that is that the body is naturally inclined to raise
itself. It seems that the earth is not drawing the body, it is something above which draws it; that is the sign of the sunrise. And
it does not depend upon the age, it depends upon the condition
of the harmony that is established between the spirit and the
body. For a mystic it is quite usual to know if a person is going
to die in three years' time, and easier still to know if a person
is to die in a year. Apart from the inner spirit, even the tendency,
the inclination of the body gives every sign.

x

There are different ways of looking at illness. One person
will look at an illness as a punishment from above; another
person looks at it as a punishment brought about by his own
misdeeds; there is another way of looking at illness, and that
is that it comes from the past karmas, that one has to pay back
by illness the karmas, the actions of the past. I have seen patients
go through their illness in the thought that as it is the debt of
the past that one has to pay, it is just as well that it should be
paid back. When we look at it critically, we find that the one
who thinks that it is a punishment that God inflicts upon a person, certainly puts God in a severe light, making Him a hard
Judge instead of a most merciful and compassionate Father and
Mother, both in one. If the earthly mother and father would
not like to inflict pain and suffering upon their child, it is hard
to think that God, whose mercy and compassion are infinitely
greater than those of the earthly parents, could send illness to
a person as a punishment for his actions. It seems more reasonable when a person says that the illness is brought about by his
own actions. But it is not always true, it is not true in every case.
Very often the most innocent and the best souls, who have nothing but good wishes and kind thoughts, will be found among
sufferers.

Thinking that it is the debt of the past life gives one the idea
of fatalism, that there is a certain suffering through which one

must pass, that there is no other way, and that therefore one must patiently endure something which is most disagreeable. I have seen a young man suffering from an illness, who most contentedly told me, on my giving him advice to do something for his health, 'I believe that this is a debt of the past that I have to pay. I might just as well pay it.' From a business point of view it is very just, but from a spiritual person's point of view it can be looked at differently. What man does not wish for himself is not for him, is not his portion. For in every soul there is the power of the Almighty, there is a spark of divine light, there is the spirit of the Creator; and therefore all that man wishes to have is his birthright. Naturally a soul does not wish to have an illness unless he is unbalanced. If the soul knew the power of his natural inclination to enjoy health, he would experience health in life in spite of all the difficulties that the conditions of life may present.

One may wonder if illness is never to be understood as being the will of God. And if not, how is it with death? Death is different from illness, for illness is worse than death. The sting of death is only momentary; the idea that one leaves one's surroundings is one moment's bitter experience, no longer; but illness is incompleteness, and that is not desirable. Is it wrong to let a person die who is suffering very much, or should one use artificial means to keep him alive? It is not advisable that a doctor, or a relation, or anyone should kill a person who is suffering very much from a disease, in order to save him from pain; for nature is wise, and every moment that one passes on this physical plane has its purpose. We human beings are too limited to judge, to decide to put an end to life and suffering. We must try to make the suffering less for that person, to do everything in our power to make that person feel better. But to use artificial means of keeping someone alive for hours or days is not a right thing to do; because that is going against nature's wisdom and the divine plan. It is as bad as killing a person. The tendency is for man always to go further than he ought to; that is where he makes a mistake.

Can astrology help to find out the cause of a disease? Is such a method to be recommended? Yes, astrology can help to find

out the cause, if it is the right astrology; but it is not to be recommended for a person who looks at a condition in which he
is helpless. In a case in which it is favourable, it works to his
advantage, it is all right; but when it is not favourable, then it
works to his disadvantage. For instance an astrologer said to
someone, 'In three years' time you will be ill, and in the end
you will die.' This man became ill and died at the end of three
years. Why must we, therefore, depend upon such things? Why
not depend upon the life and light of God which are in us?
Why not say to oneself that life lives and death dies? And why
not always hope for the best to come, never look at nor expect
the worst to come? One might say that in order to be ready to
face the worst we should look at the dark side. But by looking
at the dark side of things one focuses one's spirit on it, and so
involves oneself in all kinds of obscurities, instead of rising above
it and seeking for the light, hoping for the best to come. In that
way one prepares oneself also to face the worst if it should come.

No doubt a man is very often himself the cause of the disorder
of this physical mechanism. It is this disorder which he calls illness, whether it is physical or mental. Sometimes it is his neglect,
sometimes an unbalanced condition of his mind or body which
causes it; sometimes conditions around him cause an illness.
Nevertheless, to have a yielding attitude towards illness is not
the right thing. No doubt it is a good thing to look upon the
illness of which one has been cured as having been a trial, a test,
an ordeal through which one was passing and which one has left
behind; thinking that it was for the better, that one is now purified, that one has learned a lesson from it, that one has become
more thoughtful and considerate towards oneself and others by
an experience like this. To think, 'What I am going through is
something that I must continually bear', is not the right attitude.
The attitude should be, 'No, this is not my portion in life. I
will not have it, I must not have it. I must rise above it, I must
forget it. I must do everything in my power to overcome it,
by a thought, by a feeling, by a belief, by a good action, by
progress, by a conception, by healing, by whatever method.'
There must be no limitation.

Sometimes a person says, 'I believe only in healing, I will not touch medicine, it is material'; that is wrong also. Sometimes a person says, 'I only believe in medicine, I have no faith in healing'; that is wrong, too. To grow towards perfect health, to bring about a cure, one must heal oneself from morning till evening. One should think, 'Every ray of the sun cures me, the air heals me; the food I take has an effect upon me; with every breath I inhale something which is healing, purifying, bringing me to perfect health.' With a hopeful attitude towards a cure, towards health, towards a perfect life, a person rises above disorders, which are nothing but inharmonious conditions of mind or body, and makes himself more fit to accomplish his life's purpose.

It is not selfish to think about one's health. No doubt it is undesirable to be thinking about one's illness all the time, to worry about it, or to be too anxious about it; but to care about one's health is the most religious thing there is, because it is the health of body and mind that enables one to do service to God and to one's fellow-men, by which one accomplishes one's life's purpose. One should think, 'I come from a perfect source and I am bound for a perfect goal. The light of the perfect Being is kindled in my soul. I live, move, and have my being in God; and nothing in the world, of the past or present, has power to touch me if I rise above all.' It is this thought which will make one rise above influences of inharmony and disorder, and will bring a person to the enjoyment of the greatest bliss in life, which is health.

xi

There is a saying in the East that there is one illness for which there is no remedy, and that illness is called *Vahm*, which means imagination. In every illness the imagination plays its rôle. The greater the imagination, the greater becomes that illness. But apart from illness, in every little thing in life imagination makes mischief, exaggerates it, and makes it more difficult to bear. It is not seldom but often that one sees a person feeling tired before he has worked, at the very thought of the work. When working, that tiredness which was imagined before increases still more and before the work is finished the person is exhausted. One will often see that the head of a factory is more tired after two hours' work than the workman who has perhaps worked all day long with the engines; a superintendent of a garden becomes much more tired than the gardener who has been working on the soil all day long. Often a person in the audience becomes much more tired than the singer who has sung the whole programme of the evening. And before having walked so many miles a person may have become tired at the thought of it. Imagination always leads, illness follows.

Imagination is an automatic working of the mind. One can train imagination by training thought. We must make thoughts out of imaginations. There comes a development of mind which shows itself just like the muscular development of the physical body, for each muscle is distinct when a person exercises his body; and so every thought becomes distinct and clear before it is expressed. In that way imagination is developed and trained.

There is no doubt that he who has control over his imagination can master himself and can rise above illness. It always amused me, when seeing a lady who used to give lectures, that when the lecture was still about fifteen days ahead she began to be worried; and as the worry came, then some illness followed, doctors came to examine her, and so it went on. When the day of the lecture came the lady was quite finished. Healers had to see her, occultists had to advise her, astrologers had to make her horoscope in order to tell her she would be successful in her lecture, before she would be ready to go and deliver it. This is not rare; very often one finds that one exaggerates tiredness, confusion, pain, and trouble, and makes a mountain out of a molehill without knowing it. If that person were told, he would not accept it, would not admit it, yet at the same time it is so. Out of a hundred persons, sufferers from a certain illness, you will find ninety-nine who could be cured if their imagination allowed them to be cured.

With children pain increases with imagination, and therefore the one who understands this can stop the pain of a child more quickly than by any medicine, for the child is responsive to suggestion. A grown-up person who holds his imagination in

hand and does not let it loose, is difficult to help, but a child
can be helped in a moment. A child may be crying in pain, and
in a moment's time, if you can get its imagination away from it,
you can cure it. A fear of illness comes upon many even before
they have felt the pain, if a physician has told them that there
is something wrong with them. The physician may be mistaken,
yet the fear of the pain that is anticipated takes the place of the
disease. With the mentally deranged imagination is the main
reason at the back of their illness.

This does not mean that one should overlook the illness of
a child. That is another thing. One should neither overlook the
illness of a child nor the complaint one has oneself, for it is not
always imagination. But at the same time imagination plays a
great rôle, and it is better for a person to analyse to what extent
imagination plays a part in his complaint. And he may analyse
it by trying to forget his pain, to forget it entirely, by trying to
deny facts which stand before him as an evidence of illness.
When a person is able to do so to that extent, then he will be
able to realize how much of it is illness and how much imagination. He will also observe this phenomenon: that as soon as he
withdraws his imagination from his illness, he starves his illness
of the food which maintains it; and it is possible that by this
starvation illness will die. One must not overlook children's illnesses, but at the same time one must not exaggerate, one must
not think too much about it; because imagination has a living
effect, imagination can create an illness in a person who has not
really got one; and it would be a great mistake on the part of
the parents to worry over children's health when it is not necessary.

The body comprises a nervous system which is the main
mechanism of one's physical body; and this mechanism is much
more responsive to imagination than is flesh, bone, or skin. The
nerves instantly respond to the thought, not skin, flesh, or bone;
these only partake of the influence coming from the nerves. The
nervous system stands between the physical and mental aspects
of being. Therefore, just as imagination can cause an illness and
can maintain an illness, so imagination can also cure a person
of illness. Once illness is cured by imagination, what is left of

that illness in the body has no sustenance upon which to exist and therefore it naturally dies out. I have often made an experiment with a person who said he had got a very bad headache. I have asked him to sing, and in the end he found that he was cured. Anything that takes the mind away from the imagination of the illness cuts down the props that support that illness; then the illness cannot stand on its feet. There must be something to hold it, and that is imagination.

Self-pity is the worst enemy of man. Although sometimes it gives a tender sensation in the heart to say, 'Oh, how poorly I am', and it is soothing to hear from someone, 'Oh, I am so sorry you are not well', yet I should think that one would prefer if another thing were said in sympathy, namely, 'I am so happy to see you are so well'. In order to create that tender sensation one need not be ill; what is needed is to be thankful. We can never be too thankful. If we can appreciate the privileges of life there are endless gifts from above which we never think about and we never value. If we think of them thankfully, naturally a tenderness is felt; and it is that tenderness which is worth having.

The animal is more responsive to nature than man, and nature helps the animal to forget its illness more than it does man, because man is not responsive to nature. Every man has his little world; it may be so little sometimes that it is like a doll's house; and in that world he lives. He is not conscious of the wide world, he is not conscious of the universe; he just lives in his small world; that is all he knows, that is all he is conscious of, that is all he is interested in. And, therefore, if his world is full of misery and illness and ill-luck, he cannot get out of it, because he has made a kind of shell, as creatures in the water make a shell to live in. The world does not hold misery for him; he has made the shell of misery for himself and he likes to hide in that shell. Because he has made it he likes to live in it, it is his home, be it a shell of wickedness, of misery, of goodness, of piety, or anything else.

Because of outward evidences, a person very often builds up concentration on an illness, for no doubt there are outer signs of illness; but the mind has such a great power that if there is one sign of illness, the mind sees a thousand signs of illness. For instance, as soon as you begin to think that your friend is displeased with you, everything he does, either good or bad, seems to you to have gone all wrong; and if you think your friend is loving and kind to you, all that he does seems to support your thought.

When a person begins to think he is under an unlucky star, with everything that happens, good or bad, he will think, 'It all brings bad luck to me. From everywhere bad luck seems to be coming.' Even a good thing that person will believe to be bad, because he is looking at it in that way. And when a person is living in the thought that good luck is coming to him, everything that comes is in the form of good luck.

The more we study this question, the more we find that our mind is the master of life; and we become the possessor of the Kingdom of God as soon as we have realized the power of thought and concentration upon our life. It is because of the absence of such knowledge that one does not value that divine spark which is in oneself; and by being unconscious of it one goes down and down, till one reaches the deepest depths. No sooner has one realized this than one begins to respect oneself; and it is the self-respecting person who has respect for another, it is the one who helps himself who will help another, it is the one who can raise himself who will take another person also towards the heights. Once we have found the remedy to cure this disease which comes from the imagination, then there is no other disease which we cannot manage to get above; we only have to realize the source of perfection within ourselves.

xii

A regular life, pure diet, good sleep, a balance between activity and repose, and right breathing, all these help one to health; but the best remedy for healing oneself of all illnesses and infirmities of mind is belief. Many think that they believe, but there are very few who really believe. The belief of many is as I heard someone say, 'I believe, may God strengthen my belief.' It is an affirmation which has no meaning. If a person says, 'I believe', that does not mean that he believes, for belief in its perfection becomes faith. And what does Christ say about faith? He says, 'Faith removes mountains.' No doubt the priest speaks of faith in the Church, the clergyman of faith in the Book; but that is not the real meaning of faith. Faith is the culmination of belief, and when faith is attained to a certain degree it will grow as a plant. When belief is complete it turns into faith. Cure is brought about by faith in all cases, whether it be a sudden cure or whatever may be the nature and character of the case. Faith speeds the condition; so great as the faith is, so quick the time of healing. Without faith even medicine cannot help. No treatment can give good results where faith is lacking. Faith is the first remedy; everything else comes afterwards. All our failures, sorrows, disappointments, difficulties in life are caused by our lack of belief. Illness means lack of belief. Beyond and above all other evidences illness is the sign of the lack of belief; if one believed, there would certainly be no place for illness. But illness takes the place of belief. One cannot disbelieve in what one believes. Illness becomes one's belief; that is where the difficulty comes in. When a person says, 'I am fighting against my illness', that means, 'My imagination is fighting against my belief.' He affirms, 'I am fighting against my illness', which means he establishes illness in himself. He fights against something which he affirms to be existing. In his belief he gives the first place to the illness; the second place in his belief he gives to the imagination of curing it. Thus the power with which he wishes to remove his illness is much smaller than the power which is already established in him by illness. He fights against something which he affirms to be existing.

There are people who think that they will never fall into such an error as believing in something for which there is no evidence, and they think this is very clever. And when we search in the world of evidences, we shall find one deluding cover under another. And so one can go on, probing the depths of life, from one illusion to another, never arriving at the realization of truth. How can you rely upon evidences which are subject to change? Therefore if there is anything to rely upon it is belief. It is not evidence which gives one belief; and if evidence gives belief, that belief will not last, for evidences are not lasting.

It is that belief which stands above evidence which in the end will culminate in faith. It is people like Bayazid, whom many would consider 'in the clouds', who prove in their lives what belief means. Bayazid was going on pilgrimage to Mecca. A dervish was sitting by the way on his journey. Wanting to pay homage to a spiritual man, he went to that dervish and sat down to receive his blessing. The dervish asked him, 'Where are you going?' He said, 'I am going to Mecca.' 'On business?' He was astonished. 'No, on a pilgrimage.' 'On a pilgrimage? What do they do on the pilgrimage?' Bayazid replied, 'They walk around the holy stone of Ka'ba.' The dervish said, 'You do not need to go so far for that pilgrimage. If you will make circles round me and go back your pilgrimage is done.' Bayazid said, 'Yes, I believe this.' He circled around the man and went back home; and when people asked, 'Did you make a pilgrimage to the Ka'ba?' he said, 'Yes, I made a pilgrimage to a living Ka'ba.'

Belief is not an imagination, belief is a miracle in itself, for belief is creative. For instance a person certainly believes that he can get so many centimes for a franc, and everyone believes it, because there is evidence. He has not far to go for the evidence. He has only to go to the bank to find out. But belief is difficult when there is no evidence. It is just like building a castle in the air, but then that castle becomes paradise. If one believes in what does not exist, the belief will make it exist; if there is a condition that one believes in, even if that condition does not exist, it will be produced. The difference between the mind of the believer and the mind of the unbeliever is this, that the mind of the believer is like a torch and the mind of the unbeliever is like a light which is covered by something which does not allow it to spread its light.

Very often a man is afraid of losing his common sense. He would rather be ordinary than become extraordinary. He is afraid of losing himself, but he does not know that losing himself means gaining himself. A person may say, 'To think about these things is like moving in the air.' But if we were not in the air what would become of us? Air is the substance on which we live, more important for us than the food we eat and the water we drink. Belief, therefore, is the food of the believer;

it is the sustenance of his faith. It is on belief that he lives, not on food and water.

Faith is so sacred that it cannot be imparted, it must be discovered within oneself; but there is no one in the world who is without faith, it is only covered up. And what covers it? A kind of pessimistic outlook on life. There are people who are pessimistic outwardly, there are others who are pessimistic unconsciously, they themselves do not know that they are pessimistic. Man can fight with the whole world, but he cannot fight with his own self, he cannot break his own doubts; and the one who can disperse these clouds has accomplished a great thing in the world.

Is faith attainable by perseverance in belief? Things of heaven cannot be attained by perseverance, they are the grace of God. No perseverance is required to ask for the grace of God, to believe in the grace of God, and to open oneself for the grace of God, to trust in it. It is this which strengthens belief into faith. Everything belonging to the earth costs us more or less, we purchase it; there is only one thing which does not cost anything, because we can never pay its price, and that is the grace of God. We cannot pay for it in any form, in any way, by our goodness, by our piety, by our great qualities, merits or virtues, nothing. For what does our goodness amount to? Our lifelong goodness is nothing more than a drop of water compared with the sea. We as human beings are too poor to pay for the grace of God in order to purchase it; it is only given to us.

For God is love. What do we expect from love? Grace. The grace of God is the love of God, love of God manifesting in innumerable blessings, blessings which are known and unknown to us. Human beings live on earth in their shells, mostly unaware of all the privileges of life, and therefore ungrateful to the Giver of them. In order to see the grace of God one must open one's eyes, raising one's head from the little world that one makes around oneself, and thus see above and below, right and left, before and behind, the grace of God reaching one from everywhere in abundance. If one tries to thank, one might thank for thousands of years and it would never be enough. But if one looks in one's own little shell one does not find the grace of

God; what one finds is miseries, troubles, difficulties, injustice, hard-heartedness, coldness of the world, all ugliness from everywhere. Because when a person looks down he sees mud, but when he looks up there are beautiful stars and planets. It only depends which way one looks, upwards or downwards. What is this mortal world? What is this physical existence? What is this life of changes? If it were not for belief, what use is it all? Something which is changing, something which is not reliable, something which is liable to destruction. Therefore it is not only for the sake of truth, but for life itself that one must find belief in oneself, develop it, nurture it, allow it to grow every moment of one's life, that it may culminate in faith. It is that faith which is the mystery of life, the secret of salvation.

PART II

HEALING

CHAPTER I

THE MAIN ASPECTS OF HEALING

Balance

HEALTH depends upon the balance between activity and repose in the five senses: sight, smell, hearing, taste, and touch; and every sense, in the normal condition of health, must be able to express itself and to respond. The senses need more time for repose than for activity. Therefore the mystics go into seclusion in order to give a chance of repose to the senses, which are different in every man. Everyone passes every moment of his waking state in activity of the senses, partly by intention, partly involuntarily. For instance, the eyes look at things intentionally perhaps a hundred times a day, but nine hundred times they look at things without intention. This shows a waste of energy in an average man's life.

In order to develop healing power one must regulate and control the senses by regulating their activity and repose; and this, done with a spiritual thought, converts power of mind into divine power. A person can heal with power of mind alone, but the results will be limited; but a person with divine power can obtain through it unlimited results.

It depends on the condition of the health how much activity one can stand and how much repose is necessary; a general rule cannot be made for everyone. A normal amount of activity stimulates and strengthens the body. Therefore physical exercises are given for physical development, and exercises of concentration and studies are given for the development and repose of the mind. According to psychic law the day is natural for activity and the night for repose, and when this is not carried out it naturally works against health. It is not necessary to rest after every little exertion, but a degree of balance ought to be maintained; and it is advisable in life to take repose without allowing it to develop into laziness.

Breath

Breath is the principal and essential power that can help in healing. There is a silent healing, and a healing by focusing the glance, by holding the painful part with the fingers, by rubbing it, by waving the hand over the painful part, by touching and by not touching it; but behind these different ways there is one power working, and that is the power of the breath. This power can be developed by breathing practices, and when the breath is so developed that it creates an atmosphere around the healer, then the very presence of the healer heals. The power of the breath can be developed by physical exercises, by rhythmic exercises of the breath, by pure living and by concentration.

The power of healing is greater than the power of the channels one uses to heal, such as the finger-tips or eyes. The eyes have more power than the finger-tips. They are finer, and the power that manifests through them is radiant, while it is not so radiant in the finger-tips. But besides the power of healing one must have a clear idea of how to recognize the complaint of another person and of the best way to heal him.

Healing with the Finger-tips

Hygiene is the first subject to consider in healing with the tips of the fingers. Hands that have been engaged in any work or that are stained with any liquid must be washed for healing. The healer must first observe the hygienic rules of keeping his body, as well as his clothes, pure and clean; especially at the time of healing he must be absolutely free from all that is unhygienic. The sleeves, at the time of healing, must be rolled back, and the finger-nails must be clean and properly trimmed. After healing one should wave the hand, as it were shaking it, to shake off any fine atoms, or even vibrations, so that a poison taken from the painful part of the patient may not be given to the patient again.

There are cases in which the sensation of the body is deadened by the pain, and the pain has gone into the depth of the affected part of the body. In such cases waving the hand or touching is not enough, rubbing is necessary. When dealing with the effects of poison from the sting of a bee or scorpion, or from snake-bite or the bite of any other poisonous animal, a simple soft touch or stroking of the affected part is indicated; if the pain is more intense touch is not necessary, simply the waving of the hand close to the affected part. In the case of the bite of a mad dog one should put some lime mixed with water on a copper coin and tie it on the part that the teeth have touched, and the rest of the affected part must be healed by touching and stroking it with the tips of the fingers. Bites of mosquitoes and midges may be cured by applying butter that has been boiled and allowed to cool, and then waving the hand over the affected part. Rosewater may be used for bites of all kinds, in cases of severe inflammation.

The Tracing of Disease

The healer's work in tracing disease is subtler than healing; for in healing power is necessary, but in tracing the disease—its nature, its cause, its secret—psychic power is of no use, there inspiration is needed; and a healer without this is an incomplete healer. The patient generally does not know the real cause, nature, and secret of his complaint. He is not supposed to know; for the patient knows the effect of the poison, not its cause, nature, and secret. The healer must trace the patient's complaint from his face, expression, voice, work, and movement; everything tells. Sometimes the healer must find out the cause by asking the patient the details about his pain and the circumstances of his life, and by knowing the attitude and the inclination of the patient.

The secret of disease can be traced also by observing what a person desires in the way of food and clothing, and in what environments he prefers to be, what attitude he has towards his friends and foes, his choice of sweet and savoury and his attraction to colours. For instance a person with a complaint that originates from melancholy will have a liking for purple; a person who has lost control over his passions will show an inclination towards passion, and he will generally like red; a person who is lifeless, who has an inclination to emptiness, will have a tendency towards white; a person who has gone through a sorrow and mourned over things and weakened his heart by it, will have an inclination towards black.

So it is with sweet and savoury: the patient who shows an inclination for sweet shows weakness of heart, and by that general weakness; and the patient who shows inclination towards savoury lacks circulation.

There are many things in the patient that one can perceive not only from his inclinations but by noticing his face and features; for in this way one reads more than by any other method. The features tell his general characteristics, and therefore a person knows the weakness that may have been the origin of his complaint, and the general expression shows the thought behind it. Since mind is the cause of all causes, the healer gets at the root of the complaint as soon as he touches the mind of the patient. How true is the saying, man's face is the mirror of his heart.

The Chief Reason of Every Disease

According to the mystical point of view there is one chief root, which can be called a common cause, from which all diseases are derived, and that is disorder of rhythm. The upset of the nerves is stated by scientists to be the chief origin of all mental diseases, and their effect upon the body produces various diseases in the body. Religious people teach concentration and meditation, sitting in a prayerful attitude. The wisdom behind all this is to bring the activity of mind and body to a normal condition. For it is the nature of activity to become more active every moment; it is the activity itself that produces energy, and the consequence is that by so producing energy, its own strength throws it out of its normal rhythm.

This one can see in the burning of the fire. The activity is little at the start; but with every moment that it burns its activity increases and culminates in the end in its utmost speed. And the speed of the beginning compared with the speed of the end will prove that it is the increase of speed of the fire which has brought about the climax, when it consumes itself. In human nature we see the same tendency. When speaking one is inclined to speak more and more quickly, until the speed is so increased that one leaves out several words of the sentence without any intention of doing so. So it is in walking; the pace increases with every step until a person finds himself almost running. So it is with the imagination, and sometimes one sees the same thing with the pulsation of the body and the circulation of the blood. Uncontrolled increase of speed, in all its aspects, hastens the climax, and when unbalanced culminates in disastrous results.

A healer without this knowledge is a blind healer who does not know the cause of diseases; his healing is a chance; but the one who knows this is more than a physician and more than a healer. He will control his own activity, and the power of control thus gained will enable him to control the activity of others, in order to keep it normal, in which is the true health of mind and body.

The Reason for Tiredness

Tiredness is due to three causes: loss of energy which is the chief reason, and besides this excess of activity of mind and of body. One generally knows tiredness to be caused by excess of bodily activity, but one is apt to overlook the fact that excess of activity of mind also causes tiredness.

The activities that specially cause tiredness are worry, fear, anxiety, and pain. There is, however, one mental cause that is less obvious, and that is the thought of being tired. Among a hundred cases of tired people you will find ninety cases of this particular kind of tiredness. When a person thinks, 'I am tired', the very thought creates the feeling of tiredness in support of the thought, and reason brings forward a thousand reasons that seem to have caused the tiredness. There are some who think that the presence of people or of some people, or the presence of a particular person, tires them; some think that their energy, their life, is eaten up by some people; some think that a particular action takes away their energy; some think that their strength is taken out of them by their everyday duty in life or the work they happen to do, such as singing, speaking, doing bodily or mental work; and of course, as they think so they experience.

In truth, there is no doubt that every kind of activity must take away some energy, more or less. But by one's thought one increases the loss; by preserving the energy and using it economically one saves it to a great extent. And there is one way, which is a spiritual way, in which one can give out energy with every activity that necessitates one's giving it out, yet at the same time one can absorb much more energy than one loses, from the life within, without, around, and about one. It is for this reason that religion has given the conception of God being almighty. Those who consider Him to be far away in heaven keep away from Him, but those who realize the meaning of the teaching in the Bible that 'we live and move and have our being in God', feel Him at all times by their side. If consciousness of wealth makes one feel rich, and if consciousness of strength makes one feel strong, how much stronger and richer should he feel who is really God-conscious!

Balance

A healer often finds patients whose complaints may differ and yet may have originated in lack of balance. Balance is the most difficult thing in life to keep for anybody and everybody. Many times a healer succeeds in curing a patient by just showing him some practices by which he can attain balance. This, besides healing, brings about a most desirable effect. Balance is gained in different ways, even in ordinary actions such as sitting, lying, standing, and walking; standing with even weight on both legs, sitting cross-legged, or on one's heels, both carrying an equal part of the weight of the body; also kneeling, walking rhythmically with an even force given to the swing of both arms. By regularity of eating and drinking, working and resting, sleeping and rising, one gets balance too. The first thing a healer should consider when treating a patient is that he must give him balance.

Pain

Pain has two origins: the mind and the body. Sometimes it is caused by the mind and held by the body, and sometimes it is

caused by the body and held by the mind. If one were absent
or did not partake of the pain suggested by the other part of the
being, the pain would not exist, or if it existed it would vanish.
The body being the servant of the mind, can never refuse to
bear the pain given by the mind, having no free will of its own;
it is only the mind that could refuse, if it were trained to do so.

The doctrine that some people hold that there is no such thing
as pain, is very helpful in the training of the mind, although its
truth may be questioned. If it is true that there is no such thing
as pain, it can only be true in the sense that everything in this
world is an illusion, it has no existence of its own, it does not
exist in reality, compared with the ultimate reality that is. But
when a person says that it is only pain which does not exist, but
that joy exists and all other things exist, then he is wrong.

Among Sufis dervishes have tried to become pain-proof by
inflicting upon themselves cruel injuries, such as whipping the
bare arms or cutting the muscles of the body, or piercing the
body with knives, or taking the eyes out of their sockets and
replacing them in their sockets again, which I have seen myself.
By this they have discovered a truth and have given it to the
thinking world: that the mind can refuse to partake of the
bodily pain, and by so doing the bodily pain is felt much less
than it would otherwise be. When the mind goes forward to
receive bodily pain, out of fear or self-pity, it increases the pain
and makes it much more than it would otherwise be. The proportion that fear or self-pity add to the pain is ninety-five per
cent. And the first thing that the healer must do in curing
patients suffering from pain, is to erase the pain from the surface
of the patient's mind by suggestion and also by his healing
power. In the absence of support on the part of the mind, the
body must give up pain, for it has no power to hold it any
longer without the mind.

Healing by Medicine

Very often it happens that a healer or a believer in healing
goes to such an extreme that he does not accept healing by medicine. In reality the thought of being given medicine by a doctor

and the thought of repeating the treatment he has prescribed so many times a day, apart from its medicinal influence, is psychically helpful; and the healers of the East, considering this, have to a certain extent played the part of a physician also. With their healing power, spiritual, psychic, and magnetic, with their hypnotic suggestion and with their mesmeric influence, they gave the patient something to eat or to drink in the form of medicine. Sometimes they gave a charm to keep by him and sometimes magnetized water.

The idea is that man is more conscious of the objective world and its activity than of any other plane of existence, and by eating or drinking, or by holding or possessing a certain thing the impression upon him becomes more real. The thought of the healer, which should ease the mind, is often hindered when the external senses of the patient are not fully responsive to it; but when the patient eats or drinks something, or tastes something, or feels something applied to or touching the painful part, the senses become the medium for the healer's thought to reach the mind of the patient. Knowledge of the physical medium is most essential for a healer, for every psychic operation requires a medium, and through a distinct and responsive medium every psychical work meets with success.

CHAPTER II

THE PSYCHOLOGICAL NATURE OF DISEASES

Causes of Diseases

THE PSYCHOLOGICAL nature of diseases can be explained in a few words as being the lack of life, either because of insufficient matter in the body, or because of excess of matter which leaves no scope for the spirit; it is also the impression of pain which the mind holds. Pain is not always physical. There are physical causes; but as soon as the mind knows of discomfort, out of fear it holds it; and this is called pain.

Disease is often caused by lack of rhythm, be it in thought or feeling, in the breath, in action, or in one's everyday life. For instance, to stay up in the night when one is accustomed to sleep, to change the dinner-hour, to take a nap when one is not accustomed to, to do anything that one is not accustomed to do, puts one out of rhythm. People who are accustomed to be angry or to quarrel would become ill if they were not allowed to do that. There is a story told in India that a person who could not keep any secret was compelled to keep quiet; in the end he became ill, and the doctor had to cure him by permitting him to let it out. All this signifies rhythm; every habit forms a rhythm.

The fear of catching a disease is also a cause of illness. There are people who wonder if they are ill, and try to find out if there is something wrong with them. There are some who enjoy self-pity or the sympathy of others; these invite disease. Some entertain disease when they are to a certain extent unwell. They wish to be treated like a patient, or try to take to a lazy life. By so doing, the mind naturally holds the disease longer, since it is allowed to do so.

There are many other causes of illness. Among them the most unfortunate is the impression: 'I have got an illness that can never be cured', for this impression is worse than a disease. In reality the soul of every individual, healthy or ill, is pure from any pain or disease, and it constantly heals mind and body, and if it were not for the mind and body, which create illness, a person would always be well. It is natural to be healthy; and all illness, pain, and discomfort are unnatural.

Magnetic Power

The health of both mind and body depends upon a magnetic power which may be called in metaphysical terms the power of affinity in elements and in atoms. It may be pictured as scattered grains of rice united by being attracted to one another; and it is this power which attracted them and shaped them into a certain form. Both mind and body are made of atoms; the former of mental atoms, the latter of physical atoms; and the power that gathered them and made them into one body or one mind is the magnetic power.

Lack of this power causes all pain, discomfort, and disease, while development of this power secures health of body and mind. By physical practices this power is developed in the body, and by mental exercises the same power is improved in the mind. It is generally found that the ill lose their magnetism to a certain extent. A healthy person often seeks to escape from the presence of the sick. It is natural, because it is magnetism in a person to which mankind is attracted, and it is its lack which causes repulsion. This also explains the reason for the attraction of youth and childhood, although in childhood this magnetism is not fully developed. The lack of this is felt in age for the same reason.

In Sufi terms this magnetism is called *Quwwat-e-Maknatis*; and it springs from every atom, physical or mental. It may be called strength or energy. It is a wealth; and just as one person can enjoy wealth for a longer time if he is careful with it, and another may spend it thoughtlessly following his fancies, so does a man do with this magnetism. Either he attracts others or he is attracted to others. In one case he is better off, in the other case he loses. Man, of whatever evolution, whatever disposition, in whatever condition of life, needs this magnetism more than anything else; for health, which is the greatest of all gifts in life, depends greatly on magnetism.

Breathing

In Sanskrit breath is called *Prana*, which means life. This prana not only gives life to oneself but it gives life to another person too. Sometimes the presence of someone fills you with life, and sometimes the presence of another so to speak takes away your life from you. One feels tired and depressed and eaten up by the presence of one person, and another person's presence gives added strength, life, and vigour. This is all accounted for by the breath. The one who has more life gives life, while the one who has less life takes it from the one who has more. But there is a contrary process too. Sometimes the stronger one takes away what little life is left in the weaker one, and sometimes the weaker one gives out his life to the stronger one. A person who takes away life in fact absorbs the life from another. In the presence of that person even flowers fade sooner and plants die.

Many deaths occur and many lives are retained by the phenomena of the breath. Therefore for the healer there is no greater source of healing. He can throw his breath upon the affected part of the patient as easily as he can cast his glance upon a painful part. Even eatables and objects that a healer's breath has magnetized carry with them the power of healing. If touch makes certain finger-marks through perspiration upon a thing, why should not the breath, the very essence of life, live in an object and give the object some greater part of life, producing in it an effect which may be a greater cure than medicine?

When the breath is developed and purified it is not necessary for the healer even to make an effort to throw his breath upon the patient, but the atmosphere that his breath creates, the very presence of the healer brings about a cure, for the whole atmosphere becomes charged with magnetism.

Insanity

There are no doubt many physical causes of various aspects of insanity, but a keen study of the subject will prove that insanity is mostly due to mental causes. Some lack of balance caused by the intensity or excess of a certain thought and feeling is found to be at the root of every cause of insanity. The physician fails to cure such cases, especially he who traces the cause of insanity in its outer manifestations and in the physical body. Every cause has an external effect, and yet it is a mistake to take the effect for the cause. It is not generally medicine or even surgical operations or any external applications that can be of great use. It is more the work of a healer than of a physician to cure insanity.

Like every disease, insanity could easily be cured in its earlier stage, and it is again the work of the healer to recognize the signs of insanity in their primary state; for mostly such signs are not noticed in a person, or they are passed over as 'something funny' or 'queer'. The first step towards healing insanity is to get at the root of the complaint by association with the subject;

and as soon as the root of the complaint is touched a great relief is brought, even before healing. Naturally, insanity being a mental disease, thought-power alone is the remedy for it.

Loss of memory, confusion, puzzlement, instantaneous temper and passion, all these are signs of the beginning of insanity. Insanity is inherited from the family, but it can also be traced in several weaknesses and vices, among which drink and fondness for drugs, unnatural habits, too much worry, anxiety, and allowing melancholy thoughts to develop in the nature; these are all things that cause insanity.

The work of the healer is first to detect the primary indication of insanity, and that is loss of memory. It is caused by weakness of the mind. The mind has not sufficient power to bring forward the thought entrusted to it at the command of the will. It is this which may be called loss of memory, and it must be healed and cured in its very beginning. The primary stage is marked by an extreme activity of mind which results in extreme thoughtless anger or passion; then when its spell is passed repentance comes. This should be avoided at its beginning. Guilty conscience, fear of consequences, doubting tendencies, all such things are like fuel to the fire of insanity. A pure, thankful, useful life, a constant thought of appreciating things and avoiding blaming things and people and conditions, all these help to keep away the germ of insanity.

Spirit

There is a part of one's life which can only be called life; there is no other name appropriate for it, and the English phrase, 'to pull oneself together', means to set that part of life to work. It might be called spirit, as this part in itself is both intelligence and power. It is intelligence because any part of the body and mind or every part of both in which it dwells, it makes sensitive; and it is powerful because whatever part of the body and mind it touches, it strengthens that part.

In games and sports, when people jump down from a great height, what is it that protects them from hurt? It is this spirit, and they have made it their habit to call this spirit to their aid.

When people throw balls to each other, and even in boxing, the receiver of the blow awakens this spirit in that part on which he receives the blow. The sportsman does not know what this spirit is, though he takes refuge in it. The mystic understands it by his meditation, also by research into metaphysics. When a person awakes from a deep sleep, the first thing that rises through his mind to his body, when the tendency of stretching and contracting comes and of twisting and turning, and of gradually opening the eyes, is this spirit; it rises, so to speak, and spreads.

By the mastery of this spirit diseases are cured, age is mastered, even death is conquered. When this spirit is lacking, energy is lacking, intelligence, joy, and rest are lacking, and when there is this spirit there is hope, there is joy, there is rest; because the nature of this spirit is to hold intact the body of atoms and vibrations. Comfort lies in its being held, discomfort when that spirit is not sufficient to hold the body intact. Thus it is the lack of this spirit that is the cause of a great many diseases. By the development of this spirit in himself the healer can give a part of his spirit to another, and that becomes the best source of healing.

The Origin of Diseases

Almost every disease originates in the mind, even when one catches infectious diseases. It does not mean that it must always be wickedness of the mind; if it were so good people would never be ill; and yet it cannot be overlooked that it is a weakness of the mind, in some way or other, that allows the disease to enter. Besides this, negligence, oversight, irregularity, mental and physical, also cause diseases. Life and death are two forces, constructive and destructive, and there is continual fighting between these two forces. There are times when one power wins, and the success of that power means either better health or disease and death. The body must be ready and fit to fight this battle; but the mind has a still greater part to perform, and when the mind fails to perform its part the body with all its fitness is incapable of retaining health. But if the mind is capable of keeping health, the body to a great extent obeys it. Still, harmony of both mind and body is needed to fight the battle of life.

The Effects of Food

It is the secret of nature that life lives upon life, as all carnivorous animals live on the flesh of other animals, and sometimes on their own kind. This shows that life sustains its body by the same element of which it is made. Man's body is made of the food he eats, and it is according to the life in the food he eats that his life develops. Little insects which live on flowers create the beauty of the flower in their body. Insects that are fed on leaves sometimes become green and beautiful like a leaf, but insects living in the earth and in dirt have a similar body. This teaches that man's body depends upon the food he eats. Any decay in the vegetables he eats and any disease in the animal whose flesh he uses, all have their effect on man's health.

Brahmins, who have been the most scientific and philosophical people in the world, have always considered this subject; and one always finds in the race of Brahmins intelligent and superior minds. In the West, although there is continual scientific discovery and discussion on hygienic life, important things in regard to food are overlooked, and this can be explained in a few words as due to the lack of home-life. Many have to take their food in public places where it is impossible for special consideration to be given in this way. There are, moreover, differences in the animal foods one eats. Some animals are clean, others unclean; and their flesh differs accordingly. This has a great influence on the health and the mind of a person.

The question as to what the mind has to do with bodily food may be answered thus, that as an alcoholic drink has an effect on the mind, so every atom of food even has a particular effect. There are foods of three kinds: Sattwa which gives nourishment with calm and peace; Rajas which gives stimulus to work and move about; and Tammas which gives sleep, laziness, and confusion.

A healer must become aware of all kinds of foods and their effects so as to prescribe for the patient, and to see whether the food is the cause of the illness, which is so in many cases, and to keep himself in such a condition that he may be able to heal successfully.

Self-control

There are many people who may be said to be of nervous temperament; who have a tendency if they walk to walk quickly, if they work to work hurriedly, if they talk to talk fast, so fast that they may drop words and make the hearer confused; whose temper may rise suddenly and who are inclined to laugh or to cry easily. This condition in a way gives a kind of joy, but it weakens a person and takes away his self-control, and in the end this results in nervous diseases. It begins as indulgence in activity and ends in weakness. Many mental diseases are caused by this negative state of mind and body. From childhood there is an inclination to this, especially among children of nervous temperament; and if it can be checked at that time there is a sure result. No disease can be worse than an increasing weakness of the nerves, which is lack of self-control; for life is not worth living when control over the self is lost.

Man's Being

Man is not only constituted of matter in his being but also of spirit. However well built a body he may have with its mechanism in good working order, there is still something that is wanting in him. For the physical body is sustained by material food and drink, breath by the air, mind by thoughts and imaginations and impressions; but that is not all, there is something besides mind and body that man possesses in his being, and that is his spirit, which is light, a divine light. It is for this reason that sunshine makes one feel bright; but it is not only sunshine that is needed for the spirit. Man's soul is like a planet; and as the planet is illuminated by the sun, so man's spirit is illuminated by the light of God. In the absence of this, however healthy and joyful a man may look, he is not really healthy. He must have some spiritual touch, some opening in his heart which will let the light come in, the light of God.

CHAPTER III

THE DEVELOPMENT OF HEALING POWER

The Breath

THE BREATH is the principal power needed in healing. All the various manifestations of the magnetic current which come from the tips of the fingers, from the glance, and from the pores of the skin are indirect manifestations of the breath. It is the strength of breath which gives magnetic power in all its different aspects. Weakness of breath causes weakness of mind and body, and strength of breath is strength to both. One cannot lack energy and magnetism if one's breath is full of energy. Therefore before developing any other means of healing the power of the breath should first be developed.

There are two ways of developing the power of the breath: one way is to make it extensive, and the other way is to make it intensive. After that the breath should be mastered so that it can be directed to any desired part of one's own body; and secondly, it should be mastered so that it may be directed to any side, level, upward, downward, to the right or to the left. Just as one becomes master of aim when one is able to hit the target at any point, so one must master the breath.

There are Yogis in India who can put out a light at some distance by the power of the breath; and even the miracle of Tansen, who is said to have lighted candles by the power of his song when he sang the Dipak, can be nothing else but the power of breath in its fullest development.

Purification

Science has always admitted, and values every day more highly, the importance of cleanliness around the patient and on the part of the physician; and things of different kinds have been used as disinfectants in many cases of disease. The healer, who has to do more with the mind, must, therefore, realize how very important it is to consider purity of mind as well as of body for the purpose. No doubt it is difficult after learning the nature of things to say which is pure and which is impure; but one way of understanding it is that everything in itself is pure, and when another element is mixed with it, then its purity is polluted. Deep thought in this direction would open a vast field to a thinker.

Another way of understanding the pure and impure is that there is one thing alone that keeps things pure, and that is life, and when the life is gone out of them they are impure. There is a third way of looking at it: that death is impurity of things, but destruction is their purity. This also opens a vast scope of understanding to an observant student of life.

In short, it is necessary for a healer to observe the laws of hygienic life and to keep himself from taking the germs of disease from the patients he heals. Besides, he should avoid all thoughts of bitterness, ill-will, wrath, anger, jealousy, purify his mind from all spite or malice, and bathe so to speak in devotion to God, so that his heart may become saturated with mercy and compassion. It is not only the power of mind that heals, but the purity of mind. The mind free from all crookedness, deceit, treachery, is alone capable of emitting power, strong and pure in its nature, which can give to a patient a new life and relieve him from all pain.

Rhythm

The development of healing power depends upon the development of the breath. The breath can be developed by purification, by extension, by expansion, and by rhythm.

There are three different kinds of rhythm in the breath: the rhythm which cannot be distinguished in the continuation of inhalation and exhalation; the rhythm that can be distinguished by the two distinct swings of inhaling and exhaling; and evenness in breathing. Those who have not mastered their breath are under the influence of these three rhythms, their health, their mood, and their condition in life; but those who master the breath, can put their breath in any of these rhythms; and when mastery is acquired then the healer has the key to wind any clock. In reality every disease means something wrong with the rhythm. As a doctor says congestion is the root of diseases, so to a Sufi congestion means lack of rhythm; it may be in the circulation, in breathing, in activity, or in repose. A physician in order to find a disease examines the pulse, the beats of the heart, and the condition of the lungs. This itself is the proof that rhythm is the keeper of health, and when there is something wrong with the health the rhythm in some way or other has gone wrong, as when the tick of the clock gets out of rhythm the clock goes too fast or too slow, and it does not give the proper time.

The healer, therefore, must get his rhythm right, so that he can control the mechanism of another person's body. In India there is a custom of clapping the hands or snapping the fingers when somebody is yawning. The idea is that yawning is the sign of the falling of the rhythm, it is the rhythm of one's body that falls to a slower rate when one feels inclined to sleep, and the clapping of the hands and the snapping of the fingers set the pulsation of the other person in the same rhythm as before. It is just like shaking a person who is nodding, to bring the mechanism of his body into proper working order. When the healer is capable of regulating his own rhythm he becomes capable also of making another person's rhythm regular. It requires great knowledge and inspiration concerning the nature of the human mind and body; and the healer who knows how to work with it is like the conductor with the orchestra. The health of everyone that he heals he keeps regular, as the conductor keeps the rhythm of every musician who plays in the orchestra.

The Power of the Breath

It is the power of the breath which heals body and mind, since breath is life, and through the breath life can be imparted to the mind and body of another person. The breath is also a cord that runs through human beings, connecting them in one life. If it were not for the breath the senses would never have perceived the external world. Therefore all that one sees, smells, feels, tastes, and hears is through the channel of the breath, and therefore no medicine can have such influence on a patient as the breath. Weak breath is susceptible to all contagious diseases, and a healer with weak breath could get the disease from his patient in one healing; that is why power of breath is the most essential thing before one should attempt to heal.

Power of breath can be developed in two ways: volume and length, which make it intensive and extensive. It is dangerous to try healing before one is fully sure of the power of the breath in both ways. The development of the power of the breath is felt, and one knows when one is ready to use it in healing.

One Common Cause of All Diseases

All pain, discomfort, disease, decay, and destruction of every sort are lack of life. The word life which we use in everyday language is the name of the result of two activities working harmoniously: one, the constant life of the spirit; the other the life that matter provides for it. This is a negative and positive activity. It is the power of inner life which attracts outer life to it, and again it is the strength of external life by which it clings to the inner life. In this way the reciprocal action of both keeps the flame of life burning, and the lack of either of these activities is the cause of disease.

There are five bodies through which the soul experiences life, the physical body being the poorest of all, for it is born of matter, fed with matter, attracted to matter, finds its life in matter, and returns to matter. As it demands matter for its sustenance, so matter demands it in the end; this demand is called disease or death when this body loses its strength; and this is caused by the loss of energy of the nerves, which so to speak pull together and keep the flesh, bone, blood, and skin not only intact, but active and vigorous. It is the weakening of these nerves by exhaustion or by lack of sustenance, by lack of rest or by loss of energy in whatever manner, which is the cause of all disease.

Thus healing may be called life-giving to that part that needs life or to the body as a whole. The materialist believes that a person, however weak, can be saved and brought to life by injecting into his body the blood of another. If that is a successful remedy, how much more could the power of thought, of life, which has more power than matter, produce life in another! And even the fine essence of the healer's physical body may be passed through gases by the process of earth rising to water, water to fire, fire to air, air to ether, and sending the finest atoms of physical energy and strengthening vibrations of mental energy to a person who needs it. The difference between medicine and healing is this: instead of sending a thing by railway it is sent through the sky by an aeroplane.

One may ask if it is worth while weakening oneself by giving part of one's life to another. No doubt it would not do for a poor person to give his last penny to one who is starving, but it is the only thing for a rich man to do, to make use of his riches for the comfort and happiness of those who are in need. A spiritual healer is rich with divine strength, and his power will not be lessened if he gives it out. Therefore material healing is a failure. However successful it may seem, it is powerless compared with spiritual healing, because the spiritual healer has the power of God on his side.

Development of Power in the Finger-tips

The human form may be called materialized light, the symbol of which in mysticism is the five-pointed star, suggesting the head, arms, and feet, which make five points. The nature of light is to spread its rays, and as the human form is made of light —Nur—the hands and the feet, the fingers and the toes, the organs of the senses and the hair all represent rays. It is the knowledge of this light that one sees in the Eastern customs of blessing with the tips of the fingers on the head; and of kissing the hand or touching the feet, for the fingers and toes are the source of the radiance.

The healer, therefore, develops the power of the finger-tips. As by directing the breath in a certain way through the body and mouth one can produce a certain pitch on a certain note, so by directing the energy through the finger-tips and by developing the magnetic power of the finger-tips one develops the power of healing. Moses is known to have possessed a light in his palm, which the poets call *Yad-e-baiza**; and Zoroaster is always pictured with burning fire in his hand. Both suggest the radiance, the battery that can be developed in the human hand. When the power is developed in the palm it pours out from the tips of the fingers and it shoots out when it is directed by the will. Then by magnetic passes and by touch on the painful part the healer is able to cure diseases.

The Power of the Presence

It must be understood by a healer that his very presence must emit healing power, and in order to do this the healer must have an overflowing life, power, and magnetism. In the first place the body must be healthy, clean, and pure, so that physical magnetism may be beneficial; also purity of mind is necessary, together with sympathy for the patient and a desire to cure him instead of profiting by his cure. The soul speaks most in the form of the atmosphere; in other words, the atmosphere tells what the soul says. The development of the soul is brought about by a spiritual process and spiritual life. Therefore the development of the mind, of the body, and of the soul is necessary in order to possess a healing power and presence.

The Power of the Mind

The power of concentration is the first thing necessary to develop healing power. The healer must be able to hold steadily the thought for the cure of his patient whenever he requires. Concentration is most difficult, but if this is accomplished, there is nothing that one cannot accomplish. It is useless to try and cure the patient by any process, however successful and good it may be, if there is no power of concentration. The work of the mind in healing is much greater than in anything else, for it is using the power of the mind on matter; and matter, which has been a disobedient slave of the spirit for ages, through the mineral, through the vegetable, and even through the animal kingdom always rebels against being controlled.

* Baiza means egg; the palm is egg-shaped.

No doubt mind can control matter and do with it whatever it likes, but when mind is enfeebled by serving matter, it loses power over matter. If it were not so, every man would cure himself by controlling matter and there would be no need of a healer. One's own power has a greater influence on oneself than the power of another; besides no one can feel so much sympathy for another as one can for oneself. The nature of the mind is to slip from one's grip. Concentration is the practice which enables the mind—which, so to speak, strengthens its own fingers—to hold fast whatever it can hold. Another secret of the mind is that even with the power of concentration the mind does not hold anything that is not interesting, and it is sympathy in the mind which is the stimulus to the holding power of the mind. Therefore no one can be a successful healer unless his sympathy comes forward with its hands extended to raise the patient from his pain.

The Power of Concentration

Before a person attempts to heal another he must develop in himself the power of concentration. The concentration of a healer should be so developed that not only when sitting in meditation and closing his eyes can he visualize the desired object, but that even with his eyes open he should be able to hold fast the picture that his mind has created in spite of anything that may be before his eyes. In healing it is necessary to know what picture one should hold in one's mind. If the healer should happen to hold the picture of a wound, he would help the wound to continue instead of being healed; and so if he thought of pain it might perhaps be continued more intensely by the help of his thought. It is the cure that he should hold in mind; it is the desired thing that he must think about, not the condition. In all aspects of life this rule must be remembered; that even in trouble one must not think of the trouble and in illness one must forget about illness. Man often continues life's miseries by giving thought to them. The healer must from beginning to end hold the thought of cure and of nothing else.

Sending Power to a Distance

The greater development in healing power is to be able to send power to a distance. No land nor sea can prevent power being sent by the mind. Scientific discoveries such as wireless telegraphy prove that by means of instruments thoughts can be sent to a distance, but the mystic has always realized and practised to a great extent the sending of thought to a distance. As the whole idea of a mystic is to serve humanity by love and goodness, he naturally does not feel inclined either to prove to the world the greatness of his power or to utilize his power for any worldly end except for healing.

The Hindu metaphysical term Nada Brahma, meaning sound-God, explains the secret of life, that sound is motion and therefore nothing takes place unless first moved by some force behind. As for external action a physical movement is necessary, so for a mental action the motion must be caused by one's mind. The voice of one person may reach to the other corner of the room, and the voice of another may reach to the other end of the street, and so it is with the power of the mind. As it is necessary to develop the power of the voice by practice, so it is necessary to develop and practise the power of the mind, but it should be remembered that the gift of healing is always necessary. A gifted person may progress much further and more quickly than a person without the gift.

There are three things necessary in sending thought to a distance: first, faith in the theory; second, self-confidence, meaning confidence in one's own power; third, the power of concentration. However great the power of concentration may be, without self-confidence it is of no use; and self-confidence without faith in the theory is powerless. Healing at a distance is the last stage at which a healer arrives after long experience in healing, and attempting this at the beginning would naturally result in failure. Work gives experience, and experience gives confidence; and faith becomes firm when it is built by experience and strengthened by confidence.

CHAPTER IV

THE APPLICATION OF HEALING POWER

Healing by Charms

THERE is a great power hidden in the mystery of the repetition of a sacred word, but there is a still greater power in writing a sacred word; because the time taken to write a sacred word carefully is perhaps five times or ten times as long as the time taken to repeat a sacred word. Besides, action completes the thought-power better than speech. In writing a sacred name it is the completing of a thought which is even more powerful than uttering the word. But when a person thinks, feels, speaks, and writes, he has developed the thought through four stages and made it powerful. Sufis, therefore, give a charm to the faithful who they think believe in the healing power of the charm. They call it *Taviz*. The patient keeps it with him night and day, and links his thought with the thought of the healer, and feels at every moment that he is being healed.

In India they put a charm in a silver or gold plate, or keep a charm engraved upon stone or metal; and the very fact of realizing that he possesses something in the form of a charm that has a healing influence upon him becomes such a help to the believer that he feels that every moment of the day and night he has the healer with him, and that he is being healed.

As a gift is nothing without the giver, so a charm is nothing without a personality that gives confidence to the patient. Therefore a charm written by an ordinary person has no effect; the personality of the person who writes the charm should be impressive, his piety, his spirituality, his love, his kindness, should all help to make the charm that he gives valuable and effective.

Magnetized Water

Water is the most responsive substance; it partakes of the colour and effect of everything. The magnetism that runs through the finger-tips enters into everything that a healer holds in his hands, and thus water can be charged with that electricity more than any other substance. Again, the breath that heals is powerful enough to produce an added life in all life-giving substances. Water especially, which is a most invigorating substance, partakes of life from the breath.

Among the ancient Hindus there was a custom of giving water as a benediction to guests, which is observed even now. A Brahmin will as a rule first offer water to his guest which means not only to quench the thirst, but is like giving life to the guest. The Persians have called the water of life *Ab-e Hayat*, and in many verses one finds this word. Among Sufis everywhere in the East there is a custom that the Shaikh gives a loaf of bread or a glass of water, milk, syrup, or buttermilk, or a fruit or some sweet, which is accepted as something that heals both mind and body. No doubt it is not only the effect of the breath or touch, it has also the power of mind with it, which is hidden as a soul in the substance which is its body.

Healing by Breathing

A healer must know in the first place that breath is the very life, that breath is the giver of life, and that breath is the bringer of life. One can live without food for some time, but one cannot live without breath even for a few minutes. This shows that the sustenance that breath brings to man's life is much greater and much more important than any nourishment upon earth. Every atom of man's body is radiant; but if the body is the flame, the breath is the fire, and as the flame belongs to the fire, so the body belongs to the breath. As long as breath dwells in it, it lives, and when breath leaves it, it is dead, for all its beauty, strength, and complicated mechanism. That is why the effect of the breath of a holy person can magnetize water, bread, milk, or wine, fruit or flower.

The breath that is developed spiritually will have a healing effect upon any painful part that it falls upon. If one knows how to direct the breath there is no better process than healing with breath; and in all the different methods of healing breath is the main thing, since in breath is hidden the current of life.

Healing by Magnetic Passes

All scriptures have explained in some way or other that life is like light. In the Moslem scripture the word *Nur* is used; in the Vedanta it is called *Chaitanya*. The nature of this light is to express itself in a particular direction, and that accounts for the face and back in our forms. At the same time the tendency of the light is to spread. This can be seen in the tendency of fire or of water to spread; air shows the same tendency, and also earth and all things on earth. A deep study of every form will show that the nature of life is to spread in four directions, for instance north, south, east, and west, or head, foot, right, and left.

Life and light have their centre in the centre of every form, but express themselves through the directions in which they spread. Therefore the power of the hand has been shown in ancient symbology. Hindus have pictured the divine incarnations with four hands; this means two hands of the mind and two hands of the body, and that when four hands work together the work is fully accomplished. This shows that in healing the hands are most important. The physical hands are needed to help the hands of the mind, and when thought is directed from the mind through the hand its power becomes double and its expression fuller.

Every atom of man's being, mental or physical, is radiant and throws its rays outward; these are life itself and give life. All illness is lack of life; and it needs life to be cured. The power of electricity has been discovered by the scientist, and he believes that it cures diseases when it is used for that purpose, but the mystic has discovered ages ago the power of this hidden electricity, the life of the mind and the life of the body, and he believes and knows that its application in healing is most beneficial. There are sores and wounds and painful parts which are too tender to touch. In such cases healing by magnetic passes, in other words by waving the hands over the affected part and so allowing thought to heal, brings about a successful cure.

Healing by Touch

Every atom in man's body is in reality radiant, living and powerful compared with other objects, herbs, or drugs. By the very fact of being a living body, besides being the finest and most perfect compared with other living bodies, it has a great power. Therefore, shaking hands, speaking to a person and touching him have a certain effect. In India when a wrestler goes to a wrestling match and when he comes back his teacher pats him on the back, saying, 'Shabaz, Bravo!' This actually gives him added strength and courage and power which otherwise he would not have had. People speaking in friendship, and even disputing and arguing, hold each other's hands, which brings about a better understanding. A mother takes away the discomfort and restlessness of the child in one moment by patting it. Therefore massage is helpful when there is pain, and yet it is a poor treatment when compared with the healing treatment; for the healer operates the power of the mind through his fingers, as a musician produces his feelings on the violin. Is it everybody that can produce on the violin the same tone that an expert could? It is not the placing of the finger on a certain place on the instrument; it is the feeling of the musician's heart manifesting through his finger-tips that produces a living tone. So it is with the touch of a spiritual healer.

Healing by Glance

The eye is the most wonderful and powerful factor in the body, which conveys to another pleasure or displeasure, joy or sorrow, love or hatred, without a word being spoken. This shows that the eye is the most responsive instrument for the mind to express thought and feeling. Sometimes in an assembly two people just look at each other and there is agreement between them, and two people may stare at each other and it may have a worse effect than shooting; this again proves that both fire and water can manifest either to destroy or to inspire. To a healer, therefore, there is no better means than the eyes to send his thought of healing; and there is no better means of receiving this thought in the patient than his eyes. The healer can send the healing power through his glance to the painful part of the body, but it is more helpful still when he sends his power direct to the eyes of the patient. As there is a link between the mind and the eyes of the healer who sends the power, so there is a link between the eyes and the mind of the patient who receives it. Medicine can touch the physical body, but thought can touch the mind, where the root of every disease often is; and a suggestion that a powerful healer gives to his patient reaches his heart and destroys the germ of disease.

The eyes of every person are not capable of healing. It is the penetrating glance and stillness of the eyes, then the power of the glance and ability to aim, that are necessary. These are developed by certain exercises, though some eyes have a natural ability for this purpose. Also, concentration of mind which gives power is necessary in healing, for power of mind directed by the glance brings about a successful result.

Healing by Suggestion

There are five elements that constitute man's being: earth, water, fire, air, and ether. Air represents the voice, and it reaches the ether, which means that the voice reaches farther than anything else in the world. It touches the depths of man's heart. Therefore music is a living miracle. There is nothing that can thrill man's being through and through as sound can. This explains why suggestion is much greater and more beneficial in healing than any other remedy.

In India, where the daily life of the people is based upon psychical laws, they take great care in speaking to another person that it may not produce a bad ·effect upon his physical, mental, or spiritual self. A healer, who by the power of Zikr develops the healing power of his voice, impresses his word with the power of his heart on the heart of the patient.

The healer must be sincere in his suggestions, because all the power lies in his sincerity; he must also be self-confident; he must have psychic power developed in him; but beyond and above all he must be a good man, so that at the time no thought

of humiliation or of any sort of uneasiness should come to him.
His thoughts, feelings, and actions should be satisfactory to his
conscience; if not, any discomfort, dissatisfaction, fear, or repentance weakens his power. Then he is no longer capable of
healing, however learned and powerful he may be. When the
healer thinks he is healing, his power is as small as a drop; when
he thinks God is healing, and when owing to this thought his
own self is forgotten and he is only conscious of the self of God,
then his power becomes as large as the ocean.

Healing by Presence

There is warmth in fire, and there is a greater warmth in feeling. The presence of a person with warm feelings can create an
atmosphere of warmth, and the presence of the cold-hearted
can freeze one. No doubt warmth of heart is not the only quality
the healer needs, he must have the power to heal, besides concentration and a desire to heal; but at the same time it is the
name of Christ that is known as that of the Messiah. Messiah in
the East means healer, and for a Messiah the power of love is
the first quality, love in the form of sympathy. One sympathizes
with another, thinking perhaps, 'He is my relation, friend, or
acquaintance', but when sympathy develops to its fullest extent
one begins to see in everybody 'I', 'myself', and the pain of
everybody one begins to feel as one's own pain.

This is a sign of a true Messiah. How can he heal the wounds
of the hearts of the children of the earth and relieve them from
pains and sufferings, since life is full of them, when his sympathy
is not awakened to such a degree that he feels the pain of another even before feeling his own pain? Every healer who has
a spiritual aspiration must develop a spark of the fire of the
heart of the Messiah; and then even before trying to heal a person his very presence will heal. When a child is ill the mother
approaches it with the wish that it may be well, with a pain in
her heart for the suffering of her child. From that moment she
becomes a healer, her touch, her word, her glance do more than
medicine or any other remedy. When this mother quality is
developed in the heart of the healer, then, when he heals not for

any return except the happiness of seeing a soul released from pain, he becomes a healer who can heal merely by his presence.

Healing by Prayer

Prayer is a wonderful means of healing oneself and another, for concentration alone, without the thought of God, is powerless; it is the divine ideal which strengthens the healing power, which gives it a living spirit. Therefore a spiritual healer has more hope of success than a material healer. For the material healer directs his own thought; however powerful it may be it is limited by his own personality; but the spiritual healer who in the thought of God and His divine power forgets himself, has much greater success than the former. It does not matter what form of prayer one uses, sincere prayer in every form will bring a fruitful result.

Prayer is in reality the contemplation of God's presence, who is the power and origin of the whole creation; and it is considering oneself as nothing before Him, and placing the wish which stands before one's personality before the Almighty. Therefore naturally the result must be incomparably greater, though it depends upon the contemplation of every individual.

In the first place, he who prays for the cure of another must surely be blessed, because goodwill and love, from which his prayer rises, of necessity bring a blessing to him. Also prayer for one's own cure is not selfish, it is making oneself a fitting instrument to be more useful in the scheme of life. On the other hand, neglect of one's own health very often is a crime. Praying to God in thought is perhaps better than in speech, but it must be remembered that speech makes it concrete; therefore thought with speech makes prayer more effective than thought alone. Words without thought are vain repetitions.

Absent Healing

When a healer has practised healing for a certain time successfully, then the next step in the line of healing is to heal a patient from a distance. The method of absent healing is totally different from healing in the presence. In absent healing the power of thought alone is necessary, and those who are accustomed to use the magnetism through the tips of the fingers, through the eyes, through touch, find it difficult to direct their thought-power without an external channel. Also when the patient is not present, in the first place the beginner wonders whether his thought-power will reach the patient, and it is also difficult to hold in one's thought a patient who is not present.

The mastery of Fikr helps a healer to hold the thought of the patient before his mind, and it is Fikr that helps to heal a patient from a distance. Breath, so to speak, is an electric current that can be attached anywhere; distance makes no difference. A current of breath so established puts the ethereal waves in space into motion, and according to the healer's magnetic power the space between the healer and the patient becomes filled with a running current of healing power. There is no doubt that spiritual evolution is the first thing necessary; without this the mind power of a healer, however strong, is too feeble for the purpose.

By spiritual development is meant God-consciousness. There is a believer in God who may be called pious, but it is the God-conscious who become spiritual. It is the belief and realization that, 'I do not exist, but God', which gives power to the healer to heal from a distance; also it is this realization that gives him the belief that his thought can reach to any distance, because the knowledge of the all-pervading God gives him the realization that the Absolute is life in itself, and that even space, which means nothing to the average person, is everything; in fact, it is the very life of all things.

CHAPTER V

VARIOUS METHODS OF HEALING

The Origin of Healing

CONSCIOUSLY or unconsciously every being is capable of healing himself or others. This instinct is inborn in insects, birds, and beasts, as well as in man. All these find their own medicine and heal themselves and each other in various ways. In ancient days the doctors and healers learned much from animals about the treatment of disease. This shows that natural intuition has manifested in the lower creation as well as in the higher. The scientists of today should not, therefore, claim with pride that they are the inventors of chemical remedies, but should humbly bow their heads in prayer, seeing that each atom of this universe, conscious of its sickness, procures for itself from within or without a means for its restoration. In other words, medicines were not discovered by physicians, but were intuitively found in creation as the necessity for them arose.

The excess of man's artificial remedies has had the effect of increasing disease. This is also mainly due to the modern artificial ways of life, so different from the natural living of the ancients which is ridiculed today by so-called civilization. Today the luxuries and needs of life are obtained at the sacrifice of true health and comfort.

Healing without drugs and medicines is the most natural method, although the absolute neglect of them is inadvisable. There are cases in which surgical instruments are also permissible but only when absolutely necessary. If horses can move wagons, why should engines be used? In the same way if a disease can be cured with a simple remedy the mental power should not be wasted, for it may be used in a more serious case. If every malady were to be healed mentally then why were all drugs and herbs created? On the other hand diseases which will yield more easily to mental treatment should not be left entirely to material remedies, for their root must first be healed. So many patients recover temporarily by the help of medicine but again become sick, and in such cases healing is especially needed. It is much to be deplored that in the present age such important work as healing has been undertaken by people who are often most materially minded and do not understand its psychology, making it a profession and thus bringing discredit upon it.

Self-healing is more desirable than healing by others; the former strengthens the will, the latter weakens it. Many people think that hypnotic and psychic power alone can heal; but they do not realize how the healer must first heal himself by the practice of the strictest morality from the lowest to the highest phase of his existence. He must purify himself by *Iman*, or faith. Then only can he claim to be a healer.

There are five kinds of disease caused by various disorders on different planes of existence. Some diseases on the physical plane are contracted from without, while others spring from within. There are several supposed causes, but in reality the true cause of disease is weakness, while the cause of health is strength. This does not mean physical weakness or strength only, but strength and weakness on all planes of existence. Activity causes what is called life, while the reverse brings about death, the former causes circulation and the latter congestion. Circulation gives health, while congestion causes disease.

The scientists of today are giving electric treatment as a comparatively new discovery, and it is claimed that it is the most beneficial of all remedies. Healing is also electric treatment, and has been given throughout the different planes of life for ages. Every being has a natural gift of healing in a greater or lesser degree, but it may be developed. The physical and mental faculties should be opened in such a way that the electric vibrations on the various planes of existence are enabled to operate. Physical vibrations depend upon the purity and energy of the body, and they can be projected through the finer parts of the body such as the palms of the hands, the tips of the fingers, the soles of the feet, the cheek, the forehead, the ear, the lips, nose, and eyes. The finest of all these is the eye; it is much more useful than all the other organs, for it is through the eyes that the electric rays can be emitted. The nose has also an important part to perform, it being the very channel of breath. The ears can work when the healer is spiritually advanced, and the vibrations can also pass through the tips of the fingers.

The Oriental custom of placing the eyes upon the holy hands or feet of the sage is not only expressive of humility, but it has a still greater meaning. It signifies the healing by the holy hands or feet which illuminate the devotee. The sages who bless these aspiring souls by placing their hands upon the head, inspire them by sending forth the rays of their power through the finger-tips. In kissing the hands or feet of the Holy Ones the Orientals have the same object in view. In the same way the caress of the mother heals the child of all its pains and soothes it to sleep. Courage and consolation are given to another by placing the hands on his shoulders, the vibrations in this action give new life and courage.

Physical Healing

A patient can only be healed if he has sufficient faith in the power of healing and confidence in the healer. In the case of self-healing, self-confidence and the power of breath and concentration are most necessary. There is a well-known story that Shams-e Tabrèz, the Shiva of Persia, was once most respectfully entreated by the priests of the day to awaken the crown prince, who had just died, from his last long sleep. The Shah, his father, issued a decree that if there was any truth at all in religion his only son must be restored to life by prayer, otherwise all the mosques would be destroyed and the mullahs be put to the sword. In order to save many lives Shams-e Tabrèz complied with their request and sought the dead body of the prince. He first said to the body of the prince, 'Kun ba Ismi Allah' (Awake at the call of God). The dead body did not move. He then, under the spell of ecstasy, exclaimed, 'Kun ba Ismi" (Awake at my command). At this suggestion the prince immediately arose. The story goes on to relate that this abrupt command, although it restored the prince to life, brought the charge that he had claimed to be God against Shams-e Tabrèz, and according to the religious law, he was condemned to be flayed alive. He gladly submitted to this punishment in order to keep religion intact, as it is the only means of elevating the multitude.

By this we understand that Shams-e Tabrèz in his first suggestion to the dead spoke conventionally, entreating God as a third person, which had not the slightest effect on the dead body; but in his next command he lost his individual self from his consciousness and felt himself to be the whole Being of God. This story makes it clear that the healer must be confident of his at-oneness with God, and during the time of healing he should most assuredly feel the power of the Almighty working through him, thus absolutely losing the thought of his individual self.

The electric battery which heals is charged in three ways: by controlling the breath, by strengthening the will, and by absorbing the electricity of the sphere.

In order to make use of this healing battery it is most essential that the eyes should be made to work so that they project the electricity. They must be first cured of their nervousness, that ever moving condition to which they are addicted from birth. The eyes are naturally weakened and made tired by allowing them to respond from morning to night, to every attraction which invites their attention. The healer, in order to make use of them for healing, first trains them to be steady.

The electricity can be absorbed by striking with the fingers the finer vibrations in space; and it can be discharged in the same way by slowly passing the tips of the fingers through the space above the affected part of the patient's body. Sometimes passing the fingers closer to the body, and sometimes slightly touching the affected part is helpful. It depends upon the intensity of pain suffered by the patient and the amount of electricity required. It is very necessary that each time the fingers have passed over the affected part they should be shaken in order to disperse the poisons collected there; in other words the poisonous germs collected on the fingers should be thrown away. It is advisable to shake the fingers over a fire so that the germs may not be left on the floor, and also to have incense burning in the room. Some healers, in order to protect the fingers, make use of peacock feathers, which sweep away all such germs.

The healer can test his healing power by feeling the electric current running through his fingers as he shakes them. A healer even when playing an instrument can heal the listeners with his music. If a healer gives a gift with a good wish it brings good luck, and if he writes a word it becomes a charm, a healer in itself which heals the possessor and keeps him free from death and disaster.

Mental Healing

Mental healing is performed by suggestion. In most cases the parents are the first healers, for they convey their thought to the child by the knitting of the brow or by looking at him fixedly. Even animals can be trained in the same way.

There are many diseases of the human mind produced by self-consciousness. They develop unconsciously, and are such as love of praise and flattery, intolerance of insult, irritability, infatuation, jealousy, anger, passion, and greed, besides the craving for alcohol and drugs. In order to cure such diseases the healer must have great control over himself, or his own shortcomings may keep the patient back. The Holy Prophet was once requested by an aged woman to speak to her son, who spent all his daily wage on dates, leaving her penniless. The Prophet promised to do so after five weeks' interval. On the appointed day the boy was brought before the Prophet, who spoke to him very kindly, saying, 'You are such a sensible lad that you ought to remember that your mother has endured much suffering for your sake, sacrificing all her wages in order to bring you up; and now she is so old and you are in a position to support her, and you are squandering your money on dates. Is this just or right? I hope by the grace and mercy of Allah you will give up this habit.' The boy listened very attentively and profited by what he heard. But the disciples of the Prophet wondered, and asked why the reproof was delayed for thirty-five days. The Holy Prophet explained, saying, 'I myself am fond of dates, and I felt that I had no right to advise the lad to abstain from them until I had myself refrained from eating them for five weeks.' The healer of character should never for a single moment try to heal another of weaknesses to which he is himself addicted.

Spiritual Healing

Spiritual healing is still higher in its nature than either of the former methods. It can be performed by a single being as well as by a group of people. In this case the heart of the healer can send forth its feelings and vibrations, and in accordance with their intensity the subject is healed. In absent spiritual healing the desire spreads forth its rays and reaches the patient wherever he may be, curing him without the presence of the healer. The concentration of several people united together works still more wonderfully.

The power of the healer depends upon the warmth of his heart. Devotees by their power of concentration, by their purity of life, and by their divine love become wonderful healers; their every tear and sigh become a source of healing for themselves and those around them. Devotion is the fire in which all infirmities are consumed, and the devotee becomes illuminated within himself; and the joy of the devotee and his pain cannot possibly be compared with any other joy in life. Spiritual healing does not require the fixed gaze, the touch of the fingers, or the power of breath, but Tawajoh (a kind glance), or Do'a (a good thought) of the spiritual healer serves the purpose.

Abstract Healing

In abstract healing the soul, heart, and body are healed of all diseases and weaknesses therein. This healing is only possible during the ecstasy of the healer. The strong psychical vibrations which run through the pores of his body from his inner self naturally pierce through the bodies, hearts, and souls of all around him, who receive them in accordance with their power of receptivity. Murshids have frequently inspired their mureeds without reading or discussing, and such mureeds have reached perfection. It is a wonderful phenomenon which an exceptional mureed once in a while experiences under the guidance of his Murshid.

There is a story told of Hafiz Shirazi, who, together with ten other Hafiz, was being trained under the same Murshid. A certain time was set apart for their meditation and other practices, and a certain time for food and sleep. Hafiz Shirazi kept awake during the night in rapt contemplation of Allah. After years of patient waiting, one evening the Murshid in ecstasy called for Hafiz. The wakeful Hafiz was the only one who heard, and he answered the call and was blessed by the Murshid, who chose this ideal time to inspire all his mureeds. Each time he called for Hafiz the same Hafiz answered the call, all the others being asleep. So the wakeful one received an elevenfold blessing, his own and that of the ten others who lost this precious opportunity by their sleep. And Hafiz became the greatest spiritual healer of his time, whose every word, from that day to this, has been powerful to heal.

MENTAL PURIFICATION

CONTENTS

CHAPTER I

MENTAL PURIFICATION

INASMUCH as it is necessary to cleanse and purify the body, so necessary, or perhaps even more necessary, is it that the mind be cleansed and purified. All impurity causes diseases as well as irregularity in the working of the physical system. The same applies to the mind. There are impurities belonging to the mind which may cause different diseases, and by cleansing the mind one helps to create health both in body and mind. By health I mean the natural condition. And what is spirituality but to be natural?

Very few think like this. So many people think that to be spiritual means to be able to work wonders, to be able to see strange things, wonderful phenomena; and very few know how simple it is, that to be spiritual means to be natural.

Mental purification can be done in three different ways. The first way is the stilling of the mind, because it is very often the activity of the mind which produces impurities. The stilling of the mind removes impurities from it; it is like tuning the mind to its natural pitch. The mind can be likened to a pool of water: when the water in the pool is undisturbed, the reflection is clear; and so it is with the mind. If the mind is disturbed, one does not receive intuition, inspiration, clearly in it. Once the mind is still it takes a clear reflection, as the pool of water does when the water in the pool is still.

This condition is brought about by the practice of physical repose. By sitting in a certain posture a certain effect is created. Mystics in their science know of different ways of sitting in silence, and each way has a certain significance. And it is not only an imaginary significance; it produces a definite result. I have had, both personally and through other persons, many experiences of how a certain way of sitting changes the attitude of mind. And the ancient people knew this, and they found different ways for different persons to sit. There was the warrior's way, the student's way, the way of the meditative person, the way of the business man, of the labourer, of the lawyer, of the judge, of the inventor. Imagine, how wonderful that the mystic should have found this out and have had the experience of it for thousands of years—the great effect that sitting in a certain posture has on a person and especially on his mind.

We experience it in our everyday life, but we do not think about it. We happen to sit in a certain way and we feel restless; and we happen to sit in another way and we feel peaceful. A certain position makes us feel inspired, and another way of sitting makes us feel unenergetic, without enthusiasm. By stilling the mind with the help of a certain posture, one is able to purify it.

The second way of purifying the mind is by the way of breathing. It is very interesting for an Eastern person to see how sometimes in the West, in their inventions, people unconsciously apply the principles of the mystical realms. They have got a machine which sweeps carpets while sucking up the dust. This is the same system inside out: the proper way of breathing sucks up the dust from the mind and ejects it. The scientist goes so far as to say that a person exhales carbon dioxide; the bad gases are thrown out of the body by exhaling. The mystic goes further, saying it is not only from the body, but from the mind also. If one knew how to remove impurities, one could remove more than one would imagine. Impurities of mind can be thrown out by the right way of breathing; that is why mystics combine breathing with posture. Posture helps the stilling of mind, breathing helps the cleansing of mind; these two go together.

The third way of purifying the mind is by attitude; by the right attitude towards life. That is the moral way and the royal road to purification. A person may breathe and sit in silence in a thousand postures, but if he does not have the right attitude towards life, he will never develop; that is the principal thing. But the question is, what is the right attitude? The right attitude depends on how favourably one regards one's own shortcomings. Very often one is ready to defend oneself for one's faults and errors, and is willing to make one's wrong right. But one has not that attitude towards others. One takes them to task when it comes to judging them. It is so easy to disapprove of others! It is so easy to take a step further and to dislike others, and not at all difficult to take a step further still and to hate others. And when one is acting in this manner, one does not think one does any wrong. Although it is a condition which develops within, one only sees it without; all the badness which accumulates within, one sees in another person. Therefore man is always in an illusion; he is always pleased with himself and always blaming others. And the extraordinary thing is, that it is the most blameworthy who blames most. But it is expressed better the other way round: because one blames most, one becomes most blameworthy.

There is beauty of form, of colour, of line, of manner, of character. In some persons beauty is lacking, in other persons there is more of it; it is only the comparison that makes us think that one person is better than the other. If we did not compare, then every person would be good; it is the comparison which makes us consider one thing more beautiful than another. But if we looked more carefully we should see the beauty that is in that other one too. Very often our comparison is not right for the very reason that although today we determine in our mind what is good and beautiful, we are liable to change that conception in a month's, a year's time. That shows us that when we look at something, we are capable of appreciating it if its beauty manifests to our view.

There is nothing to be surprised at when one person arrives at the stage where he says, 'Everything I see in this world, I love it all in spite of all pains and struggles and difficulties; it is all worth while'; but another says, 'It is all miserable, life is ugly; there is no speck of beauty in this world.' Each is right from his point of view. They are both sincere. But they differ because they look at it differently. Each of these persons has his reason to approve of life or to disapprove of it. Only, the one benefits himself by the vision of beauty and the other loses by not appreciating it, by not seeing the beauty in it.

By a wrong attitude, therefore, a person accumulates in his mind undesirable impressions coming from people, since no one in this world is perfect. Everyone has a side which can be criticized and wants repairing. When one looks at that side, one accumulates impressions which make one more and more imperfect because they collect imperfection; and then that becomes one's world. And when the mind has become a sponge full of undesirable impressions, then what is emitted from it is undesirable also. No one can speak ill of another without making it his own; because the one speaking ill of others is ill himself.

Thus the purification of the mind, from a moral point of view, should be learned in one's everyday life; by trying to consider things sympathetically, favourably, by looking at others as one looks at oneself, by putting oneself in their position instead of accusing others on seeing their infirmities. Souls on earth are born imperfect and show imperfection, and from this they develop naturally, coming to perfection. If all were perfect, there would have been no purpose in their creation. And manifestation has taken place so that every being here may rise from imperfection towards perfection. That is the object and joy of life and for that this world was created. And if we expected every person to be perfect and conditions to be perfect, then there would be no joy in living and no purpose in coming here.

Purification of the mind therefore means to purify it from all undesirable impressions; not only of the shortcomings of others, but one must arrive at that stage where one forgets one's own shortcomings. I have seen righteous people who have accused themselves of their errors until they became error themselves. Concentrating all the time on error means engraving the error upon the mind. The best principle is to forget others and to forget ourselves and to set our minds upon accumulating all that is good and beautiful.

There is a very significant occupation among the street boys in India. They take the earth from a certain place and they have a way of finding in that earth some metal such as gold or silver, and all day long their hands are in the dust. But looking for what? Looking for gold and silver.

When in this world of imperfection we seek for all that is good and beautiful, there are many chances of disappointment.

But at the same time if we keep on looking for it, not looking at the dust but looking for the gold, we shall find it. And once we begin to find it we shall find more and more. There comes a time in the life of a man when he can see some good in the worst man in the world. And when he has reached that point, though the good were covered with a thousand covers, he would put his hand on what is good, because he looks for good and attracts what is good.

CHAPTER II

THE PURE MIND

THE PURE mind does not create phenomena but is a phenomenon itself.

A man who wanted a certain bracket for his room did not know where to go in the city to find it. But he had a definite idea in his mind of what it should be like, and as soon as he went out the first shop that his eyes fell upon had that bracket in it. Perhaps throughout the whole city he could not have found another, but his mind brought him straight to the object he desired. What does this come from? It comes from purity of mind.

Mind can be likened to water. Even to look at a stream of pure water running in all its purity is the greatest joy one can have, and drinking the pure water is so too. And so it is with the mind. Contact with the pure-minded is the greatest joy, whether they speak with one or not; there emanates from them a purity, a natural purity, which is not man-made but belongs to the soul and gives one the greatest pleasure and joy. There are others who have learnt to speak and entertain, and their manner is polish, their wit exaggeration, and their speech is artificial. What does it all amount to? If there is no purity of mind, nothing else can give that exquisite joy for which every soul yearns.

There is a saying that a pure-minded person very often seems too good to live and appears to be devoid of common sense; that very often the pure-minded seem not to belong to this world. It is true; but it is not the fault of the pure-minded; it is the fault of the wicked world. That world has gone from bad to worse. Anyone who shows purity of mind begins by being an outcast and appears to be incapable of doing whatever he may attempt. But what does it matter? One can just as well be pure-minded and wise at the same time. The pure-minded can also work in worldly matters as thoroughly, as capably as a worldly man; and the one without the pure mind may be able to make a success in the world, but not an everlasting success.

When we come to the question of success and failure, there is no principle upon which this is based. It is not true that one must be good and honest and pure-minded in order to make a success. Very often the opposite is more true. But at the same time one cannot say that one has to be the opposite in order to be successful. Very often dishonesty and lack of purity of mind bring great failure upon one. If there be any rule pertaining to this, that rule is that the success of the one who achieves it through honesty and through goodness, depends upon honesty and goodness. And the one who makes a success of something without honesty and goodness will have a failure the day he is honest and good. It is because their paths are different. The whole attitude of mind acts upon one's life's affairs; it is most wonderful to watch. The more you think about it, the more it will prove to you that success and failure absolutely depend upon the attitude of mind.

I was very interested in what a friend who was a salesman in a big firm of jewellers once told me. He used to come to me to talk philosophy. He said, 'It is very strange, I have seen so often on arriving at a house where I thought they were able to pay more than the actual price of things, that I was tempted to ask a much higher price than what I knew the value to be; but every time I gave in to this temptation, I did not succeed. And again I was encouraged to do the same when I saw my fellow-salesmen selling a stone to someone who took a fancy to it for a price perhaps four times its value. Why did they succeed and why do I not succeed?' I told him, 'Your way is different, their way is different. They can succeed by dishonesty; you can succeed by honesty. If you take their path you will not succeed.'

Thus sometimes he who is busy developing mentally by mental purification may have to undergo small sacrifices, minor failures. But these are only a process towards something really substantial, really worth while. If he is not discouraged by a little failure, he will certainly come to a stage when success will be his. Purity of mind sets free springs of inspiration which otherwise are kept closed. And it is through inspiration that one enjoys and appreciates all that is beautiful, and creates all that is good for the joy and pleasure of others.

Once I visited the studio of a painter who had died. I sat there for fifteen minutes, and such depression came upon me that I asked the widow of the painter, 'What was the condition of your husband?' And she answered, 'A terrible condition. His spirit was torn to pieces.' I said, 'That is what his pictures show.'

The effect was such that whoever saw those pictures underwent the same influence. If we have purity of mind we create purity. In all we do, art, politics, business, music, industry, we pour out the purity of mind to such an extent even that those around us, strangers or friends, all have part in our joy. One says that diseases are infectious. But purity of mind is infectious too, and its effect creates purity in others. Some keep it for a long time, others keep it for a short time. It depends upon the mind.

The mind is a storehouse, a storehouse of all the knowledge that one has accumulated by studies, by experiences, by impressions, through any of the five senses. In other words, every sound, even once heard, is registered there; every form that our eyes have seen, even a glimpse of it, is registered there. And when our heart is pure it projects the light of the soul just as the light is projected from a searchlight. And the most wonderful phenomenon is that the light is thrown by the power of will on that particular spot in the storehouse of the mind which we are wanting to find. For instance, we saw a person once ten years ago and he comes before us and we look at him and say, 'I have seen that person before, but where?' In that moment we will throw the light of our soul on that picture that was made on our mind on one occasion ten years ago. It is still there.

We had completely forgotten it, but the picture is there. The moment we desired to see it our soul projected its light on that particular spot; and the most wonderful thing is that there are perhaps a million pictures. Why should the light be thrown on that particular image? That is the phenomenon. It is that the inner light has a great power; it is a power which is creative by nature. And therefore when it throws light, it throws it on that particular spot.

By the word 'mind' I mean here what is often called subconscious mind. The storehouse I spoke of above is the subconscious mind. In that storehouse there are things and they live; all thoughts and impressions are living things. There is nothing in the mind that dies. It lives and it lives long; but when we are not conscious of it, it is in our subconscious mind.

For instance, a person was told that he must go and see his friend on such a day at a certain time. He had written it in his notebook, but then he forgot it. During his daily occupations there came a moment when he thought, 'I ought to be in that place! I have not gone there. I had quite forgotten. I should have been there. Why am I not there? Why did I forget it?' Now this idea that came to his memory was in his subconscious mind. And as his will wanted to know it came up; he knew without doubt that he had an engagement, that he was meant to be there. Only for the time being he had forgotten. Where was it? In that part of his mind which one calls the subconscious.

A pupil I once had who was very interested in spiritual exercises and metaphysical questions, left me and became a business man. All his time was taken up with business. He forgot me altogether. For ten years he never did his practices. One day I happened to come to the city where he lived, and he remembered his old teacher who had returned. When he heard the lecture I gave, everything which he was taught ten years before became alive in a moment; it was only too eager to come. He said, 'It is all living for me. Please tell me what to do.' He was so eager to do things now.

And so it is. All that is in the mind, all one has never thought about, all that one never troubles about, is there; and when one has leisure from worldly occupations, it all becomes living.

At death comes leisure; after death the mind comes to greater life, a life more real than here. Death is an unveiling, the removal of a cover, after which the soul will know many things in regard to its own life and in regard to the whole world which had hitherto been hidden. Therefore the realization of what is said about heaven and hell which we have accumulated in our mind, in the hereafter will be our own. Today our mind is in us; in the hereafter we shall be in our mind. And therefore that mind which is mind just now, in the hereafter will be the world. If it is heaven, it will be heaven; if it is another place, it will be the other place. It is what we have made it. No one is attracted and put there. We have made it for ourselves, for our own convenience.

What we sought after, we have collected. A costly dress, if it was really important, is there. If we find out that it is not important, that it is foolish, it is there just the same.

Even useless things take a form in the mind, as everything has a form. But it has a form akin to the source of impression. For instance, not only a painting, a picture, has a perceptible form; music also is a language; the eyes do not see it, but the ears see it. So the mind even accumulates all such forms as sour, sweet, bitter, pungent, all the different tastes. We do not see them, but they are registered in the mind in a form distinguished by us. The eyes do not see the form, but the mind sees it actually in the same way as we had once tasted it. To the mind all these forms are intelligible in the same way, exactly the same as when they come through the different senses.

Various impressions remain in the mind after death. Because what is individual? Being individual is like being in a mist. When different physical organs cannot any longer hold the spirit then they fail, and the spirit has finished with them. The body departs, the spirit remains. The spirit is as individual as the person was individual in the physical body. After the physical body has gone, the non-physical impressions are more distinct because the limitation of the physical body has fallen away. The physical body is a great limitation. When it has fallen away individuality becomes more distinct, more capable of working than on the physical plane.

CHAPTER III

UNLEARNING

IT IS most difficult to forget what one has once learned. Learning is one thing; and unlearning is another. The process of spiritual attainment is through unlearning. People consider their belief to be their religion. In reality belief is a stepping-stone to religion. Besides, if I were to picture belief, it is just like a staircase that leads on to higher realization. But instead of going up the staircase people stand on it. It is just like running water that does not flow any more. People have made their belief rigid, and therefore instead of being benefited by their belief they are going backwards. If it were not so one would have thought that all the believers in God, in truth, and the hereafter would be better than the unbelievers. But what happens is that they are worse, because they have nailed their own feet to their belief.

Very often I am in a position where I can say very little, especially when a person comes to me with his preconceived ideas and wants to take my direction, my guidance on the spiritual path; yet at the same time his first intention is to see if his thoughts fit in with mine and if my thoughts fit in with his thoughts. He cannot make himself empty for the direction given. He has not come to follow my thoughts, but wants to confirm to himself that his idea is right. Among a hundred persons who come for spiritual guidance, ninety come out of that tap. What does it show? That they do not want to give up their own idea, but they want to have it confirmed that the idea they have is right.

Spiritual attainment, from beginning to end, is unlearning what one has learnt. But how does one unlearn? What one has learnt is in oneself. One can do it by becoming wiser. The more wise one becomes, the more one is able to contradict one's own ideas. The less wisdom one has, the more one holds to one's own ideas. In the wisest person there is willingness to submit to others. And the most foolish person is always ready to stand firm to support his own ideas. The reason is that the wise person can easily give up his thought; the foolish holds on to it. That is why he does not become wise because he sticks to his own ideas; that is why he does not progress.

Mental purification therefore is the only method by which one can reach the spiritual goal. In order to accomplish this one has to look at another person's point of view. For in reality every point of view is one's own point of view. The vaster one becomes, the greater the realization that comes to one, the more one sees that every point of view is all right. If one is able to expand oneself to the consciousness of another person, one's consciousness becomes as large as two persons'. And so it can be as large as a thousand persons' when one accustoms oneself to try and see what others think.

The next step in mental purification is to be able to see the right of the wrong and the wrong of the right, and the evil of the good and the good of the evil. It is a difficult task, but once one has accomplished this, one rises above good and evil.

One must be able to see the pain in pleasure and the pleasure in pain; the gain in the loss and the loss in the gain. What generally happens is that one is blunted to one thing and that one's eyes are open to another thing; that one does not see the loss or that one does not see the gain; if one recognizes the right, one does not recognize the wrong.

Mental purification means that impressions such as good and bad, wrong and right, gain and loss, and pleasure and pain, these opposites which block the mind, must be cleared out by seeing the opposite of these things. Then one can see the enemy in the friend and the friend in the enemy. When one can recognize poison in nectar and nectar in the poison, that is the time when death and life become one too. Opposites no more remain opposites before one. That is called mental purification. And those who come to this stage are the living sages.

The third field of mental purification is to identify oneself with what one is not. By this one purifies one's mind from impressions of one's own false identity.

I will give as an example the story of a sage in India. The story begins by saying that a young man in his youth asked his mother, who was a peasant-woman living in a village, 'What is the best occupation, mother?' And the mother said, 'I do not know son, except that those who searched after the highest in life went in search of God.' 'Then where must I go, mother?' he asked. She answered, 'I do not know whether it is practical or not, but they say in the solitude, in the forest.' So he went there for a long time and lived a life of patience and solitude. And once or twice in between he came to see his mother. Sometimes his patience was exhausted, his heart broken. Sometimes he was disappointed in not finding God. And each time the mother sent him back with stronger advice. At the third visit he said, 'Now I have been there a long time.' 'Yes,' said his mother, 'now I think you are ready to go to a teacher'. So he went to see a teacher. And there were many pupils learning under that teacher. Every pupil had a little room to himself for meditation, and this pupil also was told to go into a certain room to meditate. The teacher asked, 'Is there anything you love in the world?' This young man having been away from home since childhood, having not seen anything of the world, could think of no one he knew, except of the little cow that was in his house. He said, 'I love the cow in our house.' The teacher said, 'Then think of the cow in your meditation.'

All the other pupils came and went, and sat in their room for fifteen minutes for a little meditation; then they got tired and went away; but this young man remained sitting there from the time the teacher had told him. After some time the teacher asked, 'Where is he?' The other pupils answered, 'We don't know. He must be in his room.' They went to look for him; the door was closed and there was no answer. The teacher went himself and opened the door and there he saw the pupil sitting in meditation, fully absorbed in it. And when the teacher called him by name, he answered in the sound of the cow. The teacher said, 'Come out.' He answered, 'My horns are too large to pass through the door.' Then the teacher said to his pupils, 'Look, this is the living example of meditation. You are meditating on God and you do not know where God is, but he is meditating on the cow and he has become the cow; he has lost his identity. He has identified himself with the object on which he meditates.'

All the difficulty in our life is that we cannot come out of a false conception.

I will give another example. Once I was trying to help a person who was ill, who had had rheumatism for twenty years. This woman was in bed; she could not move her joints. I came to her and told her, 'Now you will do this and I will come again in two weeks' time.' And when after two weeks I came, she had already begun to move her joints. And I said, 'In six weeks I will come back.' And in six weeks she got up from bed and had still greater hope of being cured. Nevertheless her patience was not so great as it ought to have been. One day she was lying in bed and thought, 'Can I ever be cured?' The moment she had that thought she went back to the same condition; because her soul had identified itself with a sick person. For her to see her own well-being was impossible, she could not imagine that she would ever be quite well; she could not believe her eyes that her joints were moving; she could not believe it.

People can be well in their bodies but not in their minds. Very often they hold on to an illness which they could get rid of. And the same thing happens with misery. People who are conscious of misery attract miseries. They are their own misery. It is not that misfortune is interested in them, but that they are interested in misfortune. Misfortune does not choose people; people choose misfortune. They hold that thought and that thought becomes their own. When a person is convinced that he is going downward, he goes downward; his thought is helping him to sink.

Therefore the third aspect of mental purification is to be able to identify oneself with something else. The Sufis have their own way of teaching it. Very often one holds the idea of one's spiritual teacher; and with that idea one gains the knowledge and inspiration and power that the spiritual teacher has. It is just like a heritage.

The man who cannot concentrate so much as to forget himself and go deep into the subject on which he concentrates, will not succeed in mastering concentration.

The fourth mental purification is to free oneself from a form and have the sense of the abstract. Everything suggests to the eye a form, everything; even so much that if the name of a person whom one has never seen is mentioned, one makes a form of him. Even such things as fairies and spirits and angels, as soon as they are mentioned, are always pictured in a certain form. This is a hindrance to attaining the presence of the formless; and therefore this mental purification is of very great importance. Its purpose is to be able to think of an idea without form. No doubt this is only attained by great concentration and meditation, but once it is attained it is most satisfactory.

And the fifth way is to be able to repose one's mind. In other words to relax the mind. Imagine, after having toiled for the whole day, how much the body stands in need of rest; how much more then must the mind stand in need of rest!

The mind works much faster than the body; naturally the mind is much more tired than the body. And not every person knows how to rest his mind and therefore the mind never has a rest. And then what happens after a while is that the mind becomes feeble; it loses memory, the power of action; it loses reason. The worst effects are mostly brought about by not giving the mind proper repose. If such infirmities as doubt and fear happen to enter the mind, then a person becomes restless, he can never find rest. For at night the mind continues on the track of the same impressions. Simple as it seems to be, very few know the resting of the mind and how wonderful it is in itself. And what power, what inspiration, comes as a reaction from it, and what peace does one experience by it, and how it helps the body and mind! The spirit is renewed once the mind has had its rest.

The first step towards the resting of the mind is the relaxation of the body. If one is able to relax one's muscular and nervous system at will, then the mind is automatically refreshed. Besides that, one must be able to cast away anxiety, worries, doubts, and fears by the power of will, putting oneself in a restful state; this will be accomplished by the help of proper breathing.

Great magnetism is produced by having stilled and purified the mind. And the lack of it causes lack of magnetism. The presence of those whose mind is not purified and stilled becomes a source of unrest for others as well as for themselves. And they attract little because the power of attraction is lost; everyone is tired by their presence, and their atmosphere causes uneasiness and discomfort. They are a burden to themselves and to others.

Once the mind is purified, the next step is the cultivation of the heart-quality which culminates in spiritual attainment.

CHAPTER IV

THE DISTINCTION BETWEEN THE SUBTLE AND THE GROSS

THERE is a verse in the Bible: 'It is the spirit that quickeneth, the flesh profiteth nothing.' So what we call living is subtle, what is dead is coarse; in other words: what is dense is coarse, and what is fine is subtle.

It is true as the Hindus say that there was a golden age, then a silver age, a copper age, and an iron age. Certainly we are in the iron age. Never before in any period of history was there such grossness and denseness as mankind shows today. And it has come about by the law of gravitation. When the consciousness is absorbed in the gross matter then a person gravitates towards the earth. When the consciousness is released from the gross matter then it soars towards heaven.

I do not mean to say that people were not gross 2,000 or 3,000 years ago. But when we study traditions we find that they were also very fine and subtle in perception, more than we are today. Our contact with the earth and earthly things has made us more rigid; they were more placid. And if we want proof of this we have only to study ancient languages such as Sanskrit, Zend, Persian, Hebrew, and see the manuscripts of ancient times and the way they explain things. Maybe they are quite strange to our present-day mentality and perception, yet their fineness is beyond words. And it seems we are going from bad to worse and are becoming coarser every day. If we only realized how far we are removed from what may be called fine perception!

When a person tries to understand subtle things by mathematical calculations alone, he has come into the dense sphere. He does not want to become fine, and he wants to make the spirit, which is the finest thing, gross and intelligible. Therefore it is of the greatest importance for spiritual attainment to develop fine perception. I have seen people go into a trance or dive into a deep meditation and yet lack fine perception. And then it is of no value. They are not really spiritual. A really spiritual person must have a mentality like liquid, not like a rock. A mentality that is moving, not crude and dense.

This question has also a metaphysical side to it. There are two experiences in life. One realm of experience is sensation, the other realm is exaltation; and it is by these two experiences that one tries to experience happiness. But what is experienced by sensation or in the form of sensation is not necessarily happiness; that is pleasure. It might give the appearance of happiness for a moment, but it is only a suggestion of happiness.

Exaltation is something which the mystic experiences. And those who are not mystics experience it also, but they do not know what it is; they cannot distinguish between sensation and exaltation. Sometimes exaltation may be the outcome of sensation; it is possible; but at the same time exaltation which depends upon sensation is not an independent exaltation.

There are different grades of exaltation. To the Sufi, the soul is a current that joins the physical body to the source. And the art of repose naturally makes it easier for the soul to experience freedom, inspiration, power, because it is then loosened from the grip of the physical body. As Rumi says in the Masnavi, 'Man is a captive on earth. His body and his mind are his prison bars. And the soul is unconsciously craving to experience once again the freedom which originally belonged to it.' The Platonic idea about reaching the higher source is the same: that by exaltation the soul, so to speak, rises above the fast hold of the physical body; it may be only for a few moments, but it experiences in those moments a freedom which man has never experienced before.

A moment of exaltation is a different experience at every level. The supreme exaltation is hinted at in the Bible: 'Be ye perfect even as your Father in heaven is perfect.' Many religious people will say that it is impossible for man to be perfect; but it is said in the Bible just the same. At all times the knowers and seers have understood that there is a stage at which, by touching a particular phase of existence, one feels raised above the limitations of life, and is given that power and peace and freedom, that light and life, which belong to the source of all beings. In other words, in that moment of supreme exaltation one is not only united with the source of all beings, but dissolved in it; for the source is one's self.

The source is greater than we can put into words. We can try to conceive it by comparing it with a seed, which is the source of the flower, the leaves, the stem, the branches, and the fragrance, while if we take the seed alone we do not see all those in the seed; yet they were there all the time. On the other hand we cannot really compare even the seed with the source, for the seed depends upon the sun and water and earth for its growth, whereas the ultimate source does not depend upon anything. It is all that is strong and powerful; it is beyond words and beyond our limited conception even to think of the source, except that when we get greater inspiration, peace, joy, and magnetism, we appreciate things much better. In this way we may understand a little how great the source must be. The greater we are, the closer we reach to that source. As the great Indian poet Khusrau says, 'When I become Thou and Thou becomest me, neither canst Thou say that I am different, nor canst Thou say that Thou art different.'

The different grades of exaltation are as the different notes in music. As we distinguish lower and higher notes, so it is with the different grades of the experience of exaltation. Even reading a beautiful poem can produce exaltation; good music gives exaltation, and a feeling of great joy does so too. It all breaks up congestion; there are fine cells of the nerves which become free, and the body experiences relaxation.

There is a difference between sensation and exaltation, but when we come to words, there is always confusion. One can say that exaltation is the fusion of all sensation; but if one says that through sensation exaltation is experienced, it is true also.

As much as we need sensation in life to make our experience of life concrete, so much or even more do we need exaltation in order to live life fully. The lower creation such as birds and beasts also have glimpses of exaltation. They do not only rejoice in grazing and in finding seeds, in making nests or in playing in the air, in singing and in running about in the forest. There are moments when even birds and beasts feel exaltation. And if we go into this subject more deeply we shall understand what we read in a most wonderful verse of Islamic tradition: 'There are moments when even rocks become exalted and trees fall into ecstasy.' If that be true, then man, who is created to complete the experience that any living being can have, must experience exaltation as much as he experiences sensation.

What I mean by sensation is the impression one has of line and colour; the preference one has for softness in structure; the appreciation one has of fragrance and perfume; the enjoyment one gains by tasting sweet and sour and pungent; the joy one experiences in hearing poetry, singing, and music. All these experiences are manifest in the realm of sensation. The world of sensation is one world; the world of exaltation is another; and these two worlds are made for man to experience in order to live life on earth fully. And yet, with this possibility and this opportunity in life, man continues to live a life of sensation, forgetting that there is another life as well, a life that can be experienced here on earth, and something that completes life's experience.

There is a physical aspect of exaltation which comes as a reaction or result of having seen the immensity of space, having looked at the wide horizon, or having seen the clear sky, the moonlit night and nature at dawn. Looking at the rising sun, watching the setting sun, looking at the horizon from the sea, being in the midst of nature, looking at the world from the top of a mountain, all these experiences, even such an experience as watching the little smiles of an innocent infant, these experiences lift one up and give one a feeling which one cannot call sensation. It is exaltation.

A higher aspect of exaltation is a moral exaltation—when we are sorry for having said or done something unpleasant; when

we have asked forgiveness, and humbled ourselves before someone towards whom we were inconsiderate. We have humbled
our pride then. Or when we felt a deep gratitude to someone
who had done something for us; when we have felt love, sympathy, devotion which seems endless and which seems so great
that our heart cannot accommodate it; when we have felt so
much pity for someone that we have forgotten ourselves; when
we have found a profound happiness in rendering a humble
service to someone in need; when we have said a prayer which
has come from the bottom of our heart; when we have realized
our own limitation and smallness in comparison with the greatness of God; all these experiences lift man up.

The moment we have these experiences, we are not living on
earth but in another world. The joy of such experiences is very
great, and yet they can be gained without paying anything,
whereas sensations cost something. We have to go to the theatre,
to go to all kinds of entertainments; all these cost something, they
cost more than they are worth; but exaltation which is beyond
price comes of itself, as soon as we have shown an inclination
towards it. It is only a matter of changing our attitude.

Once I visited a great sage in Bengal. I said to him, 'What
a blessed life is yours, which gives pleasure and happiness
to so many souls.' But he answered, 'How privileged I am
myself that a thousand times more pleasure and happiness come
to me.'

Exaltation is a purifying process. A moment's exaltation can
purify the evil of many years, because it is like bathing in the
Ganges, as Hindus say. It is symbolical: exaltation is the Ganges,
and if we bathe in it we are purified from all sins. It does not
take much to make us exalted: a kind attitude, a sympathetic
trend of mind, and it is already there. If we were to notice it,
we would find that our eyes shed tears in sympathy with another, we were already exalted, our soul has bathed in the
spiritual Ganges. It comes by forgetting self and by destroying
selfishness. But remember, we can never claim to be unselfish;
however unselfish we may be, we are selfish just the same. But
we can be wisely selfish, and if we are to be selfish, it is just as
well to be wisely selfish. It is the same thing as what we call

unselfishness, and it is profitable to be that instead of being foolishly selfish; because the former gains and the latter loses.

The third aspect of exaltation comes by touching the reason
of reasons and by realizing the essence of wisdom; by feeling
the depth, the profound depth of one's heart, by widening one's
outlook on life; by broadening one's conception, by deepening
one's sympathies, and by soaring upwards to those spheres where
spiritual exaltation manifests. Today a man of common sense or
a person who is called a practical man is in the habit of laughing
at the idea that someone has visions or experiences of ecstasy,
that someone goes into what is called a trance. But there is
nothing to be surprised at, nothing to laugh at. All these things
are laughable, however, when done by the undeserving; and it
is mostly such who make these claims and look for approbation
from others for their experiences. Those who really experience
these things do not need to tell people that they had this or that
experience. Their own joy is their reward. No one else should
recognize it; the less others know about it the better.

Why must we show ourselves to be different from others?
It is only vanity. And the more vanity the less progress we make
along the spiritual path. It is the worst thing on the spiritual
path to try and show oneself to be different from others; those
who are really evolved, are glad to act as everyone else acts.
To novelists it seems beautiful to describe masters as living in
caves of the Himalayas or moving about in the forest somewhere
where one cannot go and find them, always keeping aloof and
apart so that no one can reach them. But every soul has a divine
spark, and therefore if there is any higher stage of human evolution it is for human beings, not for those outside the human
world. If they are outside the human world, there is no relation
between us and them. The great spiritual souls have lived in the
world, in the midst of the world, and proved to be the greatest
masters.

Imagine the life of Abraham, of Moses, the life of Jesus Christ;
and again the life of Mohammad in war and battles, and yet as
exclusive and remote, as spiritual as anyone could be. And
Krishna, picture him in Kurukshetra fighting in the battle, giving a world-scripture. If they had all lived in mountain caves

we would not have been benefited by them. What is the use of
those holy ones who never see, never experience from morning
till evening the tests and trials of the dense world, where at every
move there are a thousand temptations and difficulties, a thousand
problems? What can they do, those who are outside the world,
for us who are exposed to a thousand difficulties at every moment
of our life? And these difficulties are increasing. With the evolution of the world life is becoming heavier, more difficult. No,
the mastery, the holiness, the evolution must be shown here on
earth. It is very easy to be evolved in the seventh heaven. But
exaltation experienced and imparted to others here on the earth
is exaltation which is more worth while.

As to the grossness and subtlety of human nature, the heroes,
kings, masters, prophets, those who have won the heart of
humanity, have been fine in perception and in character. They
have not been gross. Their fineness was simple; there was always
a simple side to it, but at the same time it was subtle, which made
it beautiful. A person who can say without saying and one who
can do without doing is a subtle person and that subtlety is worth
appreciating. The one who sees and does not see, knows and
does not know; the one who experiences and does not experience at the same time, the one who is living and yet dead, that
is the soul who experiences life fully.

CHAPTER V

MASTERY

THE PURPOSE of life is to attain to mastery; this is the
motive of the spirit, and it is through this motive at the back
of it that the whole universe is created. The different stages from
mineral to vegetable and from vegetable to the animal kingdom,
and from animal to man, are the awakening of the spirit towards
mastery. By using the mineral and the vegetable kingdoms and
controlling the animal kingdom for his service, man shows in

the first place that in him is awakened that spirit by which the whole universe was created.

His power of knowing, of understanding, of utilizing to the best advantage, is the sign of mastery. But at the same time there is one enemy that man has, and that enemy is limitation; and the spirit of limitation is always a hindrance to realizing the spirit of mastery and practising it. Those who at some time or other in their lives have realized this principal object for which man is born, have then tried to develop that spirit of mastery in order to defend themselves.

The process of going from limitation to perfection is called mysticism. Mysticism means developing from limitation to perfection. All pain and failure belong to limitation; all pleasure and success belong to perfection. In one's own surroundings, one will find that those who are unhappy and dissatisfied with life and who make others unhappy, are those who are more limited; those who can help themselves and help others, who are happy and bring pleasure into the lives of others, are nearer to perfection.

What is meant by limitation and what by perfection? These are only conditions of the consciousness. When one is conscious of limitation, one is limited; when one is conscious of perfection, one is perfect. Because he who is limited in the limited consciousness is the same as he who is perfect in the perfect consciousness. To give an example: there was a son of a rich man who had plenty of money put in his name in the bank. But he did not know this; and when he wished to spend some money he found very little in his pocket. This made him limited. In reality his father had put a large sum in the bank, but he was not conscious of it. It is exactly the same with every soul. Every soul is conscious of what it possesses and is unconscious of what is put in its name. What is within one's reach, one feels to be one's own, but what does not seem to be within one's reach one considers to be outside. This is natural. But wisdom opens a door to look out and see if that which seems outside is not meant to be known too.

Sometimes the mastery of life is known to a person; he may not be a mystic, but if his time comes, he knows it. One day

I was interested when a man, who had done nothing but business all his life and made himself so rich that he was perhaps one of the richest men in the country, wanted to show me his park, a beautiful park he had around his house. While I was his guest we were taking a walk. He said, 'It is wonderful to come here into my park in the morning and evening.' I asked him, 'How far does your park extend?' And he said, 'Do you want to know? Do you see the horizon from here?' I said, 'Yes.' He told me, 'All this land is mine and the sea besides. All that you can see.' It was a wonderful answer, and an example of the theory I have mentioned; he was not only conscious of what he possessed, but of all that was there. He did not make a dividing line between what was his own and what was beyond. It is a mystery, and it is difficult for anyone to look at life in this way. But this man who was in business, this man who never even thought of mysticism, could also arrive at that conception which the mystic discovers after years of meditation. It was a purely mystical conception.

When dervishes, who sometimes have patched sleeves or are scantily clad, who sometimes have food and sometimes not, address one another, they say, 'O King of Kings, O Emperor of Emperors'. It is the consciousness of what is king or emperor which is before them. The boundary of their kingdom is not limited. The whole universe is their kingdom. It is in this way that a soul proceeds towards perfection, by opening the consciousness and raising it higher. When the soul evolves spiritually, it rises to a height where it sees a wider horizon; therefore its possession becomes greater. You might say, 'By looking at the horizon it does not become our possession; what we possess is what we call our own.' But Columbus first saw America. He did not possess it first. The possession came afterwards. The first thing is to see, afterwards we possess; but if we do not see how can we possess? And without seeing our possession it is not our possession.

There are two different ways, two different angles from which one should look at perfection. One way is likened to a perpendicular line and the other to a horizontal line. The way which is likened to a perpendicular line is the reaching of the knowledge within. How does one reach this knowledge? First of all by concentration one reaches the knowledge within, which means one is able to see concretely and to be conscious of something which is apart from one's physical body. A person may be conscious of a poem, a word, a picture, an idea or something, and if he can be so conscious of it that he can lose the consciousness of his limited body for a moment, that is the first step.

Although it seems very easy, it is not so easy. When a person begins to do it, no sooner does he close his eyes in order to concentrate than a thousand things come before him. Also his physical body becomes restive. It says, 'This person is not conscious of me!' And then he gets nervous and twists and turns in order to be conscious of the body. The body does not like a person to be unconscious of it. It is like a dog or a cat; it likes one to take notice of it. Then a kind of nervous action arises in the body. It feels like moving, turning, scratching, or something. As soon as one wants to discipline the body, the body does not want to accept discipline.

The second stage is that instead of being conscious of a thought, one is conscious of a feeling, which is wider still; because thought is a form, and the mind even sees the form. But feeling has no form, therefore to fix one's mind on a feeling and to keep it with the intention of keeping it, is not an easy thing. If once a person has done it and has not given in to the restiveness of mind, then he certainly feels uplifted.

This is the boundary of human progress and further than that is divine progress. What is divine progress? When one goes further still, then instead of being active one becomes passive. It is a state of consciousness, to be passive. There one does not need concentration, what one needs there is meditation. There one gets in touch with that power which is audible and visible within one and of which one is yet ignorant; that power which is busy moving towards the materialization of its intended object.

Once one comes into contact with this experience, one can no longer say in later life that there is such a thing as an accident. Then one will see that all that happens is destined and prepared, when one catches it in its preparatory condition before it has manifested on the earthly plane.

And if one goes further, there is consciousness in its aspect of pure intelligence. It is knowing and yet knowing nothing. And knowing nothing means knowing all things. Because it is the knowing of things that blunts the faculty of knowledge. In other words, when a person is looking in a mirror, his reflection covers the mirror and in that mirror nothing else can be reflected. Therefore when the consciousness is conscious of anything, it is blunted; at that moment it is blunted, or in other words it is covered by something that it is conscious of. The moment that cover is taken away, it is its own self, it is pure intelligence, it is pure spirit. In that condition its power, life, magnetism, force, its capacity, are much greater, incomparably greater than one can imagine. What it is cannot be explained except that by the help of meditation one reaches that condition. And if one goes higher still, it is not even consciousness, it is a kind of omniscient condition which is the sign of inner perfection.

This is one direction of progress. There is another direction of progress; that is to see oneself reflected in another. When one is friends with another person, naturally one's sympathy, love, friendship, make one see oneself in the other, and this gives the inclination to sacrifice. No one will sacrifice for another except when he is oneself. If this feeling develops it extends further, not only with the friend, with the neighbour, but with the stranger, with the beast and bird and insect; one is in at-one-ment with all living beings, and it gives one as much insight into another as the other person has into himself. One knows as much about him as he knows, even more. This is the simplest phenomenon of this consciousness; not to work wonders. It brings a quick proof that one knows as much about another person as he knows himself.

But there is another, moral proof; that one becomes friends with the wise and foolish, with the virtuous and wicked, more and more, as if one attracted them. One cannot help it. Sympathy is so powerful that even enemies are melted sooner or later. It is not just a tale that Daniel was sent to the mountain cave and the lions were tamed. In order to see this phenomenon one need not go to the mountains; in this world there are worse

than lions: good natures and bad natures, possible and impossible
people, and if one can subdue them, one has accomplished something; for it requires a greater power than calming lions. One
can think of different ideas: agitated ones, antagonistic ones,
blunted ones, ignorant ones, ideas full of falsehood or jealousy;
how many swords and poisons there are in this world! And it
is only one power, the power of one's sympathy, that assimilates all poisonous influences. It takes away their poison and it
does not hurt oneself. One can sooner or later purify them, re-
vivify them, melt them, mould them, and direct them towards
the purpose of life.

The world seeks for complexity. If I were to give lectures
upon how to get magnetism in order to make people listen to
you, and in order to draw them to you; if I were to give twenty
exercises for doing these things, it might mean great success for
me. But if I tell you simple things like this, that it is the deepening of your sympathy, the awakening of that sympathetic spirit
in you which is every power and magnetism, and the expansion
of which means spiritual unfoldment, then there will be few to
understand. For human beings do not want simple teaching, they
want complexity.

And then there is another stage of expansion, and that is trying to look at everything from another's point of view also,
trying to think also as the other person thinks. This is not an
easy thing because from one's childhood one learns to think so
that one stands upon one's own thought. One does not move
to another's thought. The very fact that one has a thought oneself, keeps one to it. It is therefore a sign of expansion to be able
to see from the child's point of view, or from the point of view
of the foolish person, how he looks at things. And the most
interesting thing is that it brings one to being tolerant and
patient. In this way one extends one's knowledge to a degree
that no reading can give. Then one begins to receive from all
sources; one will attract knowledge from every plane as soon
as the mind becomes so pliable that it does not only stick to its
own point of view.

This process is called unlearning. If you say of a certain man,
'This is not a nice person', although you may be quite wrong

the general tendency is to stick to that idea. But the greater
evolution is to see from that man's point of view also. He has
a reason for being as he is; maybe he is too unevolved to see, or
he is more evolved and less interested in the other person. Yet,
by seeing from his point of view you do not lose your own;
your own point of view is still there; but the other point of
view is added to yours, therefore your knowledge becomes
greater. It means a greater stretching of the heart and sometimes
the heart feels pain when you stretch it. But by stretching the
heart and by making it larger and larger, you turn your heart
into the sacred Book.

And the third aspect is to feel another person. A man is very
often different from what he appears and from what he thinks.
Sometimes he acts and speaks quite differently from his feelings;
and if your feelings can know the feeling of another, this is a
high aspect. You become a highly evolved personality when
the feelings of another can tell you much more than his words
and actions can; and sometimes they can give you quite a different opinion of a person from what you would have had if
you had only seen him and heard him speak. When one has
arrived at this point, human evolution ends and divine evolution begins. Then no doubt one gets insight into what happens
in the spirit of man; if he is going to succeed or not, if he is
going to be happy or not, or what he is going to accomplish;
because there is something going on within that person, preparing his plan of tomorrow. You begin to touch it and begin
to get the impression of it, and that impression is as clear sometimes as anything visible and audible could be.

If you go further then you unite with everything. In this
consciousness distance is no longer distance; if you can extend
your consciousness so that your consciousness touches the consciousness of another, then not only the thoughts of that person
but his whole spirit is reflected in your spirit. Space does not
matter; your consciousness can touch every part of the world
and every person, at whatever distance he may be.

And if you go still further, then you can only realize that you
are connected with all beings. That there is nothing and no one
who is divided or separate from you, and that you are not only

connected by chains with those you love, but with all those you have known and do not know—connected by a consciousness which binds you faster than any chains. Naturally one then begins to see the law working in nature; one begins to see that the whole universe is a mechanism working towards a certain purpose. Therefore the right one and the wrong one, the good and the bad, are all bringing about one desired result, by wrong power and by right power, a result meant to be, which is the purpose of life.

Then naturally one holds oneself back from that dogmatic spirit: 'you are wrong' and 'you are right', and one comes to the spirit of the sage: saying nothing, knowing all, doing all, suffering all things. This makes one the friend of all and the servant of all. And with all the realizations of mystical truth and spiritual attainment, what one realizes is one thing, the only thing worth while, and that is to be of some little use to one's fellow-men.

CHAPTER VI

THE CONTROL OF THE BODY

MANY PEOPLE think that the physical has little to do with the spiritual. Why not, they ask, cast the idea of the physical aside in order to be entirely spiritual? If without the physical aspect of our being the purpose of life could be accomplished, the soul would not have taken a physical body and the spirit would not have produced the physical world. A Hindustani poet says, 'If the purpose of creation could have been fulfilled by the angels, who are entirely spiritual, God would not have created man.' That shows that there is a great purpose to be accomplished by what is called the physical body. If the light of God could have shone directly, there would not have been a manifestation such as that of Christ. It was necessary, so to speak, that God should walk on the earth in the physical body. And the conception that the physical body is made of sin, and that this is the lowest aspect of being, will very often prove to be a mistake, for it is through this physical body that the highest and the greatest purpose of life is to be achieved. A person only calls it his physical body in ignorance; once the knowledge has come to him he begins to look upon it as the sacred temple of God.

Our experience of life through the physical body has five aspects. The first aspect is health, the possession of which is heaven, and the absence of which is hell. No matter what we have in life, wealth, name or fame, power or position, comfort or convenience, without health it is all nothing. When a person is healthy he does not think about it, he does not value it. He cares about things he has not got. He tries to sacrifice his health for pleasures, for material wealth; he is ready to sacrifice his health for his intellectual fancies, for gaiety, for merriment, for a good time, for an ambition he wants to fulfil. But very often before the ambition or the desire is fulfilled the collapse comes and then he begins to realize what health means. Nothing can buy it, nothing can be compared with it. If we gather together all the blessings that can be received in life and weigh them on a scale, we will find that health weighs heaviest.

It is health which enables man to be material as well as spiritual; its lack robs him of materiality as well as of spirituality. It robs him of materiality because his condition is not in order, and of spirituality because it is the completeness of health that enables man to experience spiritual life fully. I do not mean that it is a sin to be ill and a virtue to be well; I mean that health is a virtue and illness a sin.

Another aspect of the physical existence is balance. It is balance which gives control of the body. It is by balance that man is able to stand, to walk, to move. Every action, every physical movement, is sustained by balance. And the lack of balance will always show some lack in the character of a person and at the same time in the condition of his life. In whatever form the lack of balance manifests, it always means that there is something lacking in the personality. If one studies the walk of a person, the way he moves or looks, everything he does, one sees that whenever balance is lacking something is lacking behind this

which one may not have known but which one will find out
in time. For instance, when a person is wobbling, do not believe
that it is only an outside defect; it has something to do with that
man's character. As he is wobbling in walking, so he will be
wobbling in his determination, in his belief. Just as the physician
sees the internal condition in the eyes and on the tongue of the
patient, so the wise see all that pertains to a man in his every
movement especially by watching the balance.

Many Western readers of Oriental philosophy have asked me,
'Why is it that your adepts in the East practise acrobatics, sitting in certain postures, standing on one leg, on their heads,
sitting cross-legged in one position for a long time, and many
other strange things that one would not think of a spiritual
person doing? What spirituality is there to be attained by it?
We consider that these things belong to acrobatics and athletics.'
And I have answered that all such things as sports and athletic
and acrobatic practices when done as a pastime abuse energy,
time, and work. One does not get the full benefit out of them;
but the adepts use them towards a higher purpose. There is
nothing in this world, if properly practised, which will not
prove to be beneficial in spiritual attainment.

Do not think that going to church or temple and offering
prayers, or sitting in silence with closed eyes, is the only way to
spiritual attainment. But if we turn all things we do in our everyday life towards the spiritual goal, this will help us in our spiritual attainment. Besides, going to church once a week involves
very little spiritual work; even when we say our prayers every
night before going to bed, very little spiritual work is done.
For every moment of the day we live in illusion. Everything
we do has the effect of covering our spiritual vision. That is
why every moment of the day we should have a concentration.
How can we do this if we have our business, industry, profession,
a thousand things to do in everyday life? The answer is that we
should turn all things that we do into a prayer. Then whatever
be our profession, work, occupation in daily life, it will all
help us to spiritual attainment. Then our every action will
become a prayer. Every move we make towards the South,
the North, the West, or the East will point to the spiritual goal.

Not everyone realizes to what extent he lacks balance in his life; among a hundred persons you can hardly find one really balanced. There is spiritual balance also, but this spiritual balance is attained by first balancing the physical body and its movements.

The third aspect of our physical existence is the perfecting of our body, in other words the fineness, the sensitiveness, of the body. There is a spiritual temperament, and that temperament you can see from a person's body. There are sensitive people, maybe a little bit nervous, and then there are dense people who have quite a different aspect. A sensitive person who can appreciate music, who can respond to the beauty of line and colour, who can enjoy a salt and sweet, a sour and bitter taste fully, who can feel cold and heat, who can perceive fragrance, distinguish all these, it is he who is born with a spiritual temperament. The person who has no love for music, who cannot appreciate fragrance, who cannot understand the beauty of line and colour, that person is dense, and it will take time for him to develop. Therefore the experience of all the joy and pleasure that life offers is not in materiality, it is in spirituality. It is not the material person who experiences life fully; it is the spiritual person who does so.

One might ask, 'Then what about these ascetics who lived the life of a hermit in solitude, who did not eat proper food, who kept themselves away from all the comfort and beauty of life?' These are not for everyone to follow. At the same time it is a mistake to criticize them. Such people are the ones who make experiments of life by the sacrifice of all the joy and pleasure that the earth can give. By their solitude they experiment, just as a scientist shuts himself up in his laboratory for years and years; and these ascetics who left everything in the world also attained a certain knowledge which they give us. It is not a principle for everyone to follow, for spirituality does not depend upon such things. Why are the eyes given if not to appreciate all that is beautiful; why are the ears given if one may not enjoy music; why has one been sent on to the earth if one cannot look at the earth for fear of being called materialist? Those who make spirituality out to be something like this make a bogey of God, something frightening. In point of fact spirituality is the fullness of life.

With regard to the fourth aspect of our physical existence, man wrongly identifies himself with the physical body, calling it 'myself'. And when the physical body is in pain he says, 'I am ill', because he identifies himself with something which belongs to him but which is not himself. The first thing to learn in the spiritual path is to recognize the physical body not as one's self, but as an instrument, a vehicle, through which to experience life. This instrument is so equipped that one may be able to experience all that is worth experiencing outside oneself, and also all that is worth experiencing within oneself. When a child is born and brought up, its first tendency is to enjoy and experience all that is outside itself, and the man usually gets no chance to experience what is within himself. But at the same time the body is equipped with the instrument, with the means, by which to experience both the life outside and the life within. If a person does not use his hand or his leg for many years, the outcome will be that it loses its vitality, life, energy, and will no longer be of any use. We know the use of our hands and feet which are outer parts of the physical mechanism, but there are inner and finer parts of the physical mechanism which mystics have called centres, each centre having its particular object—intuition, inspiration, impression, revelation—which are all realized through the medium of these centres.

As the organs of our senses can experience life that is around us, so the nervous centres can experience life that is within us. But when these centres are not used for many years they become blunted, not destroyed but blunted, and can no longer be put to the use for which they exist. Many who embark upon spiritual work guided by a proper teacher begin to feel a sensation in the middle of the forehead, as if something is awakening there. After some time they begin more and more to notice a sphere of which they were quite ignorant. There are some who begin to notice a feeling in the solar plexus which they did not have before. If that feeling is awakened they naturally become more intuitive. Some feel a certain sensitiveness on the top of their head, or in the centre of their throat. With their growth they feel it more and more. Among these people there will doubtless be found some who are intuitive by nature.

The difference between those whose nervous centres respond and those whose nervous centres do not respond is that of rock and plant. The rock does not respond to sympathy, but the plant does. And so the ones whose intuitive centres are awakened to some extent begin to feel intuitive, and then inspiration and revelation follow. But one should bear in mind that these things are not to be talked about. Those who know least talk most; and then if those who are not yet ready to know these secrets get hold of some theory or other of this kind, they speak about it to everybody. And then they write a book about their own wrong conceptions. They have never had the patience, perseverance, and right guidance to help them, and often they go astray; and many of them have damaged their health and got out of balance trying to awaken centres. They make light of something which is most serious, most sacred, and which leads to spiritual attainment. Others make fun of it, those of the wrong quality who cannot perceive sympathy as a plant perceives it. They do not see the possibilities in themselves and mock at those who do perceive; and in this way a science, which is the highest of all sciences, has been abused and laughed at.

In the East a teacher does not give guidance until he has full confidence in the pupil, so as not to allow that which is most sacred to be mocked and laughed at by others. When he gives an initiation the pupil takes an oath that he will not speak about these things before those unaware of their value, importance, and sacredness; and only then is he guided. Also, every individual is guided by the teacher separately.

Finally, there is the fifth aspect of our physical existence. There are two things: sensation and exaltation. Through sensation one experiences pleasure. Through exaltation one experiences joy. There is a difference between joy and pleasure. What man is accustomed to experience by the medium of his physical body is pleasure; the pleasure of eating, the pleasure of drinking, the pleasure of looking at beautiful things. Therefore everything comforting he knows is that which is experienced by the physical senses. But besides that there is a joy which does not depend upon the senses, which only depends upon exaltation; and that exaltation is also achieved by the medium of the body.

How is this achieved? There is action and its result, and there is repose and its result. It is the result of action which is called sensation, and it is the result of repose which is called exaltation. In the Masnavi of Rumi, the most wonderful poet of Persia, we read about the blessing of sleep, where he says, 'O sleep, there is no greater bliss to be compared with you; in sleep the prisoners are free from their prison, and the kings do not possess throne and crown. The suffering patients lose their pain or worries, and sorrows are forgotten.' This shows that sleep is a form of repose, automatically brought about, which lifts us up from anxieties, worries, and discomforts, from sorrows and troubles. When this condition of repose can be brought about at will, one will have an experience of mastery, for then one is not dependent upon an automatic condition. If this condition which raises us above our worries, troubles, sorrows, anxieties, pains, and suffering can be produced within ourselves, a great thing is accomplished. And the way of accomplishing it is by the practice of repose. The first thing an adept does in life is to master the five different aspects which I have mentioned, and having mastered them he is ready for the next step in the path of spiritual attainment.

CHAPTER VII

THE CONTROL OF THE MIND

THE TENDENCY to be worried over nothing, to become anxious about little things, to be fidgety and restless, to be afraid, to be confused, the tendency of moving about without any reason, the tendency of speaking without purpose, the tendency of being sad without any motive, all these things come through lack of control over the mind. Have they also any other effect besides the effect that is made upon one's own personality?

Yes; all weaknesses, errors, and mistakes that man makes against his own wish, all these come from lack of control over his own mind. And if there is a secret of success the key to it is the control of mind. Intuition, inspiration, revelation, all come when the mind is controlled. And all worries, anxieties, fears, and doubts come from lack of control.

What is mind? One part of humanity considers mind as something inexplicable, and another part of humanity considers mind as an action of the brain. It is a very limited conception of mind. The voice reaches, through the wireless, for thousands of miles, but the mind is much finer than the voice. It cannot be limited and restricted to the brain, although the brain is the medium by which thoughts are made clear. Mind according to the mystic is the real man; the body is only a garb which man wears. This word has a Sanskrit origin; in Sanskrit it is called *mana*, and from that is derived *manu*, which is nearly the same as the English word *man*. In other words, man means mind; and one sees that this is true when someone calls another person sad or downhearted or courageous or enthusiastic or well-balanced, for all these attributes belong to his mind. Man is not his body, but he is his mind. There is a saying that what you are speaks louder than what you say. This means that the voice of mind reaches further than the spoken word and has greater effect.

It is mind which creates atmosphere. One often wonders why it is that one feels uncomfortable in the presence of someone without his having done any harm; or that one feels excited in the presence of someone, or that one gets out of tune, or tired, or confused in the presence of someone else. Why is it? It is the effect of that person's mind. The mind that is on fire creates fire in the atmosphere, and everyone within its atmosphere is burning too in the same fire. The mind which is restful and peaceful gives rest and peace to those who come within the atmosphere of that mind.

Once I asked my spiritual teacher how we can recognize the godly man. And my teacher replied, 'It is not what he says and it is not what he seems to be, but it is the atmosphere that his presence creates. That is the proof. For no one can create an atmosphere which does not belong to his spirit.'

It is said in the Bible that first the earth was created and then, after the earth, the heavens, which means that the body was finished first and then the mind. An infant is born, so to speak, with a vision of mind, a skeleton of mind, and then the flesh and skin are put on it.

There is no mind without body; that is to say, before the body was made the mind was only an *Akasha*, an accommodation. The experience it has gained through the body as its vehicle has become its knowledge; and it is knowledge that makes mind. The Akasha which becomes mind after the body has been born on earth has already gathered some indistinct knowledge from several minds it has met while coming to earth; perhaps from one mind more than from other minds. In that case it has gained characteristics chiefly from one individual who has passed on from the earth. Besides, through the parents this Akasha has gained the knowledge or the mentality of their ancestry, their nation, their race, and of the particular grade of evolution of the whole of humanity at that particular time.

Some say animals have no mind. But that is a wrong conception. Wherever there is a body there is a mind; even the tree has a mind. Luther Burbank once said to me in support of this argument, 'You should watch the tendency of a plant, what is its inclination; for if you do not watch it the plant will not grow fully. I treat them as living beings. They speak to me, and I to them.'

The first thing we can learn about the mind is that the mind is independent of the body as far as its existence is concerned. But the mind is enriched by the experience man gets through his senses. There is no doubt that mind is within the body, but it is outside the body also, just like the light which is both within the lantern and without. The body is the lantern in which there is the light, but the light is not obscured by the lantern; the light is independent of the lantern. It shines out; and so does the mind. The brain is not mind, just as the piece of flesh in the breast is not the heart. Only, feeling is felt more deeply in the breast, and thought is made more clear in the brain. In other words, spectacles are not eyes; spectacles only enable one to see things more clearly; but the sight is independent of the spectacles, while the spectacles are dependent upon the sight. So the body is dependent upon the mind, but the mind is independent of the body. Body cannot exist without mind, but mind can exist without the body. The mind is the invisible being of the body. It has its seat in the physical being; and it is that seat which is called brain, as the seat of feeling is the heart.

All that the senses can perceive is outward, but all that the mind can perceive is inward. This means that imagination rises from the mind and that the mind can perceive it; feeling, memory, concentration, reason, all these are perceptions of the mind. One can call the mind more the being of man than the body; when we compare body with mind it is just like the coat a person wears.

Mind has five different aspects. The first aspect is the power of thinking. And thinking can be divided into two parts: imagination, which is an outcome of the automatic action of mind, and thought, which is a result of intentional thinking. A thoughtful man, therefore, is not necessarily imaginative, nor an imaginative man thoughtful. Both qualities have their place. A person who is accustomed to think and who is not capable of imagination is far removed from that beauty which is expressed in poetry and music, as these come from imagination. When the mind is given a free hand to do as it likes it dances as it were, and out of its gestures a picture is created, call it art, poetry, or music. In whatever form it expresses itself it is beautiful.

Many people laugh at an imaginative person. They say, 'He is in the clouds; he is dreaming.' But all works of art and music and poetry come from imagination, for imagination is the free flow of the mind, when the mind is allowed to work by itself and bring out the beauty and harmony it contains. But when it is restricted by a certain principle or rule, then it does not work freely. No doubt among artists and musicians you will find many who are dreamers and unpractical people. But that does not mean they are less gifted. Perhaps their unpracticalness in some way helps them to accomplish something that practical people cannot accomplish. One need not follow their example, but one can appreciate it just the same. Besides, no one has believed in God, no one has loved God, and no one has reached the presence of God, who has not been helped by his imagination. Those who

argue with the believer and say, 'But where is God? Can you
show me? How can you conceive God? How do you explain
God?' they are the ones without imagination; and no one can
give his own imagination to them. Can anyone believe in the
belief of another? If one can believe in anything one must do it
oneself. And of what is that belief formed? Of imagination. It
has been said: 'If you have no God make one'; and no one has
ever reached God who has not been able to make God. Those
who trouble themselves about the abstract God have no God;
they only use the word God. They have the truth, but they do
not have God.

Truth without God is not satisfying. One ought to reach truth
through God; it is that which gives satisfaction. If all the strength
that one derives from food were given in one pill it would perhaps keep a person alive, but it would not give him the joy of
eating. If one took the pill of truth, maybe a part of one's being
would be satisfied, but that is no real satisfaction. The idea of
God feeds a person; he must first make it in himself, with his
imagination; but if he is not willing to use his imagination, if
he is only waiting for God to come to him, he will have to wait
a long time.

When a person thinks, that is another kind of action. At that
time he controls his mind, either consciously or unconsciously,
and directs it according to his own will. He becomes reasonable,
exact, and thoughtful. Both an imaginative and a thinking person
may go to extremes and may fail; but keeping the balance is
what brings about desired results. A thinking person, also, may
think so hard that he becomes confused by his own thoughts.
There are many thinkers who think so hard that they become
thoughtless.

The second aspect of mind is memory. The work of memory
is not creative but perceptive. Its work is to receive impressions
and to gather them together. Some scientists say that the cells
of the brain are impressed by every impression that comes
through the senses, and it is that which is kept in the brain, to
be brought forth when one wants them. But it is not like that,
although it can be taken as a symbolic explanation. The scientist
has pictured it as it is in the inner plane, but because he does not

recognize the inner plane he wants to explain it in physical terms and calls it brain-cells. It is true in essence; but it is not in the brain, it is in the mind.

Memory can be likened to a photographic plate; the impressions it takes remain there, and when a person wishes to recollect something this faculty helps him. It is within his reach. As soon as he wants to recall an experience he puts his hand, so to speak, on that particular plate which has received the impression of a certain experience. No experience received from sight, or smell, or hearing, or touch, or taste is lost. When people say, 'My memory is not good; I cannot remember things; I am absent-minded', the reason is that they have lost control over this faculty; but the impression is there all the same. Very often a person says, 'I know it, but I cannot recall it to my memory.' In other words, in his mind he knows it, but in his brain it is not yet clear. For instance, when a person cannot remember the name or the face of someone he says, 'I think I know it but I cannot find it for the moment.' That means that his mind knows it, that it is there, but that he cannot make it clear in his brain.

Memory can also be divided into two parts. There are certain things we need not look for, but which are always clear in our memory. We have only to stretch out and put our hand on them, such as figures, names, and faces of those we know. We can recall them at any moment we wish; they are always living in our memory. But then there is the second part of memory which is sometimes called the subconscious mind, though in reality it is the bottom of the memory. In this part of the memory a photograph is made of everything we have seen or known or heard, even once just like a flash, and it remains there. There we can find it at some time or other, either with difficulty or easily, as the case may be.

Besides these two aspects of the memory there is a still deeper sphere to which our memory is linked, and that sphere is the universal memory, in other words the divine Mind, where we do not only recollect what we have seen or heard or known, but where we can even touch something we have never learnt or heard or known or seen. This can be found there also; only for this the doors of memory should be laid open.

The third aspect of the work of the mind is mind-control, the concentrating power. This is done in two ways: with the help of memory and with the help of mind. The concentration that is performed with the help of memory is a negative or passive concentration. It requires little effort to concentrate with the help of memory. The Hindus taught this by placing certain gods and goddesses before a person and telling him to look at them and then to close his eyes and think about them. By looking at a certain object the memory reflected it, and that reflection was the concentration.

But those who do not practise concentration automatically retain things of great interest, things that impressed their mind most. It is for this reason that some carry with them a fear which has perhaps been there from childhood. It is carried with them through life. Some have a sad impression of disappointment; they carry it throughout life, they retain it in their mind. The mind keeps an impression alive by revivifying it, an impression of revenge, of gratefulness, of success, of failure, of love, of admiration. It is kept there, and the mind-cells give it food to keep it alive. Sometimes this is helpful and sometimes it works against one. Now the psychologist calls it a fixed idea and is always ready to call it a form of insanity, but it is not insanity. Everyone has got it; it is one of the attributes of mind. It is the faculty, the quality of retaining a thought. No doubt it may sometimes seem to be insanity, but insanity only comes from the abuse of that faculty. Any faculty can be abused and make a person unbalanced.

Then there is the positive concentration which is creative. This concentration comes by thinking. When one thinks of a tree or a flower, the mind has to create atoms in order to make that form; therefore it is positive. It needs will-power, a greater action of mind, to concentrate upon an object which the mind has to make. The mind has to work; it is not only concentrating, but creating and concentrating.

There are some who have a natural power of concentration, and there are others who lack it. But the mystery of success in all directions of life and the secret of progress is to be found in the power of concentration. It is not only progress and success which are gained by it, but spiritual attainment is the result of concentration. And very often one sees that some make efforts to concentrate but cannot really concentrate, and others do not know that they concentrate but do it all the same. Prayer and meditation and various other exercises, religious or spiritual, are meant to develop the power of concentration.

In the East it is customary in the mosque for one man to lead the prayers and all the other worshippers stand behind him. Before offering their prayers they first focus their minds on joining the thought of their leader. Now there was a great mystic who would not go to the mosque to pray. He was always in prayer; he did not need to go to the mosque. But there was an orthodox king reigning at the time, who had decreed that everybody had to attend the prayers. So this man was compelled by the police to go and join in, but in the middle of the prayers he left, which was considered a great crime. When he was brought before the court to be judged he said, 'I could not help it. The leader in his thought went to his house because he had forgotten his keys. So while I was praying I was left without a leader in the mosque, and that is why I went out.' This shows that as long as there is spirit in a religious form, it is a beautiful form which has life in it; but if there is no spirit behind it, however beautiful the form may be it is of no use. This is what is indicated by the saying in the Bible: 'It is the spirit that quickeneth; the flesh profiteth nothing.'

The fourth aspect of the mind is reasoning. This is a mathematical faculty, a faculty which weighs and measures and sees angles, whether they are right or wrong. And it is this faculty which makes man responsible for his actions. If he is not an individual he is nothing but an atom moved by influences. Whether conditions move him, or climatic influences, or personal influences, he is nothing but an instrument. But if he is held responsible for his actions it is because of this one faculty of mind that weighs and measures and reasons things out. Nevertheless, the reasoning of one person is not the same as the reasoning of another; and the reason of one moment is not the reason of the next moment. Something that is right just now may not be right tomorrow because reasoning will change. And they who dispute over reasonings do it in vain, for the reasoning of every person is different, and the reasoning of every person is good for him at that specific time. To urge and force one's reason on the mind of another is useless. The best way to educate a person is to develop his reasoning instead of urging upon him one's own reason, which is what many do.

It is very wonderful to watch the tricks of the reasoning faculty. When another person has done something, reason says, 'Because that person is wicked and has already done ten wicked things, now he has surely done another wicked thing.' And when a person himself has done a wicked thing, reason says, 'I have done it because I could not have done otherwise. I could not help it.' Reason takes the side of the ego. Reason is a slave and a servant of the mind; it is at its beck and call. The mind has only to turn its face to reason, and reason stands there as an obedient slave. It may not be right at all, but it is always there.

Reason is the most valuable thing that exists, but it is worthless when it is a slave of the mind. It gives the mind a reason to do either right or wrong. If one went and asked criminals in jail why they had done wrong, each one would have a reason. And if we look still closer at reason we shall see that reason is nothing but a veil and a series of veils, one veil over another. Even when the veils are lifted, at the end there is reason just the same. But as one goes further one will find the more thorough and more substantial reason. It is the surface of reason which is unreliable, but the depth is most interesting; for the depth of reason is the essence of wisdom. The more one understands reason the less one will seek it, because then there is nothing to it; one knows the reason already. It is the unreasonable man who always accuses every person's reason. The more reasonable a person is the more he understands everyone else's reason; that is why the wise can get along with both the wise and the foolish. But the foolish can get along with neither the foolish nor the wise.

There is no doubt that there is always a reason behind a reason, a higher reason. And when one arrives at this higher reason one begins to unlearn, as it is called by the mystics, all that one has

once learnt. One unlearns and one begins to see quite the opposite. In other words, there is no good which has not a bad
side to it, and nothing bad which has not a good side to it. No
one rises without a fall, and no one falls without the promise
of a rise. One sees death in birth, and birth in death. It sounds
very strange, and it is a peculiar idea; but all the same it is a
stage. When one rises above what is called reason one reaches
that reason which is at the same time contradictory. This also
explains the attitude of Christ. When a criminal was taken to
him he had no other attitude towards him but that of the for-
giver. He saw no evil there. That is looking from a higher reason.
And if we penetrate the thousand veils of reason we can touch
the reason of all reasons, and we can come to an understanding
that the outer reasons cannot give. And by that we understand
all beings: those who are in the right and those who are in the
wrong. It is said that the Apostles in one moment were inspired
to speak in many languages. It was not the English language,
the Hindustani or Chinese language; it was the language of
every soul. When a person has reached that state of mind in
which it touches the essence of reason then it communicates
with every soul. It is not a great thing to know thirty languages;
a person may know a hundred languages, but if he does not
know the heart of man he knows nothing.

There is a language of the heart. Heart speaks to heart, and
that communication makes life interesting. Two persons may
not speak, but their sitting together may be an exchange of lofty
ideal and harmony. When first I became initiated at the hands
of my spiritual teacher in India I was as eager as any man could
be to assimilate, to grasp, as much as I could. Day after day I
was in the presence of my Murshid, but not once did he speak
on spiritual matters. Sometimes he spoke about herbs and plants,
at other times about milk and butter. I went there every day for
six months to see if I could hear anything about spiritual things.
After six months the teacher spoke to me one day about the two
parts of a personality, the outer and the inner. And I was over-
enthusiastic; the moment he began I took out a notebook and
pencil. But as soon as I did this my teacher changed the subject
and spoke about other things. I understood what that meant;

it meant in the first place that the teaching of the heart should be assimilated in the heart. The heart is the notebook for it; when it is written in another notebook it will remain in one's pocket, but when it is written in the heart it will remain in the soul. Besides one has to learn the lesson of patience, to wait, for all knowledge comes in its own time. I asked myself further if it was worth while to come to a place after a long journey, and go there every day for six months to hear of nothing but trees and butter. And my deepest self answered: yes, more than worth while, for there is nothing in the whole world more precious than the presence of the holy one. His teaching may not be given in theories, but it is in his atmosphere. That is a living teaching which is real upliftment.

The essence of reason is the knowledge of God. Therefore, if there is any divine knowledge to be found it is in the essence of reason that one can find it.

And the fifth aspect of the mind is feeling. If this faculty is not open, then however wise and clever a person may be he is incomplete, he is not living. Mind begins to live from the moment that feeling is wakened in it. Many use the word feeling, but few of us know it. And the more one knows it the less one speaks of it. It is so vast that if there is any sign of God it is in feeling.

Today people distinguish intellectuality from sentimentality, but in point of fact intellectuality cannot be perfect without sentimentality. Neither can the thinking power be nurtured, nor the faculty of reasoning be sustained, without a continual outflow of feeling. In this age of materialism we seem to have lost the value of feeling. We speak of heart, but we do not see its real importance, although it is the principal thing, the root of the plant of life. The heart quality is something which sustains the whole of life. All virtues such as sincerity, respect, thoughtfulness, consideration, appreciation, all these qualities come through heart-quality. If he has no heart a person is not capable of appreciating, nor of being grateful, nor capable of expressing his own soul, nor of receiving goodness and help from another. A person without heart-quality remains selfish, even foolishly selfish. If he were wisely selfish it would be worth while.

People very often say that they have no time to show their heart-quality, no time to allow the heart to develop; they are so busy. But we can be busy every minute from morning till evening and at the same time do what we do with our whole heart, express it from the depth of our heart. When the heart-quality is shut out then all one does is lifeless. Feeling is such an important thing in our lives; our whole life depends upon our feeling. A person once disheartened sometimes loses enthusiasm for his whole life. A person once disappointed loses trust completely. A person who becomes heartbroken loses his self-fidence for the rest of his life. A person once afraid sustains fear in his heart for ever. A person who has once failed keeps the impression of his failure all through life.

People love to watch a cock-fight in the East. Two men bring their birds to fight, and as soon as one of them sees that the other bird will win he takes his bird away while it is still fighting, before it can expect defeat. He prefers to admit defeat while the two birds are still fighting than to allow his bird to be impressed by defeat, for once it is so impressed it will never fight any more. That is the secret of our mind. And once one learns to take care of one's mind just as in the case of the bird, to go to any sacrifice rather than give one's mind a bad impression, one will make the best of one's life.

One can read in the lives of great heroes and great personalities, how they went through all difficulties and sorrows and troubles and yet always tried to keep their heart from being humiliated. That gave them all the necessary strength; they always avoided humiliation. They were prepared for death, wars, suffering, poverty, but not for humiliation. Once when I was in Nepal I wanted a servant. I sent for one, and he was of the warrior caste, the Kshatrias, brave fighters in the mountains. And when I asked what work he wanted to do, he said, 'Any work you like, anything you like.' I said, 'What about the pay?' 'Anything you will give', he answered. I was greatly amused to find a man willing to do any work I gave him and to accept any pay I offered. 'Well,' I said, 'then there is no condition to be made?' He said, 'One. You will never say a cross word to me.' He was ready to accept any money, willing to do any work, but not humiliation. I appreciated that spirit beyond words; it was that which made him a warrior.

Is there anyone in this world who will own that he has no feeling? And yet there are hearts of rock, of iron, of the earth, and of diamond, silver, gold, wax, and paper. There are as many kinds of hearts in this world as there are objects. There are some objects that hold fire longer, there are others which burn instantly. Some objects will become warm and in a moment they will grow cold again; others disappear as soon as the fire touches them, while one can melt others and make ornaments out of them. And so are the heart-qualities. Different people have different qualities of the heart, and the knower of the heart will treat each differently. But since we do not think about this aspect we take every man to be the same. Although every note is a sound, they differ in pitch, in vibrations; and so every man differs in the pitch, the vibrations, of his heart. According to the vibrations of his heart he is either spiritual or material, noble or common. It is not because of what he does, nor because of what he possesses in this world; he is small or great according to how his heart vibrates.

I have all my life had a great respect for those who have toiled in the world, who have striven through life and reached a certain eminence, and I have always considered it a most sacred thing to be in their presence. This being my great interest in life, I began, at first in the East, to make pilgrimages to great people, and among them were writers, sages, philosophers, and saints; but once I came in contact with a great wrestler. And this man, who had the appearance of a giant with his monstrously muscular body, had such a sympathetic expansive nature, such simplicity and gentleness that I was deeply surprised. And I thought, 'It is not his size and strength that have made him great, but that which has melted him and made him lenient; it is that which makes him great.'

Feeling is vibration. The heart which is a vehicle, an instrument of feeling, creates phenomena if one only watches life keenly. If one causes anyone pain, that pain is returned. If one causes anyone pleasure, that pleasure is returned too. If one gives love to someone, love comes back; and if one gives hatred, that hatred comes back to one in some form or other—maybe in the form of pain, illness, health, or of success, joy, happiness; in some form or other it comes, it never fails. One generally does not think about this. When a person has attained a certain position in which he can order people about and speak harshly to them, he never thinks about those things. But every little feeling that rises in one's heart and directs one's action, word, and movement, causes a certain action and rebounds; only sometimes it takes time. Could one think that one can ever hate a person and that that hatred does not come back? It surely comes, some time. On the other hand, if one has sympathy, love, affection, kind feelings, one need never tell anybody that one has it, for even then it returns in some form or other.

Someone came to me and said, 'I was very sympathetic once, but somehow I have become hardened. What is the reason for it?' I said, 'You tried to get water from the bottom of the earth. But instead of digging deep down you dug in the mud and you were disappointed. If you have patience to dig till you reach water then you will not be disappointed."

Very often a person imagines that he has feeling, that he has sympathy. But if he had it he would be the master of life; then he would want nothing any more. When this spring which is in the heart of a man is once open it makes him self-sufficient and it takes away the continual tragedy souls have to meet with in life. That tragedy is limitation. Very often it is lack of feeling that paralyses the four other aspects of mind. The person without feeling is incapable of thinking freely. Feeling is what makes one thoughtful. A man may be of powerful mind, but if he cannot feel the power of his mind is limited, for real power is in feeling, not in thinking.

Sometimes people come to me and say, 'I have thought about it and I have wanted it, but I never got it.' And I have answered, 'You have never wanted. If you had wanted you would have got it.' They do not believe this; they continue to think that they have wanted it. It may be so, but to want it enough is another thing. If a person went and stood before a bank and said, 'Let all the money in the bank come to me', would it come? He imagines that he wants it, but he has doubts, he does not believe it will come. If he believed it, it would come. Doubt is a destructive element. It may be likened to the shadow that produces dampness, that hides the sun. The sun has no chance of reaching the place which is covered by it.

There is a story of Shirin and Farhad, a very well-known story of Persia. There was a stone-cutter and he was labouring at a memorial for somebody. One day he saw a lady who was to be the future queen of the Shah; and he said to her, 'I love you.' A stone-cutter, a labourer in the street, asking for the hand of a lady who was to be the future queen! He was a man without reason; but not a man without feeling. Feeling was there, and the claim came with feeling. This lady said, 'Very well, I will wait and see if your claim is true, and tell the Shah of Persia to wait.' And to try him she told him to cut a way through the mountains. He went, one man with hammer and chisel. He did not ask if he was able to do it or not. There was no reason; there was only feeling. And he made the road which thousands of people would not have made in a year, because every time he hammered the rock he called out the name of Shirin, the one he loved. He made the way, and when the king heard that it was finished he said, 'Alas, I have lost my chance, what shall I do?' Someone in the presence of the king said, 'I will see what can be done.' He went to Farhad the stone-cutter and told him, 'How wonderful is your love and devotion! It is phenomenal. But haven't you heard that Shirin is dead?' 'Is she dead?' he said. 'Then I cannot go on living.' And he fell down lifeless.

The point of this story is the power of feeling. What is lacking at this time is the feeling quality. Everyone wishes to think with the brain, to work with the head, but not with the heart. One can neither imagine and create beautiful art, nor think and make wonderful things, nor can one keep in one's memory something beautiful, nor retain thoughts in concentration, if there is no feeling at the back of it. Besides, if there is no feeling behind all such words as gratitude, thanks, appreciation, these words are without spirit; they become mere politeness. Today fineness is so much misunderstood; people only learn the outward aspect. If there were feeling behind all they say, life would be much more worth living.

When the mind is troubled it is confused, it cannot reflect anything. It is the stillness of mind that makes one capable of receiving impressions and of reflecting them. In Persian the mind is called a mirror. Everything in front of the mirror appears in it; but when this is taken away the mirror is clear. It does not remain. It remains in the mirror as long as the mirror is focused on it, and so it is with the mind.

The quality in the mind which makes it still at times and active at other times, which makes it reflect what it sees at one time and makes it avoid every reflection at another so that no outer reflection can touch it, this quality develops by concentration, contemplation, and meditation. The mind is trained by the master-trainer by diving deep, by soaring high, by expanding widely, and by centralizing the mind on one idea. And once the mind is mastered a person becomes a master of life. Every soul from the time it is born is like a machine, subject to all influences, influences of weather and of all that works through the five senses. For instance, no one can pass through a street without seeing the placards and advertisements. A man's eyes are compelled by what is before him. He has no intention of looking, but everything outside commands the eyes. So a man is constantly under the influence of all things of the outside world that govern him unknowingly. A person says, 'I am a free man; I do what I like.' But he never does. He does what he does not like many times. His ears are always subject to hear anything that falls on them, whether it is harmonious or inharmonious, and what he sees he cannot resist. And so a man is always under the influence of life.

Then there are the planetary influences and the living influences of those around him; and yet a man says, 'I have free will; I am a free man.' If he knew to what little extent he is free he would be frightened. But then there is one consolation, and that is that in man there is a spark somewhere hidden in his heart which alone can be called a source of free will. If this spark is tended a person has greater vitality, greater energy, greater power. All he thinks will come true, all he says will make an impression, all he does will have effect. What does a mystic do? He blows this spark in order to bring it to a flame till it comes to a blaze.

This gives him the inspiration, the power which enables him to live in this world the life of free will. It is this spark which may be called the divine heritage of man, in which he sees the divine power of God, the soul of man; and to become spiritual means that by blowing upon this spark one produces light from it and sees the whole of life in this light. And by bringing the inner light to a blaze one is more able to think, to feel, and to act.

CHAPTER VIII

THE POWER OF THOUGHT

THERE are some who through life's experience have learned that thought has power, and there are others who wonder sometimes whether this is really so. There are also many who approach this subject with the preconceived idea that even if every thought has a certain power, yet it is limited. But it would be no exaggeration to say that thought has a power which is unimaginable; and in order to find proof of this we do not have to go very far. Everything that we see in this world is but a phenomenon of thought. We live in it, and we see it from morning till evening, and yet we doubt if it is so; which shows that this, our beautiful world, itself gives us a pride and vanity, making us believe that we understand things better than we do. The less a person believes in the power of thought, the more positively he thinks he stands on the earth. Nevertheless, consciously or unconsciously he feels his limitation, and searches for something that will strengthen his belief in thought.

Thought can be divided into five different aspects: imagination, thought, dream, vision, and materialization. Imagination is that action of mind which is automatic. From morning till evening a person is either working, or if he is resting his mind is working just the same through imagination. Thought is thinking with will-power behind it; in this way we distinguish between the imaginative and the thoughtful. These two kinds of people cannot be confused; for one is imaginative, which implies powerless thinking, automatic thinking, and the other is thoughtful, which means his thinking is powerful.

When this automatic action takes place in the state of sleep, it is called a dream. This is distinct and different from imagination, because while a person is imagining his senses are open to this objective world, and therefore his imagination does not take a concrete form. But when the same automatic action of mind goes on in the dream, there is no objective world to compare it with. The mystic can always see the condition of the mind of a person by knowing how he dreams, for in the dream the automatic working of his mind is much more concrete than in his imagination.

There are some who are able to read the character or the future by knowing what the person imagines. They always ask him to name a flower, a fruit, something he loves or likes, in order that they may find the stream of his imagination. From that stream of imagination they find out something about the character of that person and about his life. It is not necessary to be a character-reader or a fortune-teller; any wise and thoughtful person can understand by the way someone dresses or by his environment how his thoughts run, what his imaginings are. But since the state of dreaming enables the mind to express itself more concretely, the dream is the best way to understand what state of mind a person has. When once this is understood, there is little reason left to doubt whether the dream has any effect upon a person's life and future. Indeed, man does not know, man cannot imagine, to what an extent thought influences life.

Vision can be said to be a dream which one experiences in the wakeful state. A person who is imaginative or capable of imagination is capable of creating a thought. And when this thought which he has created becomes an object upon which his mind is focused, then all else becomes hidden from him; that particular imagination alone stands before him as a picture. The effect of this vision is certainly greater than the effect of a dream; the reason is that the imagination which can stand before one's mind in one's wakeful state is naturally stronger than the imagination which was active in one's state of sleep.

The fifth aspect of thought is materialization. And it is in the study of this subject that we find the greatest secret of life. No doubt a person will readily accept that it is by the architect's imagination that a beautiful building is built, that it is by the gardener's imagination that a beautiful garden is made. But generally when it comes to matter and all things that are connected with matter, man wonders how far imagination or thought has power over them. Nowadays, as psychology is beginning to spread throughout the Western world, people will at least listen patiently when one speaks about it. But on the other hand there are many who take a medicine with great faith, but if they are told that a thought can cure them they will smile at the idea. This shows that with all the progress that humanity seems to have made, it has gone back in one direction, the higher thought; for man today generally does not believe in the power of thought and he believes still less in what he calls emotion.

In point of fact if one can speak of the soul of a thought, that soul is the feeling which is at the back of it. One sees that people become confused when they hear only words behind which there is no feeling. What makes a thought convincing is the power behind it; and that power consists of feeling. The general tendency is to wave aside what is called imagination. When one says that a person imagines something it means that he amuses himself. One says to him, 'Oh, you only imagine it; it does not exist in reality'. But in reality when one has imagined something, that imagination is created, and what is once created exists; and if it is thought that is created, it lives longer, because thought is more powerful than imagination. In this way man today ignores that power which is the only power and the greatest power that exists, calling it sentimentality, which means nothing. It is with this power that heroes have conquered in battle; and if anyone has ever accomplished a great thing in the world, it is with this power of heart that he has accomplished it, not with the power of the brain. The music of the most wonderful composers, the poetry of the great poets of the world, have all come from the bottom of their hearts, not from their brain. And if we close the door to sentiment, to imagination, and to thought, that only means that we close the door to life.

The Sufi sees both the Creator and the creation in man. The limited part of man's being is the creation, and the innermost part of his being is the Creator. If this is true, then man is both limited and unlimited. If he wishes to be limited he can become more and more limited; if he wishes to be unlimited he can become more and more unlimited. If he cultivates in himself the illusion of being a creation, he can be that more and more. But if he cultivates in himself the knowledge of the Creator, he can also be that more and more.

With every kind of weakness, every kind of illness, every kind of misery, the more one gives in to them, the more they weigh one down. And sometimes this can happen even to the extent that the whole world falls on one's back and one is buried beneath it. Another person, however, will rise up from it. It may be difficult, but at the same time it is possible. Little by little, with courage and patience, he will rise up and stand upon that world which would otherwise have crushed him. The former is going down, the latter is rising. Both depend upon the attitude of mind; and it is the changing of this attitude which is the principal thing in life, either from a material or from a spiritual point of view. All that is taught in the Sufi esoteric studies and by Sufi practices is taught in order to arrive little by little, gradually, at that fulfilment which is called mastery.

Mastery comes from the evolution of the soul, and the sign of mastery is to conquer everything that revolts one. That is real tolerance. Souls which have attained to that spiritual mastery show it not only with people, but even with their food. There is nothing that the soul which has gained mastery would not touch, though it may not like it or approve of it.

The entire system of the Yogis, especially of the Hatha Yogis, is based upon making themselves acquainted with something their nature revolts against. No doubt by doing this they may go too far in torturing and tormenting themselves, and these extremes are not right, but all the same that is their principle.

It is not the heat which kills a person, but the acceptance of the heat. It is the same with food and medicine, for behind everything there is thought. Even now there are Yogis who could jump into the fire and not be burnt. One will find that intolerant souls are the most unhappy in the world, because everything hurts them. Why should they be so—uncomfortable in the house and restless outside? Because of this tendency of disliking, of rejecting, of prejudice. It is this tendency which must be conquered; and when it is conquered great mastery is achieved.

I remember my teacher at school telling us that the leaves of the Nīm tree had great healing qualities. That did not interest me very much, but what did interest me, as he told us also, was that these leaves were so bitter than one could not drink a brew of them. And the first thing I did was to gather some of these leaves, and nobody understood why I did it; but I made a tea of them and drank it, and to my great satisfaction I did not even make a face! For four or five days I continued this and then I forgot all about it. It is fighting against all that one cannot do that gives one mastery. But generally one does not do that; one fights against things that prevent one from getting what one wants. Man should fight only with himself, fight against the tendency of rejecting; this would lead him to mastery. As a general principle in life there is no use in forcing anything, but if we want to train ourselves, that is another thing. It is a process, not a principle.

One may say it is a great struggle. Yes, it is so; but there is struggle in both, in coming down and in going up. It is just as well to struggle and come up, instead of struggling and going down. Whenever a person goes down, it only means that he is feeble in his thought. And why is he feeble in his thought? Because he is weak in his feeling. If feeling protects thought, and if thought stands firm, whatever be the difficulty in life, it will be surmounted.

CHAPTER IX

CONCENTRATION

TO GAIN knowledge of concentration requires not only study, but balance also. Before touching this subject I would first like to explain what motive we have behind concentration. There are two aspects of life: the audible life and the silent life.

By audible life I mean all experiences, all sensations that we experience through our five senses. This is distinct from the life which I would call the silent life. And when one asks what benefit one derives from getting in touch with the silent life, the answer is that the benefit is as abstract as the silent life itself. The life of sensation is clear; its benefit is clear; and yet as limited as is the life of sensation, so limited is its benefit. That is why in the end we find all our experiences of little value. Their importance lasts as long as we experience them; but after that the importance of the life of sensation is finished.

The value of silent life is independent. We are inclined to attach a value to something which concerns our outer life. The silent life does not give us a special benefit but a general benefit. In other words, if there is a minor wound on the body an external application of a certain medicament can cure it; but there are other medicines which can cure the general condition, and this is more satisfactory than the external cure, though it is less spectacular.

One cannot say exactly what profit is gained by concentration, but in reality every kind of profit is to be attained through concentration, in all directions. There are two kinds of concentration: automatic concentration and intentional concentration. Automatic concentration is found in many people who do not know that they concentrate and yet they do. They concentrate automatically, some to their disadvantage, some to their advantage. Those who concentrate to their advantage are the ones whose mind is fixed on their business, on their art, on any occupation they have. They are the ones who because of their concentration can work more successfully; be it a composer, a writer, or a musician, according to his power of concentration so will be his success. I once had the pleasure of hearing Paderewski in his own house. He began to play gently on his piano. Every note took him into a deeper and deeper ocean of music. Any meditative person could see clearly that he was so concentrated in what he did that he knew not where he was. The works of great composers which will always live, which win the hearts of men, whence do they come? From concentration. So it is with a poet, so it is with an artist; it is concentration which brings colour and line, which makes the picture. Naturally, whether it be an artist or a writer, a musician or a poet, or somebody who is in business or industry, in the absence of concentration he can never succeed.

Sometimes concentration works to a disadvantage. There are some people who always think that they are unlucky, that everything they do will go wrong, who think that everybody dislikes them, that everybody hates them. Then some begin to think that they are unable to do anything, that they are incapable, useless. Others out of self-pity think that they are ill. In that way even if they are not ill they create illness. Some by concentration cherish illness, always think of it. No physician could be successful with them. An old physician once said, 'There are many diseases, but there are many more patients.' Once a person has become a patient through concentration, he is difficult to cure. And there are many such cases of automatic concentration to the disadvantage of man.

Intentional concentration is taught by thinkers, philosophers, and meditative people. The whole of mysticism, of esotericism, is based upon the idea of concentration. This mystical concentration can be divided into four different grades. The first is concentration, the next contemplation, the third meditation, the fourth realization.

The definition of the first grade is the fixing of one's thought upon one object. One should not concentrate upon just any object that comes along, for what one concentrates upon has an effect upon one. When one concentrates on a dead object it has the effect of deadening the soul; when one concentrates on a living object it naturally has a living effect. The secret of the teachings of all prophets and mystics is to be found in this.

This concentration is achieved in three different ways. The first way is by action. One makes a certain movement or performs an action which helps the mind to concentrate on a certain object. Another way is with the help of words. By the repetition of certain words one learns to think automatically of a certain object. The third way is with the help of memory. Memory is like a builder's yard. From this the builder takes anything he likes: tiles, pillars, bricks, whatever he wants. The man who concentrates in this way does the same as children who have bricks to build toy houses with. He collects things in his memory and with them he composes objects in order to concentrate on what he wishes.

As to contemplation, it is only when a person is advanced enough that he can contemplate; because contemplation is not on an object, it is on an idea. No doubt a man may think that he is ready to do anything, and that after concentration he can contemplate; but the nature of the mind is such that it slips out of one's hands the moment one tries to hold it. Therefore before one really starts to think the mind has already thrown off the object of concentration like a restive horse. Mind is not always so unruly; it proves to be unruly when it wants to rule itself. It is like the body: one may feel restful sitting naturally, but as soon as one keeps quite still for five minutes, the body begins to feel restless; and it is still more difficult to make the mind obey. Mystics therefore find a rope to tie the mind in a certain place where it cannot move. What is that rope? That rope is breath. It is by that rope that they bind the mind and make it stand where they wish it to stand. It is like the bird which uses its saliva to make its nest; so is it with the mystic who out of breath creates atmosphere, creates light and magnetism in which to live.

One characteristic of the mind is that it is like a gramophone-record: whatever is impressed upon it, it is able to reproduce; and another characteristic of the mind is that it does not only reproduce something, but it creates what is impressed upon it. If ugliness is recorded, it will produce disagreement, inharmony. The learning of concentration clears the record, makes it produce what we like, not what comes automatically. In this world one is so open to impressions. One goes about with eyes and ears open, but it is not only the eyes, not only the ears which are open; the lips are open to give out what the eyes and ears take in, that is the dangerous part.

The third part of concentration is meditation. In this grade one becomes communicative; one communicates with the silent life, and naturally a communication opens up with the outer life also. It is then that a man begins to realize that both the outer and the inner life, everything, in fact, is communicative. Then a man begins to learn what can never be learnt by study or from books, that the silent life is the greatest teacher and knows all things. It does not only teach, but gives that peace, that joy, that power and harmony which make life beautiful.

No one can claim to be meditative. For a meditative person need not say it with the lips. His atmosphere says so, and it is the atmosphere alone which can say whether it is true or false. Once I asked my spiritual teacher what was the sign of knowing God. He said, 'Not those who call out the Name of God, but those whose silence says it.' Many go about looking, searching for something worth while, something wonderful, but there is nothing more wonderful than the soul of man.

Realization is the result of the three other grades. In the third kind of experience man pursued meditation; but in this, meditation pursues man. In other words, it is no longer the singer who sings the song, but the song sings the singer. This fourth grade is a kind of expansion of consciousness; it is the unfoldment of the soul; it is diving deep within oneself; it is communicating with each atom of life existing in the whole world; it is realizing the real 'I' in which is the fulfilment of life's purpose.

CHAPTER X

THE WILL

WORDS such as wish, desire, love, and their like mean more or less the same thing; but the word 'will' has a greater importance than all those other words. And the reason is that will is life itself. The Bible calls God love. Love in what sense? Love in the sense of will. The Creator created the universe by what? By love? By will; love came afterwards. Love is the will when it is recognized by its manifestation; then it is called love; but in the beginning it is will. For instance, the Taj Mahal, the great building at Agra, is said to be the token of the love that the emperor had for his beloved. At the same time, when one looks at it objectively, one cannot call it an expression of love; one would sooner call it a phenomenon of will. For the beginning of the building at least, one may look at the spirit, the impulse which started it, as a phenomenon of the emperor's will; after it was finished one can say it was the expression of his love. When a person says, 'I desire it', 'I wish it', it is an incomplete will, a will which is not conscious of its strength, a will which is not sure what it wills. In that case it is called a desire, a wish. But when a person says, 'I will it', that means it is definite. A person who never can say 'I will it', has no will.

From this we may conclude that will is the source and the origin of all phenomena. Hindus have called the creation a dream of Brahma, the Creator. But a dream is a phenomenon of the unconscious will, when the will works automatically.

The will is the action of the soul. One can also call the soul the self of the will. The difference between will and soul is like the difference between a person and his action.

There is a difference between the thoughtful and the imaginative man, and the difference is that the one thinks with will, the other thinks without will. When once a person knows the value of will he then recognizes that there is nothing in the world which is more precious than will. Naturally, therefore, the question arises in the mind of the thoughtful man, 'Have I will in me? have I a strong will or have I a weak will?' And the answer is that no one can exist without will; everyone has a will.

The automatic working of the mind produces imagination, and the value of imagination depends upon the cultivation of the mind; if the mind is tuned to a higher pitch then the imagination will naturally be at a higher pitch; but if the mind is not tuned to a high pitch then naturally the imaginations will not be at a high pitch.

Imagination has its place and its value. But when? At that time when the heart is tuned to such a pitch that the imagination cannot go anywhere else but into paradise. The heart which is so tuned by love and harmony and beauty, without willing it begins to float automatically; and in this automatic movement it reacts to whatever it touches, or expresses it in some form. When it is in the form of line or colour or notes, then art, painting, music, or poetry is produced; it is then that imagination has value. But when it comes to business and science and all things which are connected with our everyday life and the world, it is better to leave imagination aside and work with thought.

As both night and day are useful, as both rest and action are necessary, so both thinking and imagination have their place in our life. For instance, if a poet used his will to direct his imagination it would become a thought and would become rigid. The natural thing for a poet is to let his mind float into space; and whatever it happens to touch to let his heart express it, and then what is expressed is an inspiration. But when a person has to attend to a business affair he must not let his heart float in the air; he must think of the things of the earth, and think about figures very carefully.

Then we come to the question of how we can maintain our will. The nature of the life we live is to rob us of our will. Not only the struggle we have to undergo in life, but also our own self, our thoughts, our desires, our wishes, our motives, weaken our will. The person who knows how our inner being is connected with the perfect Will, will find that what makes the will smaller, narrower, more limited, is our experience throughout life. Our joys rob us of our will as do our sorrows; our pleasures rob us of our will as do our pains; and the only way of maintaining the power of will is by studying the existence of will and by analysing among all the things in ourselves what will is.

It might seem that motive increases will-power, but no doubt in the end we will find that it robs us of will-power. Motive is a shadow upon the intelligence, although the higher the motive, the higher the soul, and the greater the motive, the greater the man. When the motive is beneath the ideal, then this is the fall of man; and when his motive is his ideal it is his rise. According to the width of motive man's vision is wide, and according to the power of motive man's strength is great.

Furthermore there is an English saying, 'Man proposes, God disposes.' One is always faced with a power greater than oneself which does not always support one's desire. And naturally a person with will, faced with a greater power, must sooner or later give in and be impressed by the loss of his own will. This is only one example, but a hundred examples could be given to show how one is robbed of one's will without realizing it. Very often a person thinks that by being active or determined he maintains his will, and that by being passive he loses his will. But it is not so. Where there is a battle there is an advance and there is a retreat. By a retreat one is not defeated and by an advance one has not always succeeded. A person who exerts his will all the time, strains it and exhausts it very soon. It is like being too sure of a string that one has in one's hand while rubbing it on the edge of a sharp stone. Very often one sees that people who profess great will-power fail much sooner than those who do not profess it.

There is also always a battle between will-power and wisdom; and the first and wisest thing to do is to bring about a harmony between wisdom and will-power. When a person says, 'I wish to do this, I will do this', and at the same time his sense says, 'No, you cannot do it, you must not do it', then even with all his will-power he either cannot do it or he will do something against his better judgment.

This also shows us life in another light: that those who are wise but without will are as helpless as a person with will-power but without wisdom. There is no use keeping wisdom at the front and will-power at the back; nor is there any use in keeping will-power at the front and wisdom at the back. What is necessary is to make the two as one, and this can be done by becoming conscious of the action of both in all one does. At the same time one can practise it in one's everyday life by depriving oneself of things one likes. If a person always has what he likes to have, no doubt he spoils his will, for then his will has no reaction.

A stimulus is given to the will when one deprives oneself of what one desires: then the will becomes conscious of itself, alive; it wonders why it should not have it. For instance, a person wants to have peaches, but at the same time he is very much attracted to the flower of the peach. He thinks the flower is beautiful, and then the idea comes: why not let it remain on the plant? That will make him decide not to pick it. This gives him a stimulus, because first desire wanted to take hold of it, then sense wanted to work with it; and as light comes from friction, so also does will come from friction.

The power of will is in controlling, in contrast with imagination which works without control, for if one wants to control it one spoils it. Nothing in the world, either in the sphere of the mind or on the physical plane, can move without the power of will; but while with one thing the power of will is in absolute control, with the other it is working automatically.

There is another enemy of will-power and that is the power of desire. Sometimes this robs will-power of its strength; sometimes will-power, by a conflict with desire, becomes strong. The self-denial taught in the Bible generally means the crushing of desires. It should not be taken as a principle but as a process. Those who have taken it as a principle have lost; those who have taken it as a process have gained.

The enemy of sense, of wisdom, is the lack of tranquillity of mind. When the mind is tranquil it produces the right thought, and wisdom naturally rises as a fountain. The Sufis have therefore taught different exercises, both in physical and in meditative form, in order to make the mind tranquil, so that the wisdom which is there may spring up as a fountain. It is not in disturbed water that one can see one's image reflected; it is in the still water that one can see one's image clearly. Our heart is likened to water, and when it is still wisdom springs up by itself. It is wisdom and will together that work towards a successful issue.

Will-power is systematically developed by first disciplining the body. The body must sit in the prescribed posture; it must stand in the place it is asked to stand in. The body should not become restless, tired, by what is asked of it, but it should answer the demands of the person to whom it belongs. The moment the Sufi begins to discipline the body, he begins to see how undisciplined it always was; then he finds out that this body which he has always called 'mine', 'myself', and for whose comfort he has done everything he could, that this infidel seems to be most disobedient, most faithless.

After that comes the discipline of the mind. This is done by concentration. When the mind is thinking of something else and one wishes it to think on one specific thought, then the mind becomes very restless; it does not want to remain in one spot, for it has always been without discipline. As soon as one disciplines it, it becomes like a restive horse that one has to master. The difficulty starts when one tries to concentrate; it begins to jump, while at other times it only moves about. This happens because the mind is an entity. It feels as a wild horse would feel: 'Why should I be troubled by you?' But the mind is meant to be an obedient servant, just as the body is meant to become an obedient tool to experience life with. If they are not in order, if they do not act as one wishes them to, then one cannot hope for real happiness, real comfort in life.

The will can become so strong that it controls the body, making it perfectly healthy. But, one may ask, what about death then? Death is not something foreign to will-power. Even death is caused by will-power. One thinks one does not invite one's death; indeed, one does not; but the personal will becomes feeble and the greater Will impresses this feeble will, turning it into itself. For the smaller will belongs to the greater Will. Sufis call the former *Kadr* and the latter *Kaza*. Kaza reflects upon Kadr its command, and Kadr unconsciously accepts it. On the surface a man may still want to live, but in the depth he has resigned himself to die. If man did not resign himself to death he would not die. In the depth of his being he becomes resigned to death before his life is taken away from him.

Resignation of the human will to the divine Will is the real crucifixion. After that crucifixion, follows resurrection. One can come to this by seeking the pleasure of God; and it is not difficult, once one has begun to seek the pleasure of God. It is only when one does not begin to try that one does not know what is the pleasure of God. But apart from this there is another lesson which the Sufis have taught: to seek the pleasure of one's fellowmen; and this is the very thing that man usually refuses to do. He is quite willing to do the pleasure of God, but when one asks him to seek the pleasure of his fellow-men he refuses.

In either case, however, one is seeking the pleasure of one and the same Being. One begins with resignation; but once one has learnt to be resigned in life, and when one is tuned to the divine Will, one does not need to be resigned, for one's wish becomes the divine impulse.

CHAPTER XI

MYSTIC RELAXATION (1)

MYSTIC relaxation is of the greatest importance, for the whole spiritual culture is based and built upon this one subject; and yet there is so little spoken and written about it. It has been experienced and studied by the seekers after truth of all ages, and it is by the full understanding of this subject that they attained to greater power and inspiration.

Life is rhythm. This rhythm may be divided into three stages, and at every stage this rhythm changes the nature and character of life. One rhythm is mobile, another is active, and the third is chaotic. The mobile rhythm is creative, productive, constructive, and through that rhythm all power and inspiration are gained, and peace is experienced. The further stage of that rhythm, the active rhythm, is the source of success and accomplishment, of progress and advancement, the source of joy and fulfilment. And the third stage of this rhythm, the chaotic rhythm, is the source of failure, of death, of disease and destruction, the source of all pain and sorrow.

The first kind of rhythm is slow, the second kind is faster, and the third is faster still. The direction of the first is direct, of the second even, and of the third zigzag. When one says that a person is wise and thoughtful, it means that he is in the first rhythm; when one says that a person is persevering and successful, he is in the second rhythm; and when it is said that this person has lost his head and has gone astray, he is in the third rhythm. He is either digging his own grave or the grave of his affairs; he is his own enemy. Everything he wants to accomplish, however much he wants to advance or progress, all goes down in destruction because he has taken this third rhythm, the chaotic and destructive rhythm. Therefore it is up to us to tune ourselves either to the first, to the second, or the third rhythm, and accordingly this will become our condition in life.

Have planetary influences, then, nothing to do with our life?

Yes, they have, but how do even planetary influences work on us? If we have put ourselves in a particular rhythm, these influences have no power to bring about success or failure; if we only put ourselves in that rhythm there will be a similar result, and also the environment will react in the same way. If we are in favourable or in unfavourable, in congenial or uncongenial surroundings, it all means that we have put ourselves in that particular rhythm. When we experience success, good luck or bad luck, good or bad fortune, it is according to the rhythm we have brought about.

Where is this power to be found, how is it to be realized? If a person thinks about it, he can very easily realize it physically, mentally, and spiritually. There is a time when the body is in a perfectly calm condition, and there is a time when the body is excited, when the breath has lost its rhythm, is irregular, uneven; that is a chaotic condition. And when the body has a regular circulation and proper rhythm and even breath, then a person is capable of doing things, accomplishing things. When the body is restful, comfortable, relaxed, we are able to think; inspirations, revelations come, we feel quiet, we have enthusiasm and power. In Sanskrit the first rhythm is called *Satva*, the second *Rajas* and the third *Tamas*. It is from the middle rhythm that the word Raja has come, which means the one who has persevered with his sword and made a kingdom. His rhythm is the middle rhythm. The first rhythm is sometimes called *Sand*, which makes one think of the English *saint*. From this rhythm comes goodness.

In our life at a certain time one rhythm prevails, at another the second rhythm, and at still another the third; and yet in our life one rhythm is predominating through all changes, whether a person has the third, the second, or the first rhythm.

One who has the first rhythm has always power to accomplish things. And as it is with the body, so it is with the mind. Body and mind are so closely connected that whatever rhythm the mind has, the body has; and the rhythm which is predominating in body and mind, that same rhythm is the rhythm of one's soul.

There was a king who when a certain problem was brought

to him by his ministers, used to say, 'Read it again'; and the minister would read it again. Maybe after four lines he would stop him and say, 'Read it again', and the minister would do so. And after he had heard it three times, his answer would be perfect. But what do we sometimes do when we converse with people? Before the conversation has stopped, we have answered them. So impatient are we, and eager to answer and excited about it, that only one in a hundred people stops to listen to what another has to say.

It is the wrong rhythm, the chaotic rhythm which brings about chaotic results. Where does war come from? From chaotic action. When there is chaotic action, nations become involved in war; by chaotic action the whole world may be involved in war. People doubt the religious belief of Christ having saved the whole world; they cannot understand it. They say that man saves himself. But they do not realize that one man can ruin the whole world and that one man can save it. It is by rhythm that he can save the whole world. When there is a chaotic influence it works like an intoxicating drink in thousands of people, like a germ of disease, spreading from one person to another through the whole country. If that is true mechanically, then psychologically it can be true that one person's chaotic influence can put the whole world in despair, though it is very difficult for ordinary people to understand this.

The Turkish nation was greatly depressed on every side, and the wars had made the country very poor; and with nothing but disappointment all the time it had gone down and down. And then there came one man, Kemal Pasha, and his rhythm put life into thousands and thousands of dead souls who were waiting for some result, hungry from lack of food, disappointed with every effort. And one man brought cheer to them all and picked up the whole country. We can see what happened in Italy, where every action was powerless because of so many different ideas and parties. There was no united effort, no concentration. After the fatigue of the war, there came one man, Mussolini, who lifted up the thoughts of the whole country. And this is only the outer plane; in the spiritual plane the effect is still more powerful, only those who work on the spiritual plane do not manifest to view. What happens in the political world is known, but in the spiritual world great things happen and they are not known; but their influence is most powerful because of their rhythm.

We see this in the life of Napoleon. Some appreciate his life and some do not. But nevertheless during his wars he was the inspiration and power and backbone of the whole country. It was all Napoleon's spirit. And always, even during the greatest anxieties of war, he used to have moments of silence, even sometimes on horseback; and while he was having this silence he would recuperate all the strength lost in the continual responsibilities of war, and he would feel refreshed after having closed his eyes. What was it? He had the key of relaxation. It is tuning oneself to a desired rhythm.

We should not be surprised or laugh at sages who keep one hand raised up, or stand perhaps on their head with their feet up, or sit in one posture for a long time. There is some reason for it. Those artists who know the different ways of the art of relaxation know how to bring about a relaxed condition in the body and mind. I myself, continually for about twelve years, had only three hours' sleep at night and sometimes not even that. And all those twelve years I was never ill. I had all the strength necessary and was perfectly well because of the practice of relaxation.

The question is, how does one relax? It is not by sitting silent with closed eyes; for when the mind is giving attention to the body by thought or feeling, then the body is not relaxed, because the mind is torturing the body. And when feeling is giving attention to the mind, then the mind is tortured. And this torture, even if the eyes are closed, even if we are sitting in a certain posture, does no good. With relaxation one should consider three points of view: the point of view of the physical body, the point of view of the mind, and the point of view of the feeling. The point of view of the physical body is that one must accustom oneself to get power over, or to have influence on, one's circulation and pulsation; and one can do that with the power of thought and with the power of will together with breath. By will-power one can bring about a certain condition in one's body so that one's circulation takes a certain rhythm. It is decreased according to will. One can do the same in regulating one's pulsation by the power of will. No sooner has the will taken in hand the circulation and the pulsation of the body, than the will has in hand a meditation of hours. It is for this reason that sages can meditate for hours on end, because they have mastered their circulation; they can breathe at will, slower or quicker. And when there is no tension on one's nervous or on one's muscular system, then one gets a repose that ten days' sleep cannot bring about. Therefore to have relaxation does not mean to sit quiet; it is to be able to remove tension from one's system—from one's circulation, one's pulsation, and one's nervous and muscular systems.

How does one relax the mind? The method for relaxation of the mind is first to make the mind tired. He who does not know the exercise for making the mind tired can never relax his mind. Concentration is the greatest action one can give to one's mind, because the mind is held in position on a certain thing. After that it will relax naturally and when it relaxes it will gain all power.

Relaxation of feeling is achieved by feeling deeply. The Sufis in the East in their meditation have music played that stirs up the emotions to such a degree that the poem they hear becomes a reality. Then comes the reaction, which is relaxation. All that was blocked up, every congestion, is broken down; and inspiration, power, and a feeling of joy and exaltation come to them.

It is by these three kinds of relaxation that one becomes prepared for the highest relaxation which is to relax the whole being: body in repose, mind at rest, heart at peace. It is that experience which may be called Nirwana, the ideal of thinkers and meditative souls. It is that which they want to reach, for in it there is everything. In that condition each person becomes for the time as a drop that is assimilated or submerged in its origin. And being submerged for one moment means that all that belongs to the origin is attracted by this drop, because the origin is the essence of all. The drop has taken from its origin everything it has in life. It is newly charged and has become illumined again.

CHAPTER XII

MYSTIC RELAXATION (2)

MYSTIC relaxation is really the same as meditation. Very often people are puzzled about the word meditation because it is used by so many people who sometimes have very different ideas about it. By calling it mystic relaxation the meaning becomes simple and clear.

From a physical point of view, there is the practice of contracting and stretching, which enables a man to bring out his inner vitality, whereas relaxation is a contrary action. Energy is either brought on to the outer plane or energy is put to rest in its natural, normal condition. When a person lifts something heavy, does something with determination, he charges his physical body with the energy which is within. It then expresses itself through his muscles and nerves. When a person is asleep the energy is put to rest. This energy is most valuable and precious; when it is used outwardly it brings external benefits and when it is used inwardly it brings about inner attainments.

Meditation is reached through two preliminary stages. The first stage is concentration and the next is contemplation. After these two stages comes the third, which is meditation. What comes after that is realization.

Nothing in this world can be thoroughly accomplished without concentration, whether in one's business or profession, or in spiritual work. Those who cannot make a success in their business or profession are the ones whose concentration is not right. And many of those who have succeeded in life owe this to the fact that their concentration is good. They may not know it. There have been many great inventors in the West who have produced wonderful things, yet they themselves did not know that it was due to their concentration that they were able to do so. Some are born with this as a natural gift, and it is because of it that they have made a success of whatever they have undertaken. If one is an artist, with the help of concentration one can produce wonderful works; if one is a scientist one can achieve great results in science; if one is a poet, poetry will be easy to write; if one is a mystic, mystical inspiration will flow; but without concentration, however qualified a person may be, he will not be able to make the best use of his qualifications; he can hardly be called qualified at all. It is by the power of concentration alone that he can express himself fully.

Concentration is the beginning of meditation; meditation is the end of concentration. Once concentration is fully acquired, it is easy for a person to meditate.

From a metaphysical point of view concentration can be regarded as having three aspects: reflecting, constructing, improvising. The first kind of concentration is to reflect any object that one has placed before oneself. This is the mirror-quality of mind that enables one to concentrate in this way. When one is impressed by a certain thing one has seen outside oneself, one tries to concentrate upon it, to hold it in mind. In other words, one focuses one's mind on that object with which one is impressed, and one's mind does nothing but reflect it.

The other kind of concentration is constructing or composing; for instance, when an artist has been told to make a very fanciful picture and he creates in his mind a creature with the face of a man, the horns of a buffalo and the wings of a bird. The material is there in his mind; he has only to put it together in order to produce a certain form. This is constructive concentration, visualizing, in other words making the mind produce something under the direction of the will.

All that man sees or thinks he sees is his own thought. Man can produce out of his thought an angel or a devil; he can produce God out of his thought. The building of the Tower of Babel is the making of the mind. Man's thought has great power; and when he comes to the realization that everything comes from one source and that everything is developing towards one goal, he begins to see that the source and the goal are God. Then the world of variety is no longer variety to him but unity; it is one.

The third aspect of concentration is improvising. If a poet is asked to write a poem on a rose-bud he begins to improvise. He brings into it a dewdrop, and he produces the picture of dawn; he takes a gentle stream of water and builds a beautiful background to it. This is the third kind of concentration.

Very often people think concentration means closing the eyes and sitting still in church, and that only once a week. And when they do this, although they themselves are in the church they do not know where their mind is.

When a person allows himself to be disturbed, that shows that his concentration is not good; and if his concentration is not good, that shows that his will-power fails him. The best way, therefore, to protect oneself from disturbance is to develop the power of concentration, so that the will-power develops naturally and one is able to withstand all the disturbances which arise when one has to live in the midst of the crowd.

The best remedy for a wandering mind is natural concentration; that means not forcing the mind. One should at first let the mind work naturally, thinking of things it is inclined to think about. Why should the mind think of something towards which it has no inclination? It is unnatural; it is like eating something one does not like; it will not be assimilated nor give good results. One should think about anything one loves, then one can learn to concentrate.

Sometimes one says that a person is out of his mind when he does not have it under his control. It means that his mind is working mechanically; the will has no control over it. For the will is the king and reason is his minister. When both work together the mind is under control; when reason does not help, when the will has lost control, then the mind is not one's own any more and one can say a person is out of his mind.

It happens that when a person's mind is not strong enough to hold the object which he wants to accomplish, it gives way; and sometimes the body is not in a sufficiently fit condition to hold it. But that object, when unaccomplished, is unaccomplished only according to his mind; in accordance with the scheme of nature it has died a natural, peaceful death.

The Bible speaks of self-denial. People think it means not eating, not drinking, giving up all that is beautiful and good in life, going somewhere in solitude never to appear again. It is a wrong interpretation of a true teaching. Self-denial is self-effacement; it comes from self-forgetting. If one studies one's surroundings one finds that those who are happy are so because they have less thought of self. If they are unhappy it is because they think of themselves too much. A person is more bearable when he thinks less of himself; and a person is unbearable when he is always thinking of himself. There are many miseries in life, but the greatest misery is self-pity. That person is heavier than rock, heavy for himself and heavy for others. Others cannot bear him; he cannot carry himself.

It is no easy thing to do, to forget oneself, but if one is able to, what a wonderful power one creates within oneself! It is a great mystery. It gives power over heaven and hell. Omar Khayyám says in his *Rubayat*, 'Heaven is the vision of fulfilled desire; hell is the shadow of a soul on fire.' Where is that shadow? Where is that vision? Is it not within ourselves? It is we who hold it. Therefore heaven and hell are what we have made for ourselves; it cannot be changed by anything else but concentration.

But concentration has an even greater significance than this, for it is that creative power which man possesses and which he has as a heritage of God. That creative power begins to work wonders. For instance, a person thinks, 'I should like fish for dinner', and when he comes home he finds that his housekeeper has cooked fish that evening. That is a phenomenon of concentration. He may not know it, but it worked in that way. The thought of the man struck the mind of the housekeeper, and the housekeeper served that dish to him. Imagine what a great power this is! One need not even think about one's desires; the very fact of having the desire is enough; concentration works it out and materializes it.

Such is the power of concentration. There are many stories told in the East about fakirs, dervishes, sages, Mahatmas. Many people wonder if they are true, and if they are true, how they come about. They want a scientific explanation, and it may be that one day it will be discovered by science. Nevertheless, one finds as much falsehood as truth in this, for anything can be imitated. There is gold and there is imitation gold; there is silver and there is imitation silver; and so there is imitation of truth also. What appears to be most wonderful and surprising is not all so wonderful. But at the same time there are things which are more wonderful than one can imagine, and they all belong to the power of mind. And where does this come from? From the source of all things. It is the power of God.

Even in the attainment of union with God, it is concentration which helps. The appearance of stigmata on some saints is the result of concentration; if it were not so then what would be the meaning and use of concentration? It seems out of the ordinary because only very few know what real concentration means. Someone who has mastered concentration has not very far to go; his next step will be the purpose for which he concentrated.

Contemplation is the second stage of concentration. Contemplation is the repetition of a certain idea, and this repetition materializes that idea. Those who have been able to accomplish great works in the world have been contemplative people. Often they do not know it. It is the continual repetition of a certain idea which creates that idea, which brings it into being in the physical world. For instance, those who can contemplate on health can bring about that perfect health which no medicine nor anything else can give. Those who contemplate upon inspiration will show great inspiration. Those who contemplate upon strength and power, develop strength and power. One cannot arrive at this stage until one has accomplished concentration, because concentration is the first stage, and one must proceed gradually towards the stage of contemplation. Coué's idea, that one should say, 'Every day, in every way, I am getting better and better', is something which has been known to the thinkers for thousands of years. Upon this the whole method of mysticism has been based. But he skips the first part, concentration; what he prescribes is contemplation, which is the second part.

One might ask to what extent contemplation can help. Nothing in the world is impossible for the contemplative person to accomplish if only he knows how to contemplate. No doubt this is gibberish to those who do not understand the subject. People wonder what relation man's mind has to affairs outside; perhaps one can heal oneself from illness, but if there is an affair outside which is going wrong, a money matter or a business transaction, what connection has that with the mind? The answer is that all that exists, whether it is business or anything else, all that is visible or invisible, seems to be outside, but in reality it is in our mind. It is outside because our eyes see it outside, but it is within us because the mind surrounds it. It is accommodated in our mind. Mind is an accommodation of the world which is outside.

A Hindustani poet describes this wonderfully, 'The land and sea are not too large for the heart of man to accommodate.' In other words, the heart of man is larger than the universe. If there were a thousand universes the heart of man could accommodate them. But man, unaware of his inner being, impressed by outer limitation, remains under the impression of his weakness, limitation, smallness. And that keeps him from using this great power which he can find within himself, this great light with which he can see life more clearly. It is only because he is unaware of himself.

The third stage is meditation. This stage has nothing to do with the mind. This is the experience of the consciousness. Meditation is diving deep within oneself, and soaring upwards into the higher spheres, expanding wider than the universe. It is in these experiences that one attains the bliss of meditation.

Man ought to turn every day of his life into a meditation. Whatever his work may be, he must do it, but at the same time he should meditate. Then he will get to know the secret meaning of his work, and in this way he will turn his life from a worldly life into a spiritual one. This applies to everyone, whether he works in a garden or in a factory, or elsewhere. As soon as he knows the appropriate meditation for the work he is doing he will develop, and all his work will become a meditation for him. And if he achieves this, the wages he earns will be nothing compared with the reward he will gain.

When his mind is concentrated a person does his work well, and even better than others. In a station in Rajputana I once saw a telegraph clerk accepting telegrams; while he was doing his work he was meditating at the same time. When it was my turn I said to him, 'I have come to give you this telegram, but I marvel at you, it is wonderful how you are keeping up your meditation during your work.' He looked at me and smiled; and we became friends.

If it were not for the spirit, work would be a nuisance at a time when life's needs are so great and when people have so little rest. Thus the best thing for a man is to meditate in his everyday life; if it is done properly he will reap the benefit of it not only from the earth, but from heaven. Meditation means the soul's endeavour towards spiritual unfoldment, and this endeavour may be practised in different ways in order to suit one's profession and work.

People always ask what benefit they will get; and they are more concerned with benefit today than ever before. In no age have people been so anxious to make profits as today, and they will give their life for it. It does not mean that a man today is less inclined to make a sacrifice; he is as ready to make sacrifices as a thousand years ago or even more so; only, he must be sure of what he can get by it. He is so concerned with gain that he always has gain in his view. Even when there is something that does not show immediate profit, and when he does not quite know what or how much profit there might be, he thinks, 'Well, perhaps this is something I can get without sacrifice.' It is strange. When people go to a voice-producer in order to develop their voice they work six, nine years and listen to everything the voice-producer says. They will do anything to develop their voice. But when they come to a spiritual man they ask him whether he can tell them something about concentration at the tea-table; taking tea they ask, 'What about meditation?' And they want the answer in one sentence!

But it is not gained in this way. This knowledge is attained in accordance with one's ideal about it. It is greater than religion, more sacred than anything in the world. The knowledge of self is like union with God. Self-realization is spiritual attainment. Can this be gained by a shallow conception of it? It is the deepest thing one can reach, the most valuable thing to attain to. It is for this reason that in the East a person does not look for it in a book, nor does a real teacher write a book on these things. He will write about philosophy; he prepares minds to appreciate his teaching; but he does not tell how to do it.

To my greatest surprise, while travelling in the West I saw people looking for books of this kind, wanting to buy books about Yoga, Yogis, spiritual attainment. Many have lost their mind by reading such books. They cannot keep balance. Trying to do what is in the book is just like going into the drug-store to get some Yoga-pills in order to attain spirituality! There are also many who look into the mirror to become clairvoyant, who gaze into a crystal in order to see the depth of life. They make light of something that is highest and best and most sacred.

This path can only be pursued by those who are serious. The ones who go first to some society, then to an institute, then to an occultist group, do not know what they are doing and what they are looking for. High knowledge is not to be got by going to twenty places and they will be disappointed in the end, because they went into it lightly.

There is a story of a Brahmin to whom a Moslim said, 'I am a worshipper of God who is formless, and here you are praying to this idol of God.' The Brahmin said, 'If I have faith in this idol it will answer me. But if you have no faith, even your God in heaven will not hear you.' If we do not attach ourselves seriously to things then those things laugh at us. Even as regards the things of the world, if we take them seriously we will achieve serious results.

There cannot be anything more serious than spiritual attainment. If a person takes that lightly he does not know what he is doing. It is better not to go into these things at all, rather than go and come back empty-handed. To come back disappointed from the spiritual path before reaching the final goal is the worst possible thing. To go bankrupt does not matter. One can pick up again what one has lost in the world. But the man who has embarked on the spiritual path and has turned back is to be pitied. It is the greatest loss and can never be repaired.

CHAPTER XIII

MAGNETISM

THERE is no great difference between magnetism and an electrical current. Scientists have never been able to give an answer to the question of what electricity really is; but one can say that to a certain extent electricity is magnetism and magnetism is electricity. Power of attraction is magnetism, power that gives force and energy is electricity; it is essentially the same power. But interesting as the subject of magnetism is from a scientific point of view, as interesting, or even more so, is it from a mystical point of view.

A magnet and something which is attracted to the magnet have a relationship. The magnet represents the essence, part of which is held by the object which is attracted. Very often one does not find a trace of that essence in the object that the magnet attracts, but at the same time the essence is there, and that is the logical reason why it is attracted.

The ancients used to recognize that the relationship between two persons of the same blood was influenced by that magnetism, and a deep study of this fact will certainly prove that there is an unknown attraction between two people who are blood-relations. An incident that occurred lately is an example of this. A man from Stockholm was visiting London, where he thought he had no relations or, if any, they dated from perhaps a century ago. In the street one day someone called him by name. When he turned round, the man who had called him excused himself, saying, 'I am sorry, I have made a mistake.' But he asked, 'How did you know my name? The name you said is mine!' And when they spoke together they found that they were cousins, although very distant ones.

The more attention we give to this subject, the more proof we can find of one element being drawn to its similar element. Sa'di says, 'Element attracts element, as a dove is attracted to a dove and an eagle is attracted to an eagle.' But do we not find the same thing in life every day? A gambler when he goes to another country, one does not know how, attracts another gambler very soon. And it is not only that when two persons of a similar element meet they are attracted to one another, but even conditions, life itself, brings about their meeting; life itself draws them together. And therefore it is natural that a person who is very sad attracts a miserable one to join him; the one with joy, with happiness, naturally attracts happiness. And in this way magnetism is working through the whole of creation; and in all aspects you will see the phenomena of magnetism, in the physical world as well as in the mental spheres. Of course, one cannot say that an element always attracts the same element, for the element also attracts what it lacks, what is opposite to it. When we think of friendship, we see that with some we feel inclined to be friends and from others we feel inclined to keep away. And the most interesting part is that those whom we feel disinclined to be friends with, have also some who are drawn towards them in friendship. This leads us to the truth which lies in musical harmony: how two notes have a relation to one another and their combination brings about a harmony.

Now coming to the question of the practical use of magnetism, whether you are in business or in industry, whether you are in domestic or in political work, in whatever situation, you will always find that magnetism is the secret of your progress in life; and as to qualifications, to which we give such great importance, you will find that numberless people who are most highly qualified do not make their way through life because of lack of magnetism. Very often there may be a highly qualified man, but before he speaks of his qualification the person to whom he has gone has had enough of him. Personality takes such an important place in life that even the absence of qualifications is tolerated when the personality has magnetism. In these times, when materialism is so much on the increase that personality is given much less importance in society, and when heroism has no place in life, magnetism works automatically and proves to be the most essential thing even now, and it will always prove so. But people generally do not go deeply into the subject of magnetism and only recognize personal magnetism by the attraction that they feel.

When we consider personal magnetism, we may divide it into four different classes.

One kind, the ordinary kind of magnetism, is concerned with the physical plane; and this magnetism has to do with nourishment, with hygiene, with regular living, with right breathing and the regulation of activity and repose. This magnetism also depends on the age, like the ascending and descending notes in an octave. It may be likened to the season of spring, which comes and goes; and at the same time this magnetism is dependent upon everything belonging to the physical world, since it is a physical magnetism.

Then there is the magnetism which may be called mental. A person with a sparkling intelligence naturally becomes the centre of his society. The person who has wit and a keen perception, who can express himself well, who understands quickly, that is the person who always attracts others around him and is liked by everyone. The person who has knowledge of human nature, who knows about things and conditions, naturally draws people towards him. If there is any qualification it is this; and without this qualification no other qualification can be of very great use. But a man is born with this sparkling kind of intelligence. It is he who becomes a genius, it is he who accomplishes things, and it is he who helps others to accomplish something, for on his mind others depend. It is this person who can guide himself and direct others. And with all our thought of equality in which we are so much absorbed, we shall find that it is this person who will win the battle in life, and it is this person who stands above the masses, who leads, and without whom many are lost.

The question is, how can this magnetism be developed? This magnetism is developed by study, by concentration, by a keen observation of life, and by the knowledge of repose. Very many intelligent persons, because they do not know how to concentrate and how to take repose in their lives, in time blunt their intelligence; because there is a certain fund of energy which is preserved and which is limited, and when there is too much pressure put upon that limited energy in the end what happens? A person becomes less and less intelligent, and his power of mind diminishes every day. Whenever you find a very intelligent man becoming duller every day, it always proves that the amount of energy that was there has been spent. It is, therefore, by knowing how to preserve one's energies by repose, and how to concentrate and sharpen one's intellect, that this magnetism remains in a right condition. What generally happens is that great responsibility falls on the intelligent person. Much more is asked of him than of others who lack intelligence. If he does not give his mind a rest by knowing how to repose, and if he does not concentrate and thus sharpen his intellect, naturally, just like a knife which is continually used, it will become blunted; naturally the continual use of intellect will make him short of words.

The third aspect of magnetism is perhaps a higher kind than the two which have been described above, for this magnetism is more profound and it affects another person more deeply. This is the magnetism of love, of sympathy, of friendliness. A person who by nature is sympathetic; a person who tolerates, who forgets, who forgives; a person who does not keep bitterness nor malice in his mind against anyone; a person who admires and appreciates beauty, who loves it in art, in nature, in all its forms, and who goes out to friend and foe, to the acquaintance, the stranger, to all; the person who can endure and who can suffer, and who has the power to have patience through all conditions of life, who feels the pain of another in his heart and who is always willing to become a friend, it is that person whose magnetism is greater than all the other magnetisms that we know of. We do not need to go far to see this. If only we look for good things in people we shall find this. Among our surroundings we can find many in whom we can appreciate this quality.

One day a man who had travelled very much saw an Indian mystic, and he said, 'We have heard so much and we have read so much about the saints and sages and Mahatmas and masters who live in India, but when I went there I found no one.' And the mystic told him, 'You need not have gone so far. The souls who are worth while, the souls who love one another, the saints and sages, are to be found everywhere.'

If we can appreciate them, we can find them; but if we cannot appreciate them, even if an angel came we would not be able to find these qualities in him. Nevertheless, call him a saint or a sage, call him a prophet or a Mahatma, if there is anything that draws man towards man, it is the love element that he pours out.

Now the question is, how can one develop this quality? And the answer will be: by one thing only. By studying, by knowing, by practising, and by living the life of a friend. By contemplation on this thought from morning till evening: 'Towards everyone I meet, towards those who love me and those who hate me, will I practise in my life that thought of friendliness, that outgoing, that pouring out of sympathy and love.' Apart from the magnetism that one acquires from this, when we consider life as it is, with all its limitations, with all the pain and troubles and responsibilities that it gives us, if there seems to be anything worth while it is one thing only, and that is the thought and impression that we have done our best to be gentle, to be tender to those whom we meet in our everyday life. If there is any prayer, if there is any worship, if there is any religion, it is this. For in the life hereafter there is no one to please; if there is anyone to be pleased and whose pleasure it is worth while to earn, it is here, it is man; and it is in the pleasure of man, if one understands it, that the pleasure of God resides.

The fourth aspect of magnetism is magnetism itself. Lack of magnetism means that this aspect is hidden; this magnetism is the soul of man. To define what the soul is, it may be said that the soul is the self of man. But which self? That self of which he does not know. There is a humorous Indian story about some peasants who were travelling, but it was the first time in their life that they had done so. Therefore, being worried about each other, they decided the next morning to count if all the peasants were still there. They were very upset after having counted, for they counted nineteen, and it was understood that twenty peasants had left home. And so each peasant counted and each said, 'There are nineteen'; and they could not find who was missing, for everyone was there. In the end they found that all those who had counted had forgotten to count themselves.

That is the condition of the soul. It sees all selves, but it does not see itself. And the day when the soul realizes itself, that day a new life begins, a new birth. It is the self-realized soul which grows, which expands. So long as the soul has not realized itself, it does not develop, it does not grow. Therefore it is at the moment when the soul begins to realize itself that a man really begins to live in the world. But it must be understood that the magnetism of the self-realized soul is greater than any magnetism one could ever imagine. It is power, it is wisdom, it is peace, it is intelligence, it is all. It is this magnetism that heals, heals bodies and heals minds; and it is this magnetism that raises those fallen into difficulties, in pain and sorrows. It is this magnetism that brings others out of their confusion, their darkness. It is by this magnetism that the illuminated souls spread out their love, thereby attracting all beings. It is of this magnetism that Christ said to the fishermen, 'Follow me, and I will make you fishers of men.' It is with this magnetism that the great ones, such as Buddha, such as Moses, Christ, Mohammad, came and attracted humanity. And humanity during the ages has not forgotten. It is their magnetism which, after their having left this earth, has held millions and millions of people in one bond of brotherhood, of sympathy, of friendship. The immense power that the soul-magnetism gives shows that it is divine magnetism. It is a proof of something behind the seen world.

CHAPTER XIV

THE POWER WITHIN US

ONE READS in the books from the East about the different miracles performed by great souls, and one wonders if there is some truth in them. One hears that there are people who know what is going on far away; that there are people who can send their thought from a very great distance; that there are people who can create things, produce things in a moment without having any materials; that there are people who can make things disappear. One even reads and hears that there are some who can command the rain to fall and who can make the multitude move according to their command, their will, and who can inspire the multitude in a flash; who can prevent plagues, and who can perform wonders in war.

No doubt there are many jugglers among them, but whenever there is truth, there is falsehood on the other side to laugh at it. Nevertheless, the truth remains just the same. There are stories of the wonder-workings and phenomena which occur in the East; many of those stories no doubt are of the jugglers who by sleight of hand or by some hypnotic influence can perform wonders. But there are others who are genuine. Wonders are performed during their lives, and people see them performed. But the genuine ones never say that they can perform wonders, neither do they seek such powers; these powers come naturally. Man generally is not conscious of the power he has. When a man becomes conscious of that power, he is able to do things which people cannot ordinarily accomplish.

There are two powers: one is called in Sufi terms *Kaza* and the other *Kadr*. One is individual power and the other is God-power. The individual power can work and can accomplish things as long as it is working in consonance with God's power, but the moment the individual power works contrary to God's power the man begins to realize that his strength is diminishing, that he cannot accomplish anything. Therefore the first thing that masters seek is the pleasure of God, to be in consonance with the will of God. And just as a person who has practised a gambling game or any kind of sport has learnt the way in which to practise it, so the man who has it continually in mind to do everything in consonance with God's power is helped by the will of God.

Very often people have misunderstood the will of God. They think that what they consider good is the will of God, and what they consider not good is not the will of God. But their idea of good and wrong has nothing to do with the power of God; because God's outlook is different from man's outlook. Man only sees so far and no further, whereas God sees all things.

But one wonders, if we all belong to the body of God, if

we are all as atoms of His Being, why do we not understand, why do we not readily know what is in consonance with the will of God and what not? And the answer is that each atom of our body is conscious of itself. If there is a pain in the finger, the ear does not feel it. If there is a pain in the toe, the nose does not feel it; only the toe feels it. But in both cases the man feels it because the man possesses the whole body.

Man lives in a narrow world he has made for himself. According to it he sees right and wrong, and his interests in life depend upon it. Therefore he is not always able to work in consonance with the will of God unless he makes it a habit to work in consonance with God's will.

What is man? Is man only his body? No, man is his mind, man is the soul. And therefore the power of man is greater than the power of the sun, for the sun we see is only a body, but man is body, mind, and soul. Once man has become conscious of his body, mind, and soul, his power becomes greater than the power of the sun. Because the sun is the material manifestation of the light, but man has all lights within him. The body of man is radiance; a radiance which is so great that all the invisible beings which live in space are hidden by the glow of the human form. Nothing exists which is not visible; only one thing which is more visible hides the other which is not so visible. It is the glow and radiance of the human body which is so great that it hides the beings in space. In reality they are all visible; but the radiance of man's form stands out and hides all that is less visible compared with it. When we look at life from this point of view, there is nothing that is invisible. It is only that there are things which our eyes have no power to see, but this does not mean that they are formless.

Besides man's mind has a still greater power, and that is the power of will, of mind, that can bring about change in conditions, in environments; it can have power over matter, over objects, over affairs; it can even work so wonderfully that one cannot explain it. The power of mind can work on the multitude, as the following story of Mohammad shows.

In one of the great wars that the Prophet had to fight the whole army was defeated, and there only remained ten or fifteen friends by the side of the Prophet and all the others ran away or were dead or wounded. Then the Prophet turned to his people and saw that they were all down-hearted and despairing. So he said, 'Look, before us there is an army and here are we, fifteen men. You do not see any hope; now you must retreat. But I, I will stand here whether I am to come back victorious or lose my life here on the battlefield. Now you go. Many of you have already left, so you go also.' They said, 'No, Prophet, if your life is to be ended here on the battlefield our lives will be taken first. What are our lives after all! We shall give our lives together with you, Prophet. We are not afraid of this enemy.' And then the Prophet threw away the sword he had in his hand and bowed down and took a few pebbles from the earth and threw them at the army. And the army began to run for miles and miles. They did not know what was behind them. It was only a few pebbles; but what they saw were great missiles and they began to run.

That is called power; that is man's power. It is not only that man has power over objects, but man has power over beings. It is only a little touch of power that the master of the circus uses to make the elephants work and tigers and lions dance before him. When his power is greater, he has only to look at them to make them work as he wishes them to.

When it is told in the story of Daniel that he went into the lions' den and made them all lie tamed at his feet, that is again the spiritual power. It shows what power man has; at the same time, not knowing of it, not being conscious of it, not trying to develop it, he debars himself from that great privilege and bliss that God has given; and with his limited powers he works in the world for money. In the end no money remains with him, nor has he ever known power. Power depends greatly upon the consciousness and the attitude of mind. A guilty conscience can turn lions into rabbits. They lose their power once they feel guilty; and so it is with man. When a man is impressed by what others think, if that impression is of disappointment or distress or shame, his power is diminished; but when he is inspired by a thought, a feeling, an action he performs, then he is powerful.

It is the power of truth that makes one stronger. Apart from those who know truth, even those who do not know truth, if they think rightly will have some power, the power of sincerity. Very few realize what power sincerity carries. A false man, however physically strong he is or however great is his will-power, is kept down by his falsehood; it never allows him to rise. It eats into him because it is a rust. Those who have done great things in life, in whatever walk of life it be, have done them by the power of truth, the power of sincerity, of earnestness, of conviction; when that is lacking, power is lacking. What takes away man's power is doubt. As soon as a person thinks, Is it so or not? Will it be or not be? Is it right or not right? then he is powerless. And this is so contagious that every mind catches it. You can go to a doubting person when you have great enthusiasm and hope; and he may so impress you with darkness that you end in the same boat. Doubt takes away courage and hope and optimism.

There are three grades of evolved human beings. In Sanskrit they are called *Atma*, *Mahatma* and *Paramatma*; in other words, a holy person, a divine soul and an almighty soul. In the case of the first, an illuminated soul can show five different powers. These powers are magnetic powers. The first aspect is the revivifying of the physical body. The next is brightening the intelligence. The third is deepening the love-element in the heart. The fourth is etherealizing and deepening insight; and the fifth aspect is uniting with God. With the fifth aspect the illuminated soul shows the greatest power.

The power can also be divided into two parts: one is the power of insight, the other is the power of will. The power of insight does not construct, does not make anything. It only sees; it is a passive power. The one who has the power of insight can see into human nature. He has an insight into the heart of another person, into the soul of another person, into his life, his affairs, into his past, present, and future. What inspires him in this way? What is it that he sees? He seems to understand the language of nature, the language of life. He seems to read the form, the feature, the movement, the atmosphere, the thought and feeling. Because everything has certain vibrations, a certain tendency. Therefore, to have insight is to know the language of life. And such a one can see to such an extent that the other does not know so much about himself as the one who sees. For everyone is blinded by his own affairs; when he is told he may know it, but if you do not tell him he does not know. It seems as if the knowledge of his own being is buried within himself.

Where does this science come from? Also from the knowledge of insight, at least at the beginning. Other things improve upon it; but this science which begins with intuition is insight. The great inventors of the world have insight into things. They may not believe this, but all the same they have it. They penetrate through the object and its purpose, and they utilize it towards its purpose. In that way they make use of insight for scientific inventions. If they knew, they could make use of the same insight a thousand times better.

The Mahatmas are different. It is not only that they have magnetic power but they have divine instinct, divine inspiration. Stories are told about the constructive power of Mahatmas; one is very interesting as it shows what this power can achieve.

Once a prince was sent away from his country, his father having disapproved of his conduct. And he went and lived in the forest for a long time under the training of a Guru, a teacher, and developed spiritually. And when the time came that he should be given initiation into the higher power, the Guru asked, 'My Chela, have you any relatives?' He said, 'Yes, my father and mother.' The teacher said, 'You must go to them and ask them first if you may take the initiation; because once you take it, you will have to live the life of solitude.' The teacher thought it was better than he should first go to his people and see all the possibilities of worldly life. Then, if he did not want such a life, he could come back. And the Chela was so developed at that time that he had no desire to go to his parents in that kingdom and see them again. But since the Guru told him to do it, he went. When he reached his kingdom, he went to the garden where he had lived before and which had been neglected for many years. There was nothing left in the garden. He went there and sat down and was very sorry to see his garden so neglected. He took the water in his pitcher and sprinkled it on both sides; and the garden began to flourish.

And so it was made known to the whole kingdom that a sage had arrived; that the place where he stayed for a few days had begun to flourish. The story goes on to relate that the king heard that his son was there; that he came and wanted him to take over the kingdom, to work for the country. But he refused and went away.

This story gives an example of the constructive power of the sage, it shows how constructive the soul of the Mahatma is. It is not true that Mahatmas can only be found in the caves of the Himalayas and that one cannot see them in the midst of the world. They can be found anywhere; they can be found in a palace, in the midst of riches, of comfort, and in remote places. They can be in any situation, in any position. But what comes out of the Mahatmas is a continual spreading influence of construction. They are a protection against illnesses and plagues, wars and disasters. Their constructive power is working and helping people to flourish. Today man is ready to believe that a Prime Minister or a great statesman can be such a help, that he can raise up the country, put the finances of the country in good order or guard the country against other nations; but a hidden soul which is not known can have a greater influence still on the whole country. It has been known and seen by millions of people in the East at different times when divine souls lived, that their influence spread through the whole country and uplifted it.

The third aspect of sages is Paramatma, the almighty one. He is still greater; he is no longer a person, he is God-conscious. We all are that of which we are conscious. A man in prison is conscious of the prison. A person who has a lot of money in the bank and is not conscious of it, is poor in spite of his wealth. We only have that of which we are conscious. Therefore our greatness or our smallness depends upon our consciousness. Even to become an illuminated soul is only a difference of consciousness. It is not how much good a person has done. There are many good people, but they do not always know what they themselves are.

Besides there are some who believe in God and others who love God; and there are others who are lost in God. Those who believe in God, they are on earth and God is in heaven for them. Those who love God, for them God is before them; they are face to face with their Lord. And those who are lost in God have gained their real self. They are God themselves. I know of a God-conscious soul who was once walking in the city of Baroda where the rule was that no one should go about after ten o'clock at night. And this sage was wandering about unconscious of time. A policeman asked him, 'Where are you going?' But he did not hear. Perhaps he was far away from the place where he was wandering. But when he heard the policeman say, 'Are you a thief?' he smiled and said, 'Yes.' The policeman took him to the police station and made him sit there all night long. In the morning the officer came and asked, 'What is the report?' This policeman said, 'I have caught one thief. I found him in the street.' When the officer went and saw this man, he knew that he was a great soul and that people respected him very much. He asked his pardon. 'But,' he said, 'when the policeman asked you that question, why did you say that you were a thief?' The answer was, 'What am I not? I am everything.'

We try to become spiritual, to raise our consciousness. But when it comes to an insult, we do not like it. As long as everybody flatters us we are glad to attribute those things to ourselves. But as soon as it comes to an insult, we do not like it; then we say, 'It is not me.' The Paramatma, the high soul, is united with God, he is God-conscious, all-conscious. Everyone is his own self. Whether he is a good person or a wicked person, whether he is right or wrong, he is his own self; he looks at that person as his own self. Even if he were given the name of a thief, he could say, 'Yes. All names are my names.'

In conclusion, spirituality is not a certain knowledge, spirituality is the expansion of consciousness. The wider the consciousness expands the greater is one's spiritual vision. And when once the consciousness expands so much that it embraces the whole universe, it is that which is called divine perfection.

CHAPTER XV

THE SECRET OF BREATH

IT IS clear even to those who do not know medical science that the whole mechanism of the body stops when the breath has departed. That means that however perfect the mechanism of the body may be, in the absence of breath the body is a corpse. In other words, what is living in the body, or what makes it living, is breath. And how few of us realize this fact. We go on day after day, working, busy with everyday life, absorbed in the thoughts we have, occupied with business, pursuing motives, and yet ignoring the principle upon which the whole of life is based. If someone says, 'Prayer is a very important thing', people may think, 'Yes, perhaps.' If one says, 'Meditation is a great thing', people may say, 'Yes, it is something.' But when one says, 'Breathing is a great secret', the reaction is, 'Why, I have never thought about it. What is it really?'

As far as science goes, breathing is known to be air breathed in and breathed out. When it is breathed in one gets oxygen from space, and when it is breathed out one throws carbonic acid into space. When one goes still further one knows that breathing keeps the lungs and the organs of breath going, that digestive gases are drawn in, and that one gets a greater digestive power. On the basis of that principle people are beginning to use breathing in physical exercises to make the body healthier. For some years now voice-producers have given greater importance to breath. In reality the breathing itself is voice, and the whole voice-construction depends upon breathing. Then again some physicians are beginning to see that many illnesses of the nerves, of the lungs, or of different nervous centres can often be helped by breathing. There seems to be a general awakening to the science of breath. And those who have practised breathing in connection with physical culture or for the improvement of their particular condition, illness, or weakness, have found wonderful results. It is thus far that the science of breath has reached.

But when we come to the mystery of breath, it is another domain altogether. The perceptible breath which the nostrils can feel as air drawn in and air going out, is only an effect of breathing. It is not breath. For the mystic breath is that current which carries the air out and brings the air in. The air is perceptible, not the current; the current is imperceptible. It is a kind of ethereal magnetism, a finer kind of electricity, the current of which goes in and comes out, putting the air into action. This is what the mystic calls *Nafs*, which means the self. Breath is the self, the very self of man. Also *Atman* means the soul, and in German the same word is used for breath. This shows that if there is any trace of the soul, it is to be found in breath.

Naturally, breath being the self, it is not only the air which one exhales but it is a current which, according to mystics, runs from the physical plane into the innermost plane; a current which runs through the body, mind, and soul, touching the innermost part of life and also coming back; a continual current perpetually moving in and out. This gives quite a different explanation of the breath and shows the importance of something which very few people consider important; and it makes one understand that the most important part of being is breath, which reaches the innermost part of life and also reaches outwards to the surface, which means touching the physical plane. But the direction of breath is in a dimension which the science of today does not recognize, a dimension which is recognized by mystics as being the dimension 'within'.

One day I was lecturing in England, and among the audience was a well-known scientist. After the lecture he came to me and said, 'I am very interested, but there is one thing that puzzles me. I cannot understand the word "within". What do you mean? Within the body? We can only understand inside the body.' This shows the difficulty of reaching a common understanding between science and mysticism. One day it will be overcome. It is only a temporary difficulty.

To give a philosophical explanation of this dimension, one can take as an example the simile of the eyes: what is it in these eyes of ours that can accommodate a horizon of so many miles? The size of the eyes is so small, and they can accommodate such a large horizon. Where is it accommodated? It is accommodated within. That is the only example one can give. It is a dimension which cannot be measured, but which is accommodating, which is an accommodation. The accommodation of the eye is not a recognized dimension, yet it is a dimension. In the same way there is a dimension of mind. One can think deeply and feel profoundly; one can be conscious of life and be more deeply conscious still; but one cannot point to it, because this dimension is abstract. If there is any word, it can only be called 'within'. And through that dimension a current runs from the innermost plane to the physical plane and there it keeps life living. That is why one can say that breath is the soul and soul is the breath. It is important to understand that one does not inhale like a straight line going in and coming out the same way, as one imagines it to be. The real action is that of a wheel, a circle; from the nostrils it makes a circle and the end of the circle is again in the nostrils.

The third point to understand about breath is that, just like an electric wire, it shows a glow; and as the heat and light are not confined to that glow but are around it too, in the same way the radiance of this circle of breath which goes on through the body, touches every part of the body.

Another rule to be observed is that with every direction in which the current of breath goes, it causes a different action and a different result. For instance, contracting, stretching, blinking, all these actions are the play of the breath going in different directions. So it is with every natural action one does during the day. Also coughing, yawning, heaving a deep sigh, all these are different actions of breath. Besides, the ability to eat and drink, the ability to expel all that one has in the body, are all results of different directions through which breath works. And if the breath does not work in one direction, then that particular activity of the body is stopped. It is a science that has yet to be explored by scientists and physicians. And the more it is explored the less necessity there will be for operations and many other dreadful things that doctors have to do or to give to their patients. Also the tendency to lung diseases, the pain of child-birth, and early death, all these will be avoided when the science of breath is well understood by the scientists of the day, and practised by the generality.

The picture of God and of souls is that of the sun and its rays. The rays are not different from the sun, the sun is not different from the rays. Yet there is one sun and many rays. The rays have no existence of their own; they are only an action of the sun. They are not separate from the sun, and yet the rays appear to be many different rays. The one sun gives the idea of one centre. So it is with God and man. What is God? The Spirit which projects different rays; and each ray is a soul. Therefore the breath is that current which is a ray, a ray which comes from that Sun which is the spirit of God. And this ray is the sign of life. What is the body? The body is only a cover over this ray. When this ray has withdrawn itself from this cover, the body becomes a corpse.

Then there is another cover which is the mind. The difference between mind and heart is like the surface and the bottom. It is the surface of the heart which is mind, and it is the depth of the mind which is heart. The mind expresses the faculty of thinking, the heart of feeling. This is an inner garb, a garb worn by the same thing which is called breath. Therefore, if the ray which is the breath has withdrawn itself from the body, it still exists, for it has another garb, it has a garb within. The outer garb was the body, the inner garb is the mind. The breath continues to exist, and if it is lost in that garb which is called mind, then there is another garb finer still, called the soul. Because breath runs through all three: body, mind, and soul.

Seen from this point of view one will realize that man has never been separated from God; that with every breath man touches God. He is linked with God by the current of breath. Just like people drawing water from a well, the rope in their hands and the jug of water in the well. The jug has the water, but the rope is in the hand. In so far as our soul is in the spirit of God, it is the ray of the divine sun, while the other end of it is what we call breath. We only see it reaching so far and no further, because it is only the higher part of the physical body that touches different planes. The breath goes there, but we do not see the action of breath. The action of breath in our body is limited; but in reality this current, this breath, connects the body with the divine Spirit, connecting God and man in one current.

The central current of our mind is also breath. That is why we do not only breathe through the body, but also through the mind, and through the soul too. Furthermore, death is only the departing of the body from this main current which we call breath. But when the body has departed the mind still adheres to it, and if the mind is living, the person is living also. This is what gives us the proof of the hereafter. Many will say, 'How uninteresting to live after death not as an individual, a body, but as a mind!' But it is the mind which has made this body; the mind is more self-sufficient than we can imagine. The mind is in a sphere in which it has its own body, just as this physical body belongs to the physical sphere. The body of the mind is as sufficient and even more concrete than the body we have in the physical world, for the reason that the physical body is very limited and subject to death and decay. The body of the mind which is ethereal lasts long, being less dependent upon food and water; it is maintained more by breath than by anything else. We are maintained even in this physical world chiefly by breath, although we recognize bread and water and other food as our sustenance. If we only knew that bread and water are not even a hundredth part of our sustenance compared with what breath does in our life! We cannot exist five minutes without breath; we can be without food for some days.

Since breath has such great importance, the greatest possible importance, it is clear that the way to bring order and harmony to our body, to bring order and harmony to our mind, to harmonize mind with body, and to harmonize body and mind with soul, is by the breath. It is the development of breath, knowledge of breath, practice of breath which help us to get ourselves straightened out, to put ourselves in tune, to bring order into our being. There are many who without proper guidance and knowledge practise breath. Year after year they go on and very little result is achieved. Many go out of their minds, and very often the little veins of the brain and chest are ruptured by wrong breathing. There are many who have experienced this by not knowing how to breathe. One has to be extremely careful; one must do breathing practices rightly or not do them at all.

One cannot speak fully of all that can be accomplished with the help of breath. If there are men living in the world today who while standing on the earth witness the inner planes of existence, if there are any who really can communicate with the higher spheres, if there are any who can convince themselves of the life in the hereafter and of what it will be like, it is the masters of breath, and not the students of intellectual books.

The Yogis have learnt very much about the secret of breath from the serpent; that is why they regard the serpent as the symbol of wisdom. Shiva, the Lord of Yogis, has a serpent around his neck as a necklace. It is the sign of mystery, of wisdom. There are cobras in the forests of tropical countries, specially in India, which sleep for six weeks; and then one day the cobra wakens, and it breathes because it is hungry; it wants to eat. And its thoughts attract food from wherever it may be; food is attracted from miles away by its thoughts. The breath of the cobra is so magnetic that the food is helplessly drawn; a fowl, or a deer or some other animal is drawn closer. It is so strongly drawn that it even comes down from the air, and falls into its mouth. The snake makes no effort. It just breathes; it opens its mouth, and its food comes into its mouth. And then it rests again for six weeks.

The serpent, too, is so strongly built that without wings it flies and without feet it walks. Also, if there is any animal which can be called the healthiest animal of all, it is the serpent. It is never ill; before it becomes ill it dies, yet it lives a very long time. It is said by those living in tropical countries that cobras can take revenge after as much as twelve years. If you once hit a cobra, it will always remember. That shows its memory, its mind. Music also appeals to the cobra as music appeals to intelligent men. The more unintelligent the man, the less music appeals to him; music is closely related to intelligence. This shows that every sign of intelligence, of wisdom, and of power is to be seen in the cobra.

The mystics have studied the life of the cobra and they have found two wonderful things. One is that it does not waste energy. Birds fly until they are tired; animals run here and there. The cobra does not do so. It makes a hole where it lives and rests.

It knows the best way of repose, a repose which it can continue as long as it wishes. We cannot do this. We human beings, of all creatures, know least about repose. We only know about work, not about repose. We attach every importance to work, but never to rest; this is because we do not find anything in rest but everything in work. The work of rest we do not see.

Besides, the natural breathing capacity of the cobra is such as no other creature shows. That capacity goes as a straight line throughout its body. The current which it gets from space and which runs through it, gives it lightness and energy and radiance and power. Compared with the cobra all other creatures are awkwardly built. The skin of the cobra is so very soft and of such silky texture, and in a moment's time it can shed its skin and be new, just as if born anew. The mystics have learnt from it. They say, 'We must go out of our body just as the cobra goes out of its skin; we must go out of our thoughts, ideas, feelings, just as the cobra does with its skin.' They say, 'We must be able to breathe as rhythmically, to control our breath as the cobra does. We must be able to repose and relax in the same way as the cobra can. And then it will be possible to attain all we desire.' As Christ has said, 'Seek ye first the Kingdom of God . . . and all things shall be added unto you.' The same things that are added to the cobra, all that it needs, could be added to man also if only he did not worry about them. As Sa'di has said, 'My self, you worry so much over things that you need, but know that the One who works for your needs is continually working for them. Yet you worry over them because it is your disease, your passion that makes you worry all the time!'

When we look at life more keenly, we see it is the same. Our worry about things seems to be our nature, our character; we cannot help it. It becomes such a part of our nature to worry that if we had no worry we would doubt if we were really living! Mystics, therefore, for thousands of years have practised control of the breath, its balance, its rhythm, the expanding, lengthening, broadening, and centralizing of the breath. By this great phenomena have been accomplished. All the Sufis in Persia, in Egypt, in India, have been great masters of breathing. And there are some masters who are conscious of their spiritual realization with every breath they inhale and exhale. With every breath comes the consciousness of their plane of realization.

For a person who really knows how to work with breath, if he is not lazy, there is nothing he cannot accomplish; he cannot say of anything that it is impossible. Only it requires work; it is not only a matter of knowing the theory, but it requires the understanding of it. That is why the adepts, the mystics, do not consider breathing only as a science or as an exercise; they consider it as the most sacred thing, as sacred as religion. And in order to accomplish this breathing a discipline is given by a teacher.

But there is a great difficulty. I have found sometimes in my travels, when I have been speaking about these things, that people come with preconceived ideas. They are willing to learn, but they do not want discipline. But in the army there is discipline; in the factory, in the office there is a certain discipline; in study at the university, everywhere there is discipline; yet in spiritual things people do not want it; when it comes to spiritual things they make difficulties. They think so little of it that they do not want to make any sacrifice. Because they do not know where it leads to, they have no belief. Besides there are false methods which are taught here and there, and people are commercializing that which is most sacred. In that way the highest ideal is brought down to the lowest depth; and it is time that the real thing should be introduced, seriously studied, experienced, and realized by practice.

CHAPTER XVI

THE MYSTERY OF SLEEP

IT IS very difficult to point out exactly what condition it is that may be called sleep. For when one thinks about this question one finds that one is always asleep and always wakeful. The difference is that of the particular sphere which man is conscious of when he is awake: in one sphere he thinks, 'I am awake', and when that sphere is not before his consciousness he thinks, 'I am asleep.' In reality sleep and the wakeful state are nothing but the turning of the consciousness from one side to the other, from one sphere or plane to another; and therefore according to the mystical idea man is never asleep. Although the soul is much higher than the physical body, it is the character and nature of the soul which the physical body expresses.

When a man is looking at one side he is unconscious of the other. This shows that the faculty of seeing and being conscious of what one sees can only engage itself fully with one thing at a time. A conception of musical sound which has been held for a long time in the East, and which today is recognized by scientists in the West, is that man's ears can only hear fully one sound at a time, not two or three. This indicates that each sense is capable of looking at one side only; the other is absent from the consciousness; and in order to see a particular side one has to turn one's face to it. In other words, one has to expose one's faculty of seeing to that side.

This is not only the nature of the body but also the nature of the mind; the mind cannot think of two things at the same time. Also, when the mind is at work and fully absorbed in a certain thought, a certain imagination, the outer senses may be open, but they are not fully at work. When a poet is thinking of a verse, the verse is before his mind. His eyes are open, but he does not see; and if it happens that he sees anything when he is thinking, then it is just like a moving picture. So many different pictures coming one after the other that they seem to be continuous. When the mind stops the eyes work, and when the eyes work the mind stops; and in the end it seems to make one picture, but in reality it is a separate action of the mind and of the senses. It is also true that the wakeful state of every individual is different and peculiar to himself, just as the sleep of every individual is different and peculiar to himself. One person will be what is called fast asleep, that is to say in deep sleep. Another will be half asleep. Another knows what is going on around him, and yet he is asleep. This shows that the extent of sleep is different in every experience, and no one can classify this extent of sleep.

The wakeful state also differs in every individual. Many people may be sitting in a room, but one is more conscious of what is going on in that room than another. Five people may be hearing music, and each will apply his consciousness differently to what he hears. Each will enjoy and receive the effect of the music differently, and this shows that the body and the mind are vehicles or instruments through which the soul experiences life, the soul being that part of our being which is capable of being conscious by means of mind and body. Therefore to the mystic it is that part of one's being which witnesses life through vehicles such as the mind and body which is the real being, and he calls it himself or his soul. In Sufi terms it is called *Ruh*, and in the Sanskrit or Vedantic terminology it is called *Atman*, the real being of man. By experience of life, with the help of the mind and body, this Atman or soul becomes deluded, and the delusion is that it loses consciousness of its pure self, as it is natural that when a person is poorly dressed he thinks he is poor; he never thinks it is only his dress that is poor. When he is moving in a beautiful palace he is a big man. He does not think it is the palace which is big, rather than himself.

This shows it is not what a man is, but what he believes he is, that he is related to. The soul is never ill, but when it is conscious of the illness of the body the man says, 'I am ill.' And the reason is that he cannot point out to his own consciousness his own true being; as the eyes cannot see themselves though they are able to see the whole world, so the soul cannot see itself except when it is conscious of all that is reflected in it. The soul is neither poor nor rich; it is neither sorrowful nor joyous. These are reflections which fall upon it. And as it cannot realize itself, it considers itself to be that which is reflected in it, and therefore man lives his life in his consciousness. He is at every moment that which he is conscious of; in cheerful surroundings he is pleased; in miserable surroundings he is sad. No sorrow or joy can make an everlasting impression on the soul, for the nature of the soul is like a mirror, and while all that stands before the mirror is reflected in it, nothing can stay there. When the person who stood before the mirror is removed, then the mirror is as clear as ever; and so it is with the soul.

For the sake of convenience the mystics have divided the experiences of the consciousness into five different phases. The particular phase the consciousness is most familiar with is the wakeful state in which the soul experiences through mind and body. This state in Sufi terms is called *Nasut*, and in Vedantic terms it is called *Jagrat*. As the soul only considers what it experiences through the senses with the help of the mind, the reason that many are not yet ready to believe in the soul or in the hereafter or in God is that the soul is acquainted with one sphere only, and that is the sphere which it experiences with the help of the body and mind.

An intellectual person also develops consciousness of another sphere which is called *Malakut* in Sufi terminology and *Swapna* in terms of the Vedanta. This state is experienced in two ways. When a person is absorbed in thought and is not aware of his surroundings, all he knows at that moment is the thought or imagination in which he is absorbed. This state is not dependent upon the body for its joy or its experiences of sorrow.

A person who can experience joy and sorrow by raising his consciousness to that plane can make his heaven in himself. The great poets, thinkers, writers, who have lived through difficulties, through poverty, through circumstances in which people did not understand them, opposed them, and even despised them, have lived a most happy life for the reason that they have been able to raise themselves to that plane where they could enjoy all the beauty, comfort, and joy that the ordinary man can only enjoy if it is given to him on the physical plane. And when the key of this plane comes into the hands of a man, then he is the master of his future life.

When a man's consciousness reflects heaven, that man is in heaven; and when a man is conscious of torture, pain, and suffering, he is in the place of suffering. Man makes his heaven or his hell for himself. How many in this world you will find who keep their illness by thinking about it all the time, by being conscious of it; and one sees many who might become well after having suffered pain for some years were it not for the consciousness of the pain being held by them, not as something new but as something which has always been there.

Nothing belongs to a man unless he is willing to hold it. But when he becomes accustomed to holding a certain reflection without knowing the nature of it, in time that reflection becomes his master and he becomes a slave of that reflection. And so it is with the worries and anxieties and sorrows which people have on their minds. Many say, 'I cannot forget', because they imagine it. It does not mean that that person cannot forget, but that he is holding on to something which he does not wish to throw away. If a man would only realize that it is not that someone else is holding something before him; it is he himself who holds it. Some memory, something disagreeable, something sorrowful, some severe pain, anxiety, worry, all these things a man holds in his own hands and they are reflected in his consciousness. His soul by nature is above all this. It is an illusion whose place is beneath the soul, not above, unless a man, with his own hands, raises it and looks at it.

When one considers the psychology of failure and success, failure follows failure. And why is it? Because the consciousness reflecting success is full of success, and the activity which goes out from that consciousness is creating productive activity; so if the consciousness has success before its view, then the same reflection will work and bring success; whereas if the consciousness is impressed with failure, then failure will work constantly, bringing failure after failure.

Very often pessimistic people speak against their own desire. They want to undertake some work, and they say, 'I will do this, but I don't think I shall succeed in it.' Thus they hinder themselves in their path. Man does not know that every thought makes an impression on the consciousness and on the rhythm with which the consciousness is working. According to that rhythm that reflection will come true and happen; and a man proves to be his own enemy by his ignorance of these things. The mistake of one moment's impulse creates a kind of hindrance in the path of that person all through his life.

This state of consciousness is also experienced in the dream; for the dream is the reaction of man's experiences in his wakeful state. The most wonderful thing which man can study in the dream is that the dream has a language, and a true knowledge of dream experiences teaches one that every individual has a separate language of his dream peculiar to his own nature. The dream of the poet, the dream of the man who works with his hands, the dream of the king, the dream of the poor man, all are different. There are many differences and one cannot give the same interpretation of his dream to every person; one must first know who has dreamed it. It is not the dream which can be interpreted by itself, it is the person to whom the dream came that one must know; and the interpretation is according to his state of evolution, to his occupation, to his ambitions and desires, to his present, his past, and his future, and to his spiritual aspirations.

Thus the language of dreams differs; but there is one hint which may be given, and that is that in the wakeful state man is open to outward impressions. For instance, there are moments when the mind is receptive, and there are moments when the mind is expressive. And during the moments when the mind is receptive, every impression from any person is reflected in the consciousness. Very often one finds oneself depressed and cannot find a reason, and then one finds oneself full of mirth and again cannot find the reason. As soon as a person has a certain feeling he at once looks for a reason, and reason is ready to answer him, rightly or wrongly. As soon as a person thinks, 'What makes me laugh?' there is something which his reason offers as the reason why he laughed. In reality that impression came from someone else; but he thinks the reason is something different, and so very often in the dream it happens that the reasoning faculty answers the demands of the enquiring mind, and frames and shapes the thoughts and imaginations which are going on so freely when the will-power is not controlling the mind in sleep. The mind behaves at that time just like an actor on the stage, free, without control of the will, and when that happens there may be a moment when the mind is in a receptive condition, when it receives an impression from other persons, from those who are friends or from those who are enemies, from anyone who may think of the dreamer or with whom he is connected in any way.

Those who are spiritually inclined or who are connected with souls who have passed away also feel the impressions reflected upon their souls, sometimes as guiding influences, sometimes as warnings, sometimes as instructions. They also experience what are known as initiations, and sometimes have deluding, confusing, experiences; but all takes place on that particular plane where the consciousness is experiencing life independently of the physical body and of the senses.

The third experience which the consciousness has is called in Sufi terms *Jabarut*, and in Sanskrit or Vedantic terms *Sushupti*. In this state, in which the consciousness is not very well connected with the world, it does not bring its experiences to the world except for a feeling of joy, of renewed strength or health; and all one can say after this experience is, 'I have had a very good sleep, and feel much better for it.' In point of fact, the cause is that the consciousness was freed from pain and worry and any activity or limitation of life, and even prisoners can enjoy the blessing of this state when they are fast asleep; they do not know whether they are in a palace or in a prison. They reach the experiences of that plane which is better than a palace.

Man does not realize the value of this state until the time comes when for some reason or other he is unable to receive this blessing. He cannot sleep; then he begins to think there is nothing he would not give to be able to sleep soundly. This shows that it is not only sleep he needs, but a blessing behind it. It is something which the soul has touched which is much higher and deeper, for this experience is greater than one can imagine. In this experience the consciousness touches a sphere from whence it cannot get an impression of any name or form. The impression it gets is a feeling, a feeling of illumination, of life, of joy. What message does it give? It gives a message of God which comes directly to every soul. And what is this message? God says to the soul, 'I am with you, I am your own being, and I am above all limitations, and I am life, and you are more safe, more living, more happy and more peaceful in this knowledge than in anything else in the world.'

Besides these three experiences there comes a fourth experience to those who search after it. Why does it not come to everybody? It is not that it does not come to everybody, but everybody cannot catch it. It comes and slips away from a person, and he does not know when it came and when it went. In the life of every man there is a moment during the wakeful state, a moment when he rises above all limitations of life, but so swiftly does it come and go, in the twinkling of an eye, that he cannot catch it, that he does not realize it.

It is just like a bird which came and flew away, and you only heard the flutter of its wings. But those who wish to catch this bird, who wish to see where this bird goes, and when it comes and when it goes, look out for it and sit waiting and watching for the moment when it comes; and that watching is called meditation. Meditation does not mean closing the eyes and sitting; anyone can close his eyes and sit, but he may sit for hours, or he may sit all his life, and still not know what came and what went. It is looking out for what comes, and not only looking out for it, but preparing oneself by making one's senses keen, by making one's body and mind a receptacle for the vibrations, so that when the bird makes a vibration one feels that it has come.

It is this which is expressed in the Christian symbolism of the dove. In other words, it is the moment which approaches one's consciousness rapidly of such bliss that one, so to speak, touches the depths of the whole of life and reaches above the sphere of action, even above the sphere of feeling. 'But,' one will say, 'what does one's consciousness receive from it?' It receives a kind of illumination which is like a torch lighting another light; this inner life, touching the consciousness, produces a sort of illumination which makes man's life clear. Every moment after this experience is unveiled because of this moment. It charges man's life with new life and new light. That is why in the East Yogis sit in Samadhi, in a certain posture for so many hours, or go into the forest and sit in the solitude; and they have always done so in order to catch this light which is symbolized by a dove.

There is one step even higher than this, which in the terms of the Sufis is *Hahut*, or *Samadhi* in Vedantic terms, the fifth sphere which consciousness experiences. In this the consciousness touches the innermost depth of its own being; it is like touching the feet of God. That is the communion which is spoken of in the Christian symbolism. It is just like touching the Presence of God, when one's consciousness has become so light and so liberated and free that it can raise itself and dive and touch the depths of one's being.

This is the secret of all mysticism and religion and philosophy. The process of this experience is like the process of alchemy, which is not given freely except to those who are ready and who feel there is some truth in it. It takes time for a person to become familiar with things of this nature or even to think there is some truth in them and that it is not only talk and imagination. Even one who has felt the truth of the mystical state may question if it is worth while to go on with this quest; but if he does so he must accept the guidance of someone who has knowledge of this matter, in whom he can put his trust and confidence. But it must be understood that the path of discipleship, or the path of initiation, is not such that the teacher gives some knowledge to his pupil, tells him something new which he has not heard before, or shows him some miracle; if he does he is not a true teacher. Man is really his own teacher; in himself is the secret of his being. The teacher's word is only to help him to find himself. Nothing that can be learned from books, nothing that can be explained in language, nothing that can be pointed out with a finger, is truth. If a man is sure of himself he can go further, but when he is confused in himself he cannot go further, and no teacher can help him. Therefore, although in this path the teacher is necessary and his help is valuable, self-help is the principal thing; and the one who is ready to realize his own nature and to learn from himself, is he who is the true initiate. And it is from that initiation that he will go forward, step by step, finding the realization and conviction that he seeks; and all that comes to him throughout his life will but deepen that realization of truth.

CHAPTER XVII

SILENCE

THERE is a saying that words are valuable but silence is more precious. This saying will always prove true. The more we understand the meaning of it, the more we realize its truth. How many times we find during the day that we have said something which would have been better left unsaid! How many times we disturb the peace of our surroundings, without meaning it, by lack of silence! How often we make our limitations, our narrowness, our smallness come out, which we would rather have concealed, because we did not keep silent! How very often, though desiring to respect others, we cannot manage to do so because we do not keep silent! And a great danger lies in wait for a man in the life of this world, the danger of confiding in a person in whom he did not wish to confide. We run that danger by not keeping silent. That great interpreter of life, the Persian poet Sa'di, says, 'What value is sense, if it does not come to my rescue before I utter a word!' This shows us that in spite of whatever wisdom we may have, we can make a mistake if we have no control over our words. And we can easily find examples of this truth: those who talk much have less power than those who talk little. For a talkative person may not be able to express an idea in a thousand words which those who are masters of silence express in one word. Everyone can speak, but not every word has the same power. Besides, a word says much less than silence can express. The keynote to harmonious life is silence.

In everyday life we are confronted with a thousand troubles that we are not always evolved enough to meet, and then only silence can help us. For if there is any religion, if there is any practice of religion, it is to have regard for the pleasure of God by regarding the pleasure of man. The essence of religion is to understand. And this religion we cannot live without having power over the word, without having realized the power of silence. There are so very many occasions when we repent after hurting friends, which could have been avoided if there had been control over our words. Silence is the shield of the ignorant and the protection of the wise. For the ignorant does not prove his ignorance if he keeps silent, and the wise man does not throw pearls before swine if he knows the worth of silence.

What gives power over words? What gives the power that can be attained by silence? The answer is: it is will-power which gives the control over words; it is silence which gives one the power of silence. It is restlessness when a person speaks too much. The more words are used to express an idea, the less powerful they become. It is a great pity that man so often thinks of saving pennies and never thinks of sparing words. It is like saving pebbles and throwing away pearls. An Indian poet says, 'Pearl-shell, what gives you your precious contents? Silence; for years my lips were closed.'

For a moment it is a struggle with oneself; it is controlling an impulse; but afterwards the same thing becomes a power.

And now coming to the more scientific, metaphysical, explanation of silence. There is a certain amount of energy spent by words; and breath, which has to bring new life in the body, is hindered in its regular rhythm when man speaks all the time. It is not that a nervous person speaks too much, but much speaking makes him nervous. Where did the great power attained by Yogis and faqirs come from? It was gained by having learned and practised the art of silence. And that is the reason why in the East, in the houses where faqirs meditated, and even at the court, there was silence. There were times during different civilizations of the world when people were taught, whenever they were collected together for a feast, to keep silence for a certain time. It is the greatest pity that at this time we have so neglected that question; we think so little about it. It is a question which affects health, which touches the soul, the spirit, life. The more we think about this subject, the more we see that we are continually involved in a kind of action. Where does it lead us and what is the result of it? As far as we can see, it leads us to greater struggle, competition, disagreeableness. If we think of the result, we see that it leads us to greater care, worry, and struggle in life. There is a saying of the Hindus, 'The more one seeks for happiness, the more unhappiness one finds.' And the reason is that when happiness is sought in a wrong direction, it leads to unhappiness. Our experience in life is sufficient to teach us this, yet life is intoxicating, it absorbs us in action so that we never stop to think of it.

It seems that the world is awakening to spiritual ideals, but in spite of this there is more activity; not only outer activity, but also activity of mind. In reality mankind has shattered its nerves by the lack of silence, by the over-activity of body and mind. When the body is resting, man calls it sleep. But his mind is going on, on the same record as during the day. In this world of competition every man is a hundred times more busy than he ever was. Naturally his life needs rest and quietude and peace more than that of people who live in the forest, who can call all the time their own. When activity is increased and the art of silence is lost, then what can we expect?

Where do we learn thoughtfulness? In silence. And where do we practise patience? In silence. Silence practised in meditation is something apart, but silence means that we should consider every word and every action we do; that is the first lesson to learn. If there is a meditative person, he has learned to use that silence naturally in everyday life. The one who has learned silence in everyday life has already learned to meditate. Besides a person may have reserved half an hour every day for meditation, but when there is half an hour of meditation and twelve or fifteen hours of activity, the activity takes away all the power of the meditation. Therefore both things must go together. A person who wishes to learn the art of silence must decide, however much work he has to do, to keep the thought of silence in his mind. When one does not consider this, then one will not reap the full benefit of meditation. It is just like a person who goes to church once a week and the other six days he keeps the thought of church as far away as possible.

A very devout Persian king was asked by his prime minister, 'You are spending most of the night in meditation and all day long you work. How can that go on?' The Shah said, 'During the night I pursue God; during the day God follows me.' It is the same with silence: he who seeks silence is followed by silence.

So it is with all things we wish for; when we seek after them sufficiently, they follow us in time by themselves.

There are many who do not mind if they hurt anyone as long as they think they have told the truth. They feel so justified that they do not care if the other one cries or laughs. There is, however, a difference between fact and truth. Fact is that which can be spoken of; truth is that which cannot be put into words. The claim, 'I tell the truth', falls flat when the difference is realized between fact and truth. People discuss dogmas, beliefs, moral principles as they know them. But there comes a time in a man's life when he has touched truth, of which he cannot speak in words; and at that time all dispute, discussion, argument ends. It is then that the man says, 'If you have done wrong or if I have done wrong, it does not matter. What I want just now is to right the wrong.' There comes a time when the continual question which arises in the active mind: what is what and which is which? comes to an end, for the answer rises from the soul and is received in silence.

The general attitude of man is that of listening to all that comes from outside; and not only are the ears open to the external world, but even the heart is attached to the ears. The heart which is listening to the voices coming from the external world should turn its back on all that comes from there, and wait patiently until it becomes capable of hearing the voice from within.

There is an audible voice and an inaudible voice, from the living and from those who are not living, from all life. What man can say in words always expresses little. Can one speak about gratefulness, about devotion, about admiration? Never, there will always be a lack of words. Every deep feeling has its own voice; it cannot be expressed in outer words. This voice comes from every soul; every soul is only audible to the heart. And how is the heart prepared? Through silence.

We need not be surprised that some have sought the mountains and the forest, and preferred the wilderness to the comforts of worldly life. They sought something valuable. They have passed on something of the experience gained by their sacrifice. But it is not necessary to follow them to the forest or to the cave of the mountain. One can learn that art of silence every-where; throughout a busy life one can maintain silence.

Silence is something which consciously or unconsciously we are seeking every moment of our lives. We are seeking silence and running away from it, both at the same time. Where is the word of God heard? In silence. The seers, the saints, the sages, the prophets, the masters, they have heard that voice which comes from within by making themselves silent. I do not mean by this that because one has silence one will be spoken to; I mean that once one is silent one will hear the word which is constantly coming from within. When the mind has been made still, a person also communicates with everyone he meets. He does not need many words: when the glance meets he under-stands. Two persons may talk and discuss all their lives and yet never understand one another; and two others with still minds look at one another and in one moment a communication is established between them.

Where do the differences between people come from? From within. From their activity. And how does agreement come? By the stillness of the mind. It is noise which hinders a voice that we hear from a distance, and it is the troubled waters of a pool which hinder us seeing our own image reflected in the water. When the water is still it takes a clear reflection; and when our atmosphere is still then we hear that voice which is con-stantly coming to the heart of every person. We are looking for guidance, we all of us search for truth, we search for the mystery. The mystery is in ourselves; the guidance is in our own souls.

Very often one meets a person whose contact makes one rest-less, nervous. The reason is that that person is not restful, not tranquil, and it is not easy to remain calm and to keep one's tranquillity in the presence of a restless, agitated person. The teaching of Christ is, 'Resist not evil', and that means, 'Respond not to the troubled condition of a restless person.' It is just like partaking of the fire which will burn one.

The way to develop the power in oneself to withstand all dis-turbing influences in everyday life is to quieten oneself by means of concentration. Our mind is like a boat in the water, moved by the waves and influenced by the wind. The waves are our own emotions and passions, thoughts and imaginations; and the wind is the outer influences which we have to cope with. In order to stop the boat one should have an anchor, an anchor to make the boat lie still. Now this anchor is the object we concentrate upon; if it is heavy and weighty then it will stop the boat, but if this anchor is light the boat will continue to move and not be still, for it is partly in the water, and partly in the air.

But in this way we only control the boat; utilizing the boat is another question again. The boat is not made to remain motionless; it is made for a purpose. All of us do not seem to know this, but finally this boat has to be made to go from one port to another. And for the boat to be able to sail, various conditions must be fulfilled; for instance, that it is not more heavily laden than its capacity. Thus our heart should not be heavily laden with the things that we attach ourselves to, because then the boat will not float. Also the boat should not be tied to this one port, for then it is held back and will not go to the port for which it is bound.

Furthermore, the boat must have that responsiveness to the wind which will take it to that port; and this is the feeling a soul gets from the spiritual side of life. That feeling, that wind, helps one to go forward to the port for which we are all bound. Once it is fully concentrated, the mind should become like a compass in a boat, always pointing in the same direction. A man whose interest takes a thousand different directions is not ready to travel in this boat. It is the man who has one thing in his mind, and who considers all other things secondary, who can travel from this port to the other. This is the journey which is called mysticism.

CHAPTER XVIII

DREAMS AND REVELATIONS

ALTHOUGH dreams are something which is known to everybody, the study of them leads to the deeper side of life; for it is from the meaning of the dream that one begins to realize two things: that something is active when the body is asleep, and to the deep thinker this gives faith in the life hereafter. For the dream is the proof that when the body is not active, a person is active all the same, and seems to be no less active than in the physical body. If one detects any difference, it is a difference of time, for in dreams a man may pass from one land to another in a flash instead of taking a month. In no way is he hindered as on the physical plane. In dreams he flies.

The facility of the plane of dreams is much greater. There is no difficulty in changing one's condition from illness to health, from failure to success, in one moment. People say it is only imagination, a working of the mind. But what is mind? Mind is that in which the world is reflected. Heaven and earth are accommodated in it. Is that a small thing? What is the physical body compared with the mind which is a world in itself? The physical body is only like a drop in the ocean.

It is only because of ignorance that a man does not know the kingdom in himself. Why is he not conscious of it? Because he wishes to be able to hold something; only then does it exist for him. He does not wish to admit to himself the existence of sentiment: he says that it is of no account, there is nothing to it; and so of the dream, it is only imagination, it is nothing. But science and art spring from imagination, from the mind, not from a rock, not from the physical body. The source from which all knowledge comes is the mind, not an object. Mind means 'I'. It is the mind which identifies; the body is an illusion. When the mind is depressed, we say, 'I am sad.' Not the body, but the mind was depressed; so the real identification is with the mind, not the body.

When in a dream man is able to see himself, what does that

show? That after what is called death, man is still not formless; that nothing is lost, but only that freedom is gained which was lost. The absence of this knowledge makes man afraid of losing this physical body, makes him have a horror of death. But what is death? Nothing but a sleep; a sleep of the body which was a cloak. One can take it away and yet be living. Man will realize after all talk about death that he is alive, that he has not lost but gained. Man is in the physical world to learn, and the dream teaches that a law is working; that all that seems surprising, accidental, a sudden happening, was not sudden, not an accident. It seemed accidental because it was not connected with the conditions.

Nothing happens which does not go through the mind. Man has turned his back to it; he is open only to manifestation. Did they not say in every country when the war came: we did not know? Yes, it was so for those who slept, but the awakened ones had seen the preparation. In all things we see this. Every accident, pleasant or unpleasant, is preceded by a long preparation. First it exists in the mind, then on the physical plane.

A dream shows the depths of life; through a dream we see things. Has every dream a meaning? Yes; only there are always people in a country who do not know its language, and so it is with minds. Some minds are not yet capable of expressing themselves, so the dreams are upside-down, a chaos. One sees a goat with the ears of an elephant. The mind wants to express itself. There is a meaning in what the child says, but it has not yet learned to speak, it has no words; it can only cry or make a sound; yet this has a meaning. So it is with dreams which are not expressed correctly. There is nothing without meaning; it is our lack of understanding of its meaning that keeps us in darkness.

But what about the quite meaningless dreams one sometimes has? They are due to the condition of the mind. If the condition of the mind is not harmonious, if its rhythm is not regular, then the dream is so mixed up that one cannot read it. It is just like a letter written in the dark; when a person could not see what he was writing. But all the same it is a written letter, it has an idea behind it. Even if the very person who wrote it in the dark room is not able to read it, it still remains a letter. When man

cannot understand the meaning of his dream it is not that his
dream has no significance; it only means that his own letter
has become so confused that he cannot read it himself.

One may say, how can the mind learn to express itself? It
has to become itself. Often the mind is disturbed, inharmonious,
restless. When a person is drunk he wants to say yes, and he says
no. So is the expression of the mind in a dream. It is a marvellous
thing to study the science of dreams. How wonderful that the
dream of a poet should be poetical, of a musician harmonious.
Why is this? Because their mind is trained; their mind has become individual. Their mind expresses itself in their own realm.
Sometimes one marvels at the dreams one hears experienced by
poetic souls; one sees the sequence from the first act till the last,
and that every little action has a certain meaning.

More interesting still is the symbolical dream: to see the meaning behind it. It is wonderful to think that a simple dream comes
to a simple person, but when the person is confused then the
dream is confused. And in the straight dream, in the dream with
fear, with joy, with grief, one can see what a person is. Then
the dream does not seem a dream; it is as real as life on the physical plane. But is this life not a dream? Are the eyes not closed?
The king has forgotten his palace. We say, 'Oh, it is only a
dream, it is nothing.' But this dream can show our whole past
life; this dream can be tomorrow. It is only on the physical plane
that it is a dream; it is made a dream by the condition in which
the mind is.

We say, 'Yes, but when we awake we find a house; that,
therefore, is reality. If we dream of a palace, we find no palace.'
This is true and not true. The palaces which are built in that
world are as much our own, are really much more our own.
When the body dies, these remain; they will always be there.
If it was a dream of pleasure, the pleasure will come. If it was
a dream of light, of love, then all is there. It is a treasure you can
depend upon; death cannot take it away. It gives a glimpse of
that idea of which the Bible says, 'Where your treasure is, there
will your heart be also.' We can find glimpses of it too when we
compare dreams with the wakeful state. Whatever we hold, the
longer we have held it the more firmly it is established; then we

create a world to live in. This is the secret of the whole of life. But how can words explain this?

Another form of dream is the vision. Therein a person sees clearly what will happen, or what has happened perhaps many years ago. It is like a flash. When does one get this? When the heart is focused to the divine mind, for all is there like a moving picture. There was a poet of Persia, Firdausi, who was asked by the king to write the history of the country. The king promised him a gold coin for every verse. Firdausi went into the solitude and wrote down the traditions of centuries; characters, lives, deeds, he saw it all as a play, and he wrote of it in verse. When he returned to the court, the king was most impressed; he thought it wonderful. But there are always many in the world who will reject such things. The truth is only accepted by the few. At the court he was much criticized and many showed scepticism. It went so far that they told the king that it was all Firdausi's imagination. It hurt him terribly. He took the one who had spoken most against him and held his hand upon his head, and said to him, 'Now, close your eyes and look.' And what this man saw was like a moving picture and he exclaimed, 'I have seen!' But the poet's heart was wounded and he would not accept the gold coins.

What was the message given by the great ones, by the prophets and masters, by Rama, by Krishna? It was not imagination. It was that record which can be found by diving deep, that prophecy given to the world as a lesson, living in the world, like a scripture. It is direct communion given by all masters.

A vision is more clear in the sleeping state than in the wakeful state. The reason is that when a person is asleep he lives in a world of his own, but when a person is awake he is only partly in that world and mostly in the outer world. Every phenomenon needs accommodation. It is not only the sound which is audible, but also the ears make it possible to hear the sound. The mind is the accommodation to receive the impressions, just as the ears are the accommodation to receive the sound. That is why a natural state of sleep is like a profound concentration, like a deep meditation; and that is why everything that comes as a dream has a significance.

Lastly there is another step forward, and that is revelation. It needs a certain amount of spiritual progress to believe that there is such a thing as revelation. Life is revealing, nature is revealing, and so is God; that is why God is called Khuda in Persian, which means self-revealing. All science and art, and all culture known to man have come originally, and still come, by revelation. In other words a person does not only learn by studying, but he also draws knowledge from humanity. A child not only inherits his father's or his ancestors' qualities but also the qualities of his nation, of his race, so that one can say that man inherits the qualities of the entire human race. If one realized profoundly that storehouse of knowledge which exists behind the veil which covers it, one would find that one has a right to this heritage; and this gives one a key, a key to understand the secret of life: that knowledge is not only gained from outside but also from within. Thus one may call knowledge that one learns from outer life learning, but knowledge that one draws from within may be called revelation.

Revelation comes from within. It makes the heart self-revealing; it is just like a new birth of the soul. When one has come to this state, then everything and every being is living; a rock, a tree, the air, the sky, the stars, all are living. Then a person begins to communicate with all things and all beings. Wherever his glance falls, on nature, on characters, he reads their history, he sees their future. Every person he meets, before he has spoken one word with him he begins to communicate with his soul. Before he has asked any question, the soul begins to tell its own history. Every person and every object stand before him as an open book. Then there no longer exists in him that continual 'why' one finds so often in people. 'Why' no longer exists, for he finds the answer to every question in himself. And as long as that answer is not created, in spite of all the learning of this world that is taught to man, that continual 'why' will exist.

Again one may ask, how does one arrive at this revelation? And the answer is that there is nothing in the whole of the universe which is not to be found in man if he only cares to discover it. But if he will not find it out no one will give it to him, for truth is not learned; truth is discovered.

It is with this belief that sages of the East went into the solitude and sat meditating in order to give that revelation an opportunity to arise. No doubt as life is at present there is hardly time for a man to go into the solitude. But that does not mean that man should remain ignorant of the best that is within himself; for compared with this great bliss which is revelation, all other treasures of the earth are nothing; they cannot be compared. Revelation is the magic lamp of Aladdin; once discovered it throws its light to the right and to the left, and all things become clear.

CHAPTER XIX

INSIGHT (1)

INSIGHT may be likened to the view one obtains through a telescope. From a distance one can see a wide horizon, but when one is close to things one gets a limited horizon. By getting this smaller horizon things become clearer because one sees them in detail; when there is a larger horizon things are not seen in detail but then there is a general outlook. And the same law can be applied to insight. When one looks at a person one gets a glimpse of his character, and when one looks at an assembly one gets a feeling of the assembly.

The heart is the telescope of the soul, and the eyes are the telescope of the heart. Just as when seeing through spectacles it is the eyes that see, not the spectacles, so when seeing through the heart and through the eyes, what sees is the soul. The eyes have no power to see; the eyes have only the power to help the soul to see. The moment the soul departs the eyes do not see. And so even the heart is a telescope which helps one to perceive and to conceive all that one seeks. Yet at the same time the heart does not see; it is the soul that sees.

Just as there are some who have short sight and others who have long sight, so there are some who see things at a far distance with the eye of their mind but who cannot see what is near them.

They have long sight. Then there are others who have short sight; they see all that is near them, but they cannot see further. It is said that there is a third eye that sees. It is true, but sometimes that third eye sees through these two eyes and then the same eyes see things more clearly than they would otherwise. By the help of the third eye one's eyes can penetrate through the wall of physical existence and see into the minds of people, into the words of people, and even further. When one begins to see, what happens first is that everything one's eyes see has a deeper meaning, a greater significance than one knew before. Every movement, every gesture, the form, features, voice, words, expression, atmosphere, all become expressive of the person's nature and character. Not knowing this secret, many people want to study physiognomy or phrenology, handwriting or palmistry. But in comparison with the clear vision all these different sciences are limited. They have a meaning, but at the same time when one compares these limited sciences with the insight that man has, they prove to be too small. Besides character-reading is not learnt, it is discovered. It is a sense that awakens. One does not need to learn it. One knows it.

This is one kind of insight, but there is another insight which is insight in affairs. Be it a business affair, a professional affair, a condition, a situation in life, once the insight is clear one has a grasp of the situation. For what makes things difficult in life is lack of knowledge. There may be a small problem, but when one does not know it, it becomes the heaviest and worst of all problems, because one cannot understand it. And one may analyse a problem and reason it out, but without insight it will always remain puzzling. It is the development of insight that gives one a clear vision in affairs, conditions, and the problems of life.

The faculty of seeing needs direction. For instance, in order to look to the right or the left, or before or behind, one must direct the eyes; and this directing is the work of the will. In the twenty-four hours of the day and night it is perhaps at most for five minutes or fifteen minutes that one sees under the direction of the will; all the rest of the time one sees automatically. In other words one's eyes are open, one's heart is subject to all that can be seen, and one catches unknowingly the different things that attract the eyes and mind. All that one sees during the day and night is not what one intended to see, but what one is compelled by the life around us to see. That is why the thinkers and sages of the East in ancient times used to have mantles put over their heads, so that they did not see anything or anybody and could control their sight. The Sufis of ancient times used to keep their heads covered like this for many years, and in doing so they developed such powers that their one glance would penetrate rocks and mountains. It is only control of the sight. Yogis in all ages have worked not only with their minds but even with their eyes, attaining such a stability of glance that they could direct their sight to anything they wished to examine or penetrate. Eyes, therefore, are the representatives of the soul at the surface, and they speak to a person more clearly than words can speak; to one who can read they are the signs of the plane of evolution a person is on. A person does not need to speak to one; his eyes tell one whether he is pleased or not, willing or unwilling, whether he is favourably inclined or unfavourably inclined. Love or hate, pride or modesty, all can be seen in the eyes; even wisdom and ignorance, everything, manifests through the eyes. The one who can trace the condition and character in the eyes certainly communicates with the soul of another person.

Not very long ago in Hyderabad there was a mureed, rather an intellectual pupil, and he liked to talk. His teacher was interested in his intelligent inquiries, and so he encouraged him to talk, whereas it is the custom in the East for the pupil to remain silent before his teacher. One day the teacher was in a condition of exaltation and his pupil as usual wanted to discuss and argue, which was not agreeable to the teacher at that time. He said in Persian, 'Khamush', which means silence. And the pupil became silent; he went home and remained silent. And no one heard him speak after that, no one in the house nor outside; he never spoke anywhere. Years passed by and the man still kept silent. But there came a time when his silence began to speak aloud. His silent thought would manifest, and his silent wish would become granted; his silent glance would heal, his silent look would inspire. His silence became living. It was the spoken words which had kept him dead all this time. The moment the lips were closed the silence in him began to live. His presence was living. In Hyderabad people called him Shaikh Khamush, the king of silence, or the silent king. By this I wish to imply that everyone has eyes, but to make the eyes living takes a long time. For eyes see so far and no further; it is the heart connected with the eyes that can see further, and if the soul sees through them it sees further still.

An entirely different question is how to get the eyes focused. If one wishes to look at the moon one must look at the sky instead of looking at the earth; and so if one wants to seek heaven one must change the direction of looking. That is where many make a mistake. Today in the West, where there is a very large number of students eagerly engaged in looking for the truth, many among them are mistaken in this particular respect; in order to see what can be seen within they want to look without. It is, however, a natural tendency. As a person looks without for anything he wants, he naturally looks for inner attainment also on the outside.

How can we look within and what shall we see? In the first place, to a material person 'within' means in the body, inside the body. In reality 'within' means not only inside, but also outside the body. This can be seen by the light inside a lamp: the light is inside the globe, and it is outside the globe too. So is the soul; it is inside and outside too. So is the mind; it is inside and outside, it is not confined inside the body. In other words, the heart is larger than the body, and the soul is larger still. At the same time the soul is accommodated within the heart, and the heart is accommodated within the body; this is the greatest phenomenon and is very difficult to explain in words. There are intuitive centres; and in order to see into the intuitive centres one has to turn the eyes back, turn the eyes within; then the same eyes which are able to see without are able to see within. But that is only one phase of seeing. The other phase of seeing within cannot be seen by the eyes; it is the heart that sees. And when one is able to see that way, the pain and pleasure and joy and sorrow of every person that comes before one manifest in one's own heart; one actually sees it. One sees it even

more clearly than one's eyes can see. But that is the language of
the heart. The eyes do not know it.

Sages in the East used to be called *Balakush*, which means
'He who took the draught of all difficulties.' They regarded the
difficulties of life as a wine to drink; once you drink, they have
gone. They were not afraid of it, they did not want to keep out
of it. They said, 'If we keep out this time, next time it will meet
us; it will meet us one day. If we escape one moment, another
moment it will meet us. So let it come such as it is and
let us drink it as wine.' The principle of Mahadeva, of the dervishes, of the great faqirs of all ages is this one principle: to
drink all difficulties as a wine. Then there is no more difficulty.
When one is in tune with life, life becomes revealing, for then
one is friends with life. Before that, one was a stranger to it.
Attitude makes a great difference, and it is the difference of attitude that makes a person spiritual or material. Nothing else need
be changed, only the attitude.

The lesson we learn from the developing of our insight is not to
become excited by any influence that tries to bring us out of rhythm,
but to keep in rhythm under all conditions of life; to keep our
equilibrium, our tranquillity under all circumstances. It is sometimes
very difficult to keep our equilibrium when the influences of life are
shaking us, and to keep our poise through it all; it is difficult in
the face of influences which are opposed to keeping a friendly
attitude. But at the same time, because it is difficult it is a great
attainment. To attain anything valuable and worth while we
have to go through difficulty. But we do not pay for it; we
learn without paying for it. It is something that we can practise
in everyday life because from morning till evening we are continually among jarring effects from all sides. There is plenty of
opportunity for practising this lesson of keeping a friendly attitude towards everyone, of meeting every condition courageously,
and of taking upon ourselves all influences that come along. It
is in this way that a greater insight into life is attained.

If there is anything that can make our comprehension clear, it
is reason on one side and feeling on the other. A man in whom
feeling is not awakened is awake and asleep at the same time.
That which is living is not reason, it is feeling. Many think when

the brain is working it is something tangible; one does not notice it working in feeling. But in reality feeling takes the part of the engineer and the brain is like the mechanism. The mechanism cannot work without the engineer; so the brain cannot work without the feeling behind it. These two things are needed to make knowledge clear. When a person cannot understand himself, his own imagination, his own problems deeply, then how can he understand the problems of others? Then there is no communication between one person and another. Today friendship often means only a professional interest; human relations are formed by certain interests, worldly interests. Therefore man does not know what feeling is. The alliances of nations, the unions of working men, all these things are being formed on the basis of self-interest. I am your friend if you defend my case! Therefore when feeling, which alone is divine in man, which is the proof and sign of the spirit, and which is a divine heritage, becomes blunted, then naturally whatever life may be it cannot be civilization, even if one calls it civilized.

The day will come when man will live a fuller life, a more complete life of high ideals and great principles, when feeling in man will be as much awakened as reason. When that day comes the knowledge will be spiritual knowledge, not book-learning. One can feel everywhere, in colleges, in societies, in clubs, in any of the professions, that every person is seeking directly or indirectly for some knowledge; man feels that there is a knowledge which is more real. Every person seems to be disappointed with his experience of life. He may be most successful in the world, it does not matter. He may be a rich man, he may have a high position, but he is disappointed, he is longing for something which will satisfy him. What is it? It is not outside. It is within himself. He will find it on the day when he awakens to the reality of life. Once a soul is awakened to the reality of life, all other things matter little. What matters is that he understands clearly that what satisfies is within.

Besides, when once the heart begins to live, another world is open for experience. For generally what one experiences in one's everyday life is only what the senses can perceive and nothing beyond it. But when once a person begins to feel and experience the subtle feelings of the heart he lives in another world, walking on the same earth and living under the same sun. Therefore be not surprised if you find beings who are living in another world while walking on this earth. It is as natural as anything can be for man to live in his heart instead of only living on the earth. The people in the East call it *Saheb-e-dil*, that is the master-mind.

And then if one goes still deeper within, one begins to live in the soul. Inspiration, intuition, vision, revelation are natural to this person. The soul begins to become conscious of its own domain. And it is the same kingdom of which it is said in the Bible: 'Seek ye first the kingdom of God . . .'. It is the soul which begins to see.

And one can see still further. What enables one to attain to this stage is the way of meditation under the guidance of the right teacher.

The first thing to do is to get control of the glance. The next is to get control of the feelings. And the third is to get control of the consciousness. If these three things are attained then one begins to look within. Looking within helps a person very much in looking outside; then the same power with which the heart and eyes are charged begins to manifest outwardly. And the one who looks within finds, when he looks without, that all that is within manifests without. His influence is healing and consoling, uplifting and soothing. His sight, too, becomes penetrating, so that not only human beings but even objects begin to disclose to him their nature, character, and secret.

CHAPTER XX

INSIGHT (2)

INSIGHT shows itself in different aspects: in impression, intuition, inspiration, dream, and revelation.

How does one get impressions? All impressions reach the brain through the nerve centres. They are mostly taken in by the breath; but by this one does not mean the breath inhaled through the nostrils. He who is able to get an impression of a person need not wait to see how he will turn out; he knows it instantly. Very often one may have a feeling at first sight, whether someone will be one's friend or prove unfriendly.

When someone comes and tells me, 'I am very interested in your philosophy, but before I take it up I want to study it', he may study for a thousand years and he will not get to that insight. It is the first moment: either you are my friend or not my friend. When two persons meet a confidence is established; one does not need years in order to develop friendship.

Everyone receives an impression on seeing a certain person or looking at a certain situation. One may not believe that impression, but all the same it is there. The first impression tells a man whether he will be successful or not, whether a person is right or not, whether there will be friendship between two people or not. And when this faculty is developed, a person can get an impression of a place and of persons and of conditions. Impressions come to those whose mind is still; those whose mind is active cannot take impressions. For the mind is like water: when the pool of water is disturbed, one cannot see any reflection in it. Thus purity of mind is necessary. In which sense? All that is called wrong is not necessarily wrong; some things are called wrong because of a certain moral, a certain principle, originated by the mechanical action of the mind. When the mind is kept pure from all activity that disturbs it, then it becomes like pure water. Very often the water of the mind is polluted, but when the mind is in its pure condition, then naturally it can take impressions.

The mind may be likened to a photographic plate. If several impressions have been made upon it, then there can be no other impressions. That is why the mind should be kept pure from all undesirable impressions in order that every impression may be clear.

Intuition is still deeper, for by intuition one gets a warning. Intuitively one feels: this person will one day deceive me, or turn against me; or he will prove faithful to me, sincere, to be relied upon. Or in this particular business I will have success or failure. One knows it. But the difficulty is in distinguishing the right intuition; that is the great question; for as soon as intuition springs up, reason, its competitor, rises also and says, 'No, it is not so', and then there is conflict in the mind and it is hard to distinguish, because there are two feelings at the same time. If one makes a habit of catching the first intuition and saving it from being destroyed by reason, then intuition is stronger and one can benefit by it. There are many intuitive people, but they cannot always distinguish between intuition and reason and sometimes they mix them up, for very often the second thought, being the last, is more clear to one than the first. Therefore the intuition is forgotten and reason remembered. Then a person calls it intuition and it is not so. Reason and intuition are two competitors, and yet both have their place, their importance, and their value. The best thing would be first to try and catch the intuition and distinguish and know and recognize it as intuition; and then to reason it out.

Besides, those who doubt intuition, their intuition doubts them. In other words, the doubt becomes a wall between themselves and their intuitive faculty. And there is a psychological action: as soon as intuition has sprung up, doubt and reason have sprung up too, so that the vision becomes blurred. One should develop self-confidence. Even if one proves to be wrong once or twice or thrice one should still continue; in time one will develop trust in one's intuition and then intuition will be clear.

Women are naturally more intuitive than men. The reason is that a woman is more responsive by nature and more sympathetic; therefore she can perceive intuition more clearly. Very often a man may reason and think and yet not come to a conclusion, to a clear understanding, while a woman, or any more intuitive person, in one moment is clear about a certain question, a certain point. That comes from intuition. Intuition is a faculty of the heart that feels deeply, be it of a man or a woman; the quality of intuition belongs to a sympathetic heart.

The intuition of dogs and cats and of horses sometimes seems to be more clear than that of man. They know when there is going to be an accident, when death is going to occur in the family. They know beforehand and give people warning. But people are so busy in their daily occupations that they do not respond to the intuition of the animals. People in the East believe that small insects know about happenings and give a warning to those who can understand it; and it is true. Besides, birds always give a warning of storm and wind, and of rain and the absence of rain. Mankind naturally is more capable of intuition, but because his mind is absorbed by a hundred things, his deep feelings become so blunted in everyday life that he ignores the existence of intuition or inspiration, and so this faculty itself becomes blunted and he feels and knows less than the animals. The human body is a vehicle, a telescope, an instrument by which one can perceive the knowledge of one's self within, of conditions, of others, and of everything outside.

The question is, how does one develop this faculty of intuition? The first thing is self-confidence. When there is no self-confidence one cannot develop this faculty of intuition, because it comes more and more by believing in it. When a person doubts and says, 'Is this an intuition, will this really help me, or shall I be deceived by my own intuition?' then naturally reason produces confusion in the mind and intuition is destroyed. There are many intuitive people, and their intuition has been destroyed only by this doubt which arises in their mind, whether their intuition is right or wrong. That is why they lose this faculty of intuition. Every faculty needs nurturing; if it is not nurtured it becomes blunted and destroyed; one can make no more use of it. Besides, a person may underestimate the value of this faculty in his life; he then naturally destroys it; and this faculty disappears also by a too speedy action of the mind. When a person thinks of a thousand things in a short time, the mind becomes too active and then one cannot perceive intuition, which needs a certain rhythm, a certain concentration.

A further aspect of insight is inspiration. The difference between inspiration and instinct is that what we recognize in the lower creation as instinct is the same as that which works through the human mind in the form of intuition or inspiration. One may say from a biological point of view that the lower creatures are born with a certain instinct such as the inclination to fly, to defend themselves with their horns or to bite with their teeth.

All the faculties they show are born with them; they are not only the heritage brought from their ancestors, they do not belong to their family only, they are a property of the spirit. And from the spirit all living beings get guidance in the form of an inclination. What we recognize as instinct in the lower creations is inspiration in mankind. Today, as science is increasing and as materialism prevails, man is forgetting the heritage that he has from the spirit, and attributes all knowledge and experience to the material existence of the physical world. In this way he deprives himself of those gifts which could be called his own and without which man cannot live a fuller life.

Inspiration comes to poets, writers, inventors, scientists. Where does it come from, what is its source? Why does not the inspiration of a musician come to a poet, why does not a poet's inspiration come to a musician? Why should it reach the person to whom it belongs? The reason is that there is a mind behind all minds; that there is a heart which is the source of all hearts, and that there is a Spirit which collects and accumulates all the knowledge that every living being has had. No knowledge or discovery that has ever been made is lost. It all accumulates and collects in that mind as an eternal reservoir. This is what is recognized by the seers as the divine mind. From this mind all vision can be drawn. The mind of the poet is naturally exalted, that is why it becomes enlightened by the divine mind. From the divine mind all that is needed manifests. It may be that a poet works without inspiration for six months on a poem, and it gives satisfaction neither to the poet nor to others, who find it mechanical. And there is another one who receives the inspiration in a moment and puts it down. He can never correct what he has written, he can never change it. No one can change it. If it is changed, it is spoiled. It is something that comes in a moment and it is perfect in itself, it is a piece of art, it is an example of beauty; and it comes so easily. That is inspiration.

Many have tried to imitate inspired people, in poetry or in scientific inventions. They tried, but they never reached that perfection which came in a moment's time. Those who were inspired never searched after it, it came in a mood. All that comes from inspiration is living, it always keeps its value. There are

writings of such poets in the East as Rumi of Persia, as Kalidasa
of India; and now, after thousands of years, their writings are
read by people and they are never old and people never tire of
them. It is the same with Shakespeare. He has made a living
world. The more time passes, the more it lives, the more it is
appreciated. It is for ever living. That is the character of inspiration; and it only comes to the one whose mind is still and whose
thought is absorbed in the beauty of the work upon which he
is contemplating. The mind of the musician who knows little
of this world except music, is concentrated and focused on the
beauty of his art. Naturally he will draw inspiration. So it is
with the poet. But when the mind is absorbed in a thousand
things, then it is not focused, then it cannot receive inspiration.

How is inspiration developed? By concentration. An inspired
poet is he whose mind is fully fixed on the idea he wishes to
express; he is floating, so to speak, in the beauty of it; his mind
becomes focused and inspiration mechanically comes to him.
A person who troubles about inspiration, who wants to drag
it towards him, cannot get it; it does not belong to him. In
order to get it he must float in the idea, he must merge all his
heart in its beauty. He must be so positively focused to that
spirit of beauty that inspiration may naturally flow into him.

The dream or vision is another aspect of insight. Very often
people consider a dream as an automatic action of the mind.
But this is not always the case. There is no movement in the
mind which is meaningless. Every motion and action has a meaning behind it, every motion is directed towards something either
with intention or without. There is no movement, there is no
action which is not directed from some source or other.

There are three kinds of dreams. In the first a person sees his
mind working along the same lines as it did during the day, at
the same time suggesting the past, present, or future. Then
there is another kind of dream when the mind sees in everything
quite the opposite of what is going to happen. And there is a
third type of dream in which one sees something out of the past
actually happening, or what is going to happen in the future.
This proves that everything on the physical plane is first formed
in the inner planes and then registered on the mind in the dream.

When one is concentrated one sees the happening more clearly.

There is also a state of dream in which one sees a vision. This happens in a meditative condition. A vision is more communicative, more expressive; it may be a warning which is given for the future, or an incident of the past may be made known. In the vision one can go still further and communicate with the unseen world. But a vision only comes to those who are born with that faculty or have developed that faculty in the mind by becoming fully concentrated.

A dream may be symbolical, and this is the most interesting type of dream. The greater the person, the subtler the symbolism of his dream will be. When someone is gross the symbolism will be gross. The more evolved the person is, the more fine, artistic, and subtle the dream will be. For instance, for a poet there will be poetic symbols; and the dream of a musician will have musical symbols; in the dream of the artist there will be symbols of art.

In the realistic dream one actually sees what is going to happen. All that we call accident is only our conception; because we did not know it beforehand we call it accident. This also gives us insight into what we call fate. But there is a plan; it is all planned out and known beforehand to the spirit and to those who know. There are sages who know of their death a year before. There is no such thing as accident. When a person does not know, it means he does not see; but it is there.

Revelation is still greater. It is the perfection of insight. It means a higher development when one has revelation, and it begins when a person feels in tune with everybody, everything, and every condition. But in order to come to that stage one must develop according to it. The heart must be tuned to the stage and the pitch where one feels at-one-ment with persons, objects, and conditions. For instance, when one cannot bear the climate, it only means that one is not in harmony with the climate; when one cannot get on with persons, that one is not in harmony with them; when one cannot get on with certain affairs, that one is not in harmony with those affairs. If conditions seem hard, it shows that one is not in harmony with the conditions.

Revelation came to the saints and saviours of humanity. It is not just a tale when we hear that the saints spoke with trees and plants in the wilderness, that a voice from the sea rose and the saints heard it, that masters talked with the sun, moon, and stars. For the deeper a person dives into life, the more he is convinced that all is living, whether beings or objects, whether art or nature; whatever he sees, whatever he perceives through the senses, whatever he can touch, all that is intelligible to him. It may not be seen and it may not be known by anybody else, but everything is communicating. Once a person begins to communicate with nature, with art, he begins to have the proof of this, for everything begins to speak. As the great poet of Persia, Sa'di, has said, 'Every leaf of the tree becomes a page of the Book when once the heart is opened and it has learnt to read.'

When revelation begins, a man does not need to converse; before talking, he knows what the other wishes to say. The condition of the person or the persons before him is revealed; it is like reading a letter. The person may speak to him, but without speaking he knows. This is not thought-reading, not telepathy, not psychometry or clairvoyance as people think. Revelation is all the phenomena there are. What is it? It is a fuller development of inspiration. When the intuitive faculty is fully developed, man receives revelation. All dumb creatures and mute things begin to speak. For what are words? Are they not covers over the idea? No feeling can ever be expressed in words, no idea be put fully into verse. A true glimpse of ideas and feelings can only be perceived in that plane which is feeling itself.

Revelation depends upon purity of mind. Very often someone who is worldly-wise is not really wise. Intellectuality is one thing, wisdom is another thing. Not all the knowledge learnt from books and from experiences in the world and collected in the mind as learning is wisdom. When the light from within is thrown upon this knowledge, then the knowledge from outer life and the light coming from within make a perfect wisdom; and it is that wisdom which guides man on the path of life.

Those who received revelation have given us sacred books such as the Bible, the Qur'an, the Bhagavad Gita; hundreds and thousands of years have passed and their sacred teachings have remained alive even now. But at the same time we must know that what they have given in the form of preaching, in the form of teachings, is the interpretation of the living wisdom which cannot be fully expressed in words. One can only know that living knowledge when one has experienced it oneself by the opening of the heart. It is then that the purpose of life is fulfilled.

CHAPTER XXI

THE EXPANSION OF CONSCIOUSNESS

THE consciousness is the intelligence; the intelligence is the soul; the soul is the spirit ; and the spirit is God. Therefore consciousness is the divine element, consciousness is the God-part in us. And it is through consciousness that we become small or great, and through consciousness we either rise or fall, and through consciousness we become narrow or we expand. One finds in Greek mystical symbology and also elsewhere the two wings of an eagle, and this symbol is the symbol of consciousness. When the wings are open it means the expansion of consciousness, which can also be called the unfoldment of the soul. In any path you take, when you wish to go further in the spiritual journey, be it religion, occultism, philosophy, or mysticism, you have to come to the expansion of consciousness.

What is consciousness? When we say: 'a loaded gun', we mean that there is a bullet in it. Consciousness means the loaded intelligence, intelligence charged with knowledge, with impressions carrying ideas. When we speak of moving pictures, where are they? On the screen; but we do not see the screen, we see moving pictures. Consciousness is pure intelligence which is impregnated with some idea, which is conscious of something. And what is intelligence? Intelligence is the soul; there is no other trace of the soul to be found except the intelligence. Very often people, not understanding, say the seat of the soul is in the heart, or in the right or left side of man; but in reality there is something more expressive than any side of man's body, and that is intelligence.

There is a story which demonstrates the idea of the universal or general consciousness apart from individual consciousness. There was a magician who imagined that he was fluid, liquid, moving, rising and falling, and turning into the sea. Then he imagined, 'Now I am solid.' Atoms grouped together, froze and turned into ice. Then he thought, 'I am not so cold. I can try and be stable, and will not melt'; and he turned into stone. Next he said, 'Now I want to change. I do not want to remain stone.' And he became a tree. 'But,' he said, 'still I am not moving, not working'; and he twisted and moved, and turned into an insect. But the magician thought, 'How helpless it is to live as an insect! I should like to play and sing'; and he turned into a bird. Then he said, 'I want to be more gross and dense, and feel myself more intelligent'; and he turned into an animal. Finally he said, 'I want to stand on my hind legs, to stretch my spine'; and he turned into man.

This is the phenomenon of a magician who wanted, who imagined, something and who became it. One finds this idea also in the scriptures. In the Qur'an it is said, 'Be, and it became.' It was the magician's work: what he was conscious of, he became. First there was the consciousness, and then the idea it held turned into something.

But there is another question: if the magician was so powerful as to think and turn into something, then why did he himself become obscured? The answer is this, that when a man has said, 'I would like to rest, to go to sleep', naturally he has lost his activity. Turning into something made that consciousness, which is divine or universal consciousness, limited; and this limitation robbed it of its own consciousness. This is the deepest point of metaphysics. For instance, when the consciousness thought, 'I will turn into a rock, I am a rock', it became a rock. The consciousness did not lose its fluid substance, but intelligence no longer knew its own existence. And yet when the magician thought, 'I will turn into a rock', what went into the rock? Just one little thought of the magician. Only, because of that thought he could not express himself, nor feel as he felt in the condition of being a magician. When he turned into a rock he did not feel through this thought, he felt nothing.

The more we understand this idea, the more we shall see that consciousness is to be considered in two different aspects. In one aspect the consciousness is buried under the dense forms of creation such as mountains, rocks, trees, plants, earth, and sea; and yet the tendency of consciousness is, even through these dense forms, to come out, to express itself. One can see that tendency by getting in touch with nature. For instance, those who sit before the rocks, in the caves of the mountains, in the midst of the forest, and those who get in touch with nature and whose mind is free from the worries and anxieties and troubles of the world, they get a sort of peace first; and after having experienced peace and rest, the second thing that comes to them is a kind of communication between themselves and nature. And what does nature express to them? With every action, with the rising and falling of the waves, with the upward reaching tendency of the mountains, with the moving of the graceful branches of the tree, with the blowing of the wind and the fluttering of leaves, every little movement of nature seems to whisper in their ears. That is the consciousness that wants to emerge; through trees and rocks, water and plants it wants to unfold itself, to express itself; because it is not dead, but living, though buried in the rock, in the tree, in the plant, in water, earth, and air. Every living being tries to make itself audible and intelligible; it wants to communicate, trying for years and years to break through this dense imprisonment, to emerge towards its original source, just like the magician who wanted to break through, to come out and see himself. And what did he turn into? Into man.

There is a saying of the Sufis that 'God slept in the rock, God dreamed in the tree, God became self-conscious in the animal, but God sought Himself and recognized Himself in man.' That denotes clearly man's main purpose: that whatever be his occupation, whatever may please him, whatever he may admire, there is only one motive, the one motive which is working towards his unfoldment, and that is to feel, 'What I have made, how great it is, and how wonderful. How beautiful it is to recognize it, to see it.' It is that inclination which is working through every soul. Whether a person wants to become spiritual

or not, yet unconsciously every soul is striving towards the unfoldment of the soul.

As to human consciousness, naturally when consciousness has
turned into something it has limited itself. Although in comparison with trees and plants and rocks and mountains the consciousness of man is fully awakened, yet every human being is
not awakened; most are still in captivity. As Rumi says in the
Masnavi, 'Man is captive in an imprisonment'; and his every
effort, his every desire, is to break through in order to realize
inspiration, greatness, beauty, happiness, peace, independently of
all things of this world.

Everyone comes to this sooner or later, but there is a continual yearning; wise and foolish, everyone is striving for it consciously or unconsciously. There is one person who is perhaps
very interested in himself, his health, his mind, his thoughts or
feelings, or his affairs; his consciousness does not go any further than
that little horizon. It does not mean that in that way he is not
right. He occupies that much space in the sphere of consciousness.
There is another person who has forgotten himself; he says,
'There is my family, my friends, I love them', and so his consciousness is larger. Another will say, 'I work for my fellow-
citizens, for my country, for the education of the children of
my country, for the good health of the people in my town';
his consciousness is larger still. It does not really mean that his
consciousness is larger, but he occupies a larger horizon in the
sphere of consciousness. And so do not be surprised if a poet
like Nizami says, 'If the heart is large enough, it can contain the
whole universe.' That consciousness is such that the universe is
small compared with it. The sphere of that consciousness is the
Absolute.

There is no piece of consciousness cut out for man, but man
occupies a certain horizon, as far as he can expand; for him the
Absolute can be his consciousness. Therefore on the outside he
is individual, but in reality one cannot say what he is.

It is this idea that is hinted at in the Bible when it is said, 'Be
ye perfect as your Father in heaven is perfect.' What does it
mean? That the absolute Consciousness is the sign of perfection,
and we are not excluded from it. All move and live in it. But we

Mental Purification 233

occupy only as much horizon as is within our consciousness, or as much as we are conscious of. This shows us that every individual has his own world; and the world of one individual is as tiny as a grain of lentil, and that of another as large as the whole world. Yet on the outside all human beings are more or less equal in size, one somewhat taller than the other; but in his own world there is no comparison, so different can one person be from another. There can be as many varieties of worlds in human beings as there are of creatures from ant to elephant.

There is the question of what has been called in the scriptures heaven and hell. What are they? Heaven and hell are our world, our consciousness, that in which we live day after day and year after year, and which continues in another world. Whatever we have made our world, we are experiencing it today. And what is said by the prophets, that after death all will be brought into evidence, only means that in this earthly plane we are so little conscious of our world, so absorbed in the outer world, that we do not know what world we have created within ourselves. We are so much occupied with the outer world, with our desires, ambitions, and striving, that we hardly know our own world, like the man who works in the factory: he is tired at night, and when he comes home he reads his newspaper.

It is the same with everyone. In every person's life there is so much of the outside world all day long to attract him, thousands of advertisements, shops sparkling with electricity. There will come a time when his eyes will be closed to the outside world which now occupies all his mind, to become conscious of the world within. This is the meaning of the saying of the scriptures, 'One will find what one has made.' One need not say, 'What will become of me tomorrow?' If one can direct one's mind into oneself, one can see what is within the consciousness, what it is composed of, what it contains; then one will know today what the hereafter will be.

The Sufis in all ages have tried their best to train their consciousness. How did they train it? The first training is analysis, and the second training is synthesis. The analytical striving is to analyse and examine one's own consciousness, in other words one's own conscience; to ask one's conscience, addressing it, 'My

friend, all my happiness depends on you, and my unhappiness
also. If you are pleased, I am happy. Now tell me truly if what
I like and what I do not is in accordance with your approval.'
One should speak to one's conscience as a man going to the
priest to make his confession, 'Look what I have done. Maybe
it is wrong, maybe it is right; but you know it, you have your
share of it; its influence on you and your condition is my condition, your realization is my realization. If you are happy, only
then can I be happy. Now I want to make you happy; how can
I do it?' At once a voice of guidance will come from the conscience, 'You should do this, and not that; say this and not that.
In this way you should act, and not in that way.' And conscience
can give you better guidance that any teacher or book. It is a
living teacher awakened in oneself, one's own conscience. The
teachers, the Gurus, the Murshids, their way is to awaken the
conscience in the pupil; to make clear what has become unclear,
confused.

Sometimes they adopt such a wonderful way, such a gentle
way that even the pupil does not realize it. Once a man went
to a teacher and said ,'Will you take me as your pupil?' The
teacher first looked at him, and then said, 'Yes, with great
pleasure.' But the man said, 'Think about it before you tell me
yes. There are many bad things in me.' The teacher said, 'What
are these bad things?' The man said, 'I like to drink.' The teacher
said, 'That does not matter.' 'But,' the man said, 'I like to gamble.'
The teacher said, 'That does not matter.' 'But,' he said, 'there
are many other things, there are numberless things.' The teacher
said, 'That does not matter.' The man was very glad. 'But,' the
teacher said, 'now that I have disregarded all the bad things you
have said about yourself you must agree to one condition. Do
not do any of these things which you consider wrong in my
presence.' The pupil said, 'That is easy', and went away.

As the days and months passed, this pupil, who was very
deep and developed and keen, came back beaming, his soul unfolding every moment of the day, and happy to thank the teacher.
The teacher said, 'Well, how have you been?' 'Very well', he
said. The teacher said, 'Have you done your practices I have
given you?' 'Yes,' he said, 'very faithfully.' 'But what about

the habits you had of going to different places?' the teacher asked. 'Well,' he said, 'very often I tried to go to gamble or to drink, but wherever I went I saw you. You did not leave me alone; whenever I wanted to drink I saw your face before me. I could not do it.'

That is the gentle way in which teachers handle their disciples. They do not say, 'You must not drink, you must not gamble'; they never do. The wonderful way of the teacher is to teach without words, to correct a person without saying anything. What the teacher wants to say he says without saying; when it is put into words it is lost.

Then there is the most important subject of the expansion of consciousness. There are two directions or dimensions in which to expand. The one is the outward, the other the inner dimension. One dimension is pictured as a horizontal, the other as a perpendicular line. These two dimensions together form a cross, the symbol of the Christian religion. But before the Christian religion it existed in Egypt and Tibet; and in the ancient Buddhist and Tibetan symbolical pictures you will also find the symbol of the cross.

The way of expanding within is to close the eyes and mind from the outer world, and, instead of reaching out, to try to reach within. The action of the soul is to reach out and upwards and straight forward or sideways or backwards or in an ellipse. It is like the sun; its light reaches out in all directions, it sends currents out. So the soul sends currents out through the five senses. But when the five senses are controlled, when the breath is thrown within, the ears do not hear any more and the mouth does not speak. Then the five senses are directed within. And when once the senses are closed by the help of meditation, then the soul, which has been accustomed to reach outward, begins to reach within; and in the same way that one gets experience and power from the outer world, one gets experience and power from the inner world. And so the soul can reach further and further and further within until it has reached its original source, and that is the Spirit of God. That is one way, the way of reaching within.

Then there is the way of reaching without; that is expanding which comes by changing the outlook. Because we are narrow our outlook is narrow. We think, 'I am different, he is different.' We are making barriers of our own conceptions. If we lived and communicated with the souls of all people, of all beings, our horizon would naturally expand so much that we would occupy the sphere unseen. It is in this way that spiritual perfection is attained. Spiritual perfection, in other words, is the expansion of consciousness.

The question is sometimes asked: what is cosmic consciousness, what is the nature of that state? It is a state which cannot be very well explained in words. And if an explanation can be given, it is only by saying that when we see we do not hear and when we hear fully we do not see. In this way every sense is only doing its work fully when that sense alone is active. When we are seeing something while somebody is speaking to us, we do not see fully. I have known a child most interested in music, who used to close its eyes when music was played; then only it could enjoy hearing fully. But to listen to music while drinking lemonade and eating ice-cream is something different.

The condition of meditation is different from that; it is not limited by a rule. When meditating every sense is evenly balanced. In meditation every sense is awakened and yet every sense is asleep. To be closed from outside and yet to be awakened evenly, that experience is something which cannot be told in words; it must be experienced.

Practice of meditation is prescribed individually; the method for one may not be good for another. There is an Oriental symbol, a kind of toy, three monkeys, one covering its eyes, the other its ears, and the third its mouth. This is the keynote to meditation, the key to inner expansion. But also in everyday life we can see this symbol ethically, from a moral point of view, and that is: hear no evil, see no evil, and speak no evil. And if one can take that vow it can achieve a great deal; it can take one very far on the way if these three things are practised in everyday life; never speak against anyone, never hear what is spoken against anyone, and never see any evil. If we close our eyes without closing our ears and without closing our lips, we cannot accomplish anything.

Does the development of the inner consciousness, one may ask, tend to personal isolation, to separation from the world? We are in the world, and therefore, however much we try to run away to spiritual spheres, we are thrown back to earth again. We are bound here as long as we have this earthly body. And so the best thing is to follow the process in another way: to gain inner expansion of consciousness, and no doubt at that time one must go within, one must close oneself to the outer world; but at the same time one should strive to practise the outer expansion of consciousness. In this way there is balance.

Those who only evolve spiritually become one-sided; they expand only the inner consciousness and not the outward one. Then they become unbalanced. Maybe spiritually they have extraordinary powers, but they have no balance. For this reason many people think of a spiritual person as somebody who has something wrong with his brain. If that is the understanding of the world, we should be most conscientious in order not to give the world a wrong impression. If we have a profession, if we are in business, in industry, we should do it fully, proving to the world that we can be as practical as everybody else, and also economical, regular in every way, systematic, persevering, enthusiastic. All these qualities we must show and at the same time evolve spiritually; but it is these qualities which must give the proof of our spirituality.

THE MIND-WORLD

THE MIND-WORLD in the terms of the Sufi poets is called *'Aina Khana*, which means the Palace of Mirrors. One knows very little of the phenomena that this Palace of Mirrors has in it. Not only among human beings, but also in the lower creation one finds the phenomena of reflection. In the first place, one wonders how the small germs and worms, little insects who live on other small lives, reach their food, attract their food. In fact, their mind becomes reflected upon the little lives, which then become their food. The scientist says that the animals have no mind. It is true up to a certain point. They have no mind, not what the scientist calls mind, according to his terminology; but according to the mystic, the same intelligence which is in man is to be found to a lesser degree in the lower creatures. They have a mind, but not such a clear one; and therefore, comparatively speaking, one might say it is the same thing as having no mind. But at the same time, for the mystic, who calls the mind a mirror, it may not be so clear, yet it is a mirror.

Friendship, hostility, the fights which take place among birds and animals, their becoming mates, all this takes place not as thought or imagination, but as reflection from one mirror to the other. What does it show? It shows that the language of the lower creation is more natural than the language man has made, and he has gone far away from that natural intuitive way of expression. You may ask any rider about the joy of riding, which he considers greater and better than any other form of sport or enjoyment. He may not be able to give the reason for it, but the reason is this phenomenon of reflection—when the reflection of his thought has fallen upon the mind of the horse, when the two minds are focused on each other and the horse knows where the rider wishes to go; the more sympathy there is between the rider and the horse, the greater joy one experiences in riding. After riding on horseback, instead of feeling tired one feels exalted; the joy is greater than the tiredness. And the greater communication there is between the mind of the horse and the rider, the greater the joy the rider derives from it, and so does the horse. The horse begins to feel sympathy with his rider in time.

A story is told of an Arab rider who fell on the battlefield. There was no one near to take care of his dead body, and his horse stood there for three days in the scorching sun without eating, till people came and found the dead body. The horse was guarding its master's body from vultures. There is a story of a dog that howled for three days after the death of its mate, and died at the end of the third day. That is the reflection by which they communicate with one another.

Often one sees circus horses and other animals working wonderfully according to the commands given to them. Is it their mind; have they learned it? No, they have not learned it, it is not in their minds. It is at the instant when the man stands there with his whip that the reflection from his mind is mirrored upon their minds. If they were left alone they would not work, they would not think about it. The reason is as it is said in the Qur'an, that man has been made chief of creation. This means that all creatures around him, large or small, are attracted to his magnetism; they are all attracted to him, they all look up to him, for he is the representative of the divine, and they unconsciously know it and surrender to it. Elephants in Burma work in the forests, carrying logs of wood, but it is the thought of the man who trains them, mirrored upon them, that makes them do the work. When one studies it minutely one finds that it is not a training, it is a reflection; that what man thinks in his mind, the animals do. They, so to speak, become the hands and legs of their master. Two beings become one in thought; as the Persian verse expresses it, when two hearts become one, they make a way through mountains. A relationship can be established between a man and an animal, but it is difficult to establish that oneness among human beings.

There is the story of Daniel, who entered the den of lions, and the lions were tamed instantly. Did he will them to be so? No. It was the calm and peace of the heart of Daniel reflected upon the lions that made them quiet like him. His own peace became their peace; they became peaceful. One might ask if after Daniel had left the lions' den, they remained the same. It is open to doubt, though this does not mean that something was not left there; but the predisposition of the lions remained, and no sooner was Daniel out of the den than the lions woke to lionhood again.

Very often birds and animals give warning of death in the family. One might think that they know from somewhere, or that they have a mind that thinks about it. The condition is reflected upon them. The condition of the person who is dying, the thought of those who are around him, the condition of the cosmos at that time, the whole environment, everything there is reflected on their mind. And they know, they begin to express their feeling, and they become a warning of the coming death.

Do animals project their thought and feeling upon the human being? Can man reflect the feeling of an animal? Yes, sometimes human beings who are in sympathy with a pet animal feel its pain, without any other reason. The animal cannot explain its pain, but they feel how the animal is suffering. Besides, the most curious thing is that on farms one sees shepherds, reflecting the feelings of the animals; they make noises, sing, or dance in a way that resembles animals' sounds and movements, and show in many ways the traits of animals.

It is most interesting to watch how the phenomenon of reflection between animals and man manifests to the view of one who observes it keenly; and it explains to us that language is an external means by which we communicate with one another, but the natural language is this reflection which is projected and reflected from one to another. And this is the universal language; and once this language is understood not only can one communicate with human beings, but even with the lower creation. It was not a fantasy when people said that the saints in ancient times used to speak with animals and birds; it was the truth. Only, they did not speak with them in language such as we use in our everyday life; they spoke in that natural language in which all souls communicate with one another.

Other instances are to be found in the bull-fights that take place in Spain and the elephant-fights that are known in India. It is not often that elephants fight in the forest. It is the mind of the spectators, who wish the elephants to fight, which gives a stimulus to their fighting nature; and that desire reflected upon the animals makes them inclined to fight, the instant they are free. Thousands of persons who watch these sports all expect them to fight, and the expectation of so many minds being reflected upon these poor animals gives them all the strength and desire for fighting.

There are snake-charmers who are supposed to attract snakes from their holes. Indeed, it is the music of the flute; but it is not always the music, it is the mind of the snake-charmer reflected upon the snakes that attracts the snakes out of their holes. The music becomes an excuse, a medium.

There are men who know a magic to drive certain flies from a house or from a garden; and it has been known to happen that one of these men was able to drive all the flies from a place in one day. It was his mind reflecting upon their little insignificant minds. The power of affecting the mind of insects is an evidence of power, not a peculiarity. No doubt the human mind is incomparably greater in power and concentration, and naturally it projects its thought upon the objects it chooses to project upon. It is only the one who knows how to focus his mind who can do so. If a man drives away flies from a place, it does not mean that he has in his mind a fly element; only that he can focus his mind upon flies, which another man would not be able to do, because a person does not generally give his thought to it. He does not imagine that such a thing could happen; and as he does not believe it, he cannot concentrate his mind on it. And even if he did reflect just for an experiment, he would not succeed.

The will-power develops by focusing one's thought on a certain object of one's concentration; and therefore one can develop that particular thing better than any other thing by one's will-power. For instance, those who play brass instruments in a band naturally develop the power of blowing instruments, and they will also be able to play the wood instruments, clarionet or flute;

but at the same time if they have practised the horn, they can play the horn yet better than the flute; because, although there is blowing in both, they are accustomed to that special instrument.

So with concentration. For instance, if a snake-charmer with all his power of attracting snakes went near the bank and wanted to attract a purse, he could not very well do it. He can attract snakes, but he cannot attract a purse. At the same time, once the will-power is developed in any direction, it will prove to be useful in all things one does.

There have been cases of horses having been able to give the answer to complicated mathematical problems to which those who put the question to them did not know the answer. It is the reflection of the teacher's mind projected upon the mind of the horse, for the horse is not capable of doing mathematics, nor can it be made to be. In a kind of mediumistic process, a mathematical idea is projected upon the mind of the horse. It is possible that even the person who does it does not know it; but his very effort to make the horse do mathematics has produced the result. The power of projection can be increased with the increase of will-power. It can be developed by the development of will, of thought, of feeling. There is so much that we could learn in little things, which can reveal to us the greatest secret of life, if only our eyes were open and if we were eager to observe the phenomena.

CHAPTER II

THE phenomenon of reflection differs in its nature and character, especially by reason of the nature of different personalities. In the first place, the person whose thought becomes reflected in the heart of another may have a concrete form in his thought, may be able to hold it as one design or a picture. In that case the reflection falls in the heart of another man clearly; but if the mind is so weak that it cannot hold a thought properly, then the thought is moving and it cannot reflect the mind of another properly. If the mind of the person is not in good condition, then the picture there is not clear. If a person's mind is not clear, if it is upset or too active, then that mind cannot convey the reflection fully.

The mind can be likened to a lake. If there is a wind blowing and the water is disturbed, then the reflection will not be clear; but when the water is still the reflection is clear. And so it is with the mind: the mind which is still is capable of receiving reflection. The mind which is powerful, capable of making a thought, a picture, holding a thought, can project its thought beyond any boundaries that may be standing there to hinder it.

Does the heart reflect the mind or the mind the heart? In the first place it should be known that the mind is the surface of the heart, and the heart is the depth of the mind. Therefore mind and heart are one and the same thing. If you call it a mirror, then the mind is the surface of the mirror and the heart its depth; in the same mirror all is reflected. 'Mirror' is a very good word, because it applies to both the mind and the heart. If the reflection comes from the surface of the heart, it touches the surface; if it comes from the depth of the heart, it reaches the depth. Just like the voice of the insincere person: it comes from the surface and it reaches the ears. The voice of the sincere person comes from the depth and goes to the depth. What comes from the depth enters the depth, and what comes from the surface remains on the surface.

Nothing can separate two minds which are focused on one another. No person with an affectionate heart, with tender feeling, will deny that two sympathetic souls communicate with one another. Distance is never a bar to this phenomenon. Have we not seen in the recent war the womenfolk of the soldiers, their mothers, their wives, their children, linked with their dear ones fighting at the front and feeling their conditions and knowing when a soldier was wounded or killed? Many will say that it is the thought which reaches. But at the same time even the thought vibrations in the profound depth become a picture, a design. One thought, one particular design, one particular picture becomes reflected, and because it is so mirrored upon him, the other person feels it in an instant. Reflection is not like a conversation. In a conversation every word unfolds the idea more, and so the idea gradually becomes manifested; but in the reflection, in one instant the whole idea is reflected, because the whole idea is there in the form of a picture, and it is mirrored in the mind which has received it.

This theory helps to reveal the mystery that lies in the connection between the living and the dead. The idea of obsession may be thus explained, that a reflection of the thought of someone on the other side, held fast by a living creature on the earth, becomes an obsession. Very often it may happen that when a young anarchist has assassinated someone, in the end one finds that there was no great enmity between him and the person whom he killed. The mystery behind it is that some enemy of the person who was killed, on the other side, reflected his thought in the passive mind of this young man, who through his enthusiasm and strength felt inclined to kill someone, himself not knowing the reason. One finds such cases among anarchists especially. Owing to their extreme points of view their heart is in a condition to be receptive; they can receive a good reflection or a bad reflection, and act accordingly.

Is it possible for a person living on the earth to project his thought on those who are on the other side? Every religion has taught this lesson; but the intellectual evolution of these times has not grasped it fully. For instance, among Hindus there is a custom today of offering to the dead all that they loved in the form of flowers and colours, in the form of natural environment, river, stream, mountain, tree. Of all that their dear one loved, they make an offering to him.

Among some peoples there is a custom of making delicious dishes, of burning incense, and preparing flowers and perfume; and then after offering it to the dead, they partake of it themselves. Because, however strange it may seem, if they partake of it, it is their experience which is reflected; and therefore it is right for them to partake of it though it is offered to the dead, because it is through them that the dead receive it; they are the medium for the offering. It is the only way in which they can give it.

This teaches another idea, that those who mourn over their dear ones certainly continue to give pain to those who have departed; because from this world, instead of having a better experience and reflecting it to them, they gather pain and offer it to their dead. The wisest thing that one could do for those who have passed is to project the thought of joy and happiness, of love and beauty, of calm and peace. It is in this way that one can help the dead best. One may ask if one can influence a soul that has passed beyond this world to such an extent as to make him exert a special action on the mind of another person on earth. It is a thing possible in theory, but why trouble that spirit? If you are able to influence that spirit, why not influence this person who is on earth?

At the present time, when materialism is increasingly prevalent, very few recognize the cases of obsession. Very often those who are obsessed are sent to the insane asylum, where they are given medicines or different treatments, the physicians thinking that there is something wrong with the brain of the person, with his mind; that something has gone wrong with his nerves. But in many cases this is not so; it is only the outcome of it. When once a person is obsessed, naturally he has lost his rhythm, his tone, and therefore he does not feel himself, he feels queer. A continual discomfort causes a disorder in his nervous system, causing thereby different diseases. But at the root of it there is obsession.

Obsession can be caused not only by the dead, but also by a living person; in the case of the former it is called obsession, in the case of the latter it is called impression. But what generally happens is that the souls who are attached to the earth are either earth-bound, or the inspirers or the protectors of the earth. The love of those inspirers and protectors of the earth comes like a stream. No doubt it could come to individuals, but actually it is mostly for the multitude; therefore it cannot be classed with what we call obsession; it can be called a blessing. But the other souls, who are earth-bound, when they reflect it is for the reason of a want; and however great a reason or a want may be, it is imperfection, because it is limited. Besides, creation is a phenomenon whereby every individual must have his freedom, to which he has the right. When he is deprived of that freedom by obsession, however much helped, that person remains in a limited condition. Furthermore, it is possible that obsession may become most interesting, and if the obsessed one is cured of his obsession he does not feel himself. He feels that some life that he has experienced for a long time has been taken away from him.

The inclination for automatic writing comes from a mediumistic tendency. A person who has a mediumistic tendency is naturally inclined to automatic writing. The reason is that by automatic writing he begins to feel in connection, he forms a connection with souls floating in the air. It does not matter what soul he contacts, from that soul he begins to take the reflection; and then he begins to put it on paper. There are some who, if once they have become interested in a soul on the other side, focus their attention on this particular soul. Then a connection is formed, and it is natural that day and night, or on many occasions, communication is established. But there is danger in this play. It is interesting to begin with, but later it can be most difficult to get rid of.

The story is known of a person who had put himself in spirit communication so profoundly that the spirits would not leave him alone for one moment. It was just like a telephone ringing at any time of the day. And the most curious thing was that he used to live with them; he used to say, 'I don't want you. Go away, go away.' But they came again. Day and night the poor man was exposed to the telephone ringing. He could not protect himself once he had laid himself open to them. He had focused himself on the other world, and then he could not close the doors.

Besides this, it is a great strain on the nerves because the nerves must be fine in order to get a communication. The intuitive centres in the body are made of fine nerves, finer than one can imagine. They are not matter, they are not spirit; they are between. When once these fine nerves have become sensitive, then the communication is open with the other side. But then the difficulty is that the gross vibrations of this earth are too hard on the nerves; and the nerves cannot answer the demands of this gross world, this material world; they become too fine. The result is a nervous illness.

It was for the benefit of some mediums who were used by the great explorers of spiritualism that I showed my disapproval of that line; not as an unbeliever nor as someone who makes fun of

250 The Sufi Message

these things, only for the welfare of those simple ones who are made use of, and whose lives are ruined in order that the others may find out some secret of it. But what secret do they find after all? Nothing. It is not the spectator who will find the secret of a play, it is the player himself. That is where the joy is. If they want to experience, they must experience themselves and take the consequences. But this way of taking a young, inexperienced, mediumistic person and profiting by his ruin neither brings a blessing nor does it bring the knowledge which they seek. In short, either a communication between living beings or a communication between the living and the souls who have passed from this earth is in the reflection, a reflection which depends upon the power and clearness of mind.

CHAPTER III

A THOUGHT may be compared with a moving picture projected upon a curtain. It is not one picture, but it is the several parts of this picture that, changing every moment, complete the picture. And so it is with the thought. Everybody does not always hold a picture in his mind. As a rule a person makes a picture by a gradual process of completing it. In other words, the thought picture is made in parts, and when the thought is completed the parts meet to form one picture.

It is according to this theory that the mystics have made *Mantra Shastra*, the science of the psychological phenomena of words, which the Sufis have called *Wazifa*, because for a concentration of thought the holding of a thought in mind is not sufficient. In the first place, it is not possible for everybody; only some people can hold a thought as a picture. If there is any possibility of completing a thought, it is only by repetition. Eastern art also shows this tendency for the same reason. If a border around a wall is made of roses, it is a rose repeated 20,000 times, in order that the picture of a complete rose may be had when one glance is cast over it. If there are many objects before one, no single object can be held in thought. Therefore the best way of contemplating that the mystics adopted was to repeat a word suggestive of a certain thought, a word that caused the picture of a certain idea by its repetition.

Yet repetition alone is not sufficient for the purpose. In order to engrave a certain figure upon a stone, a line drawn with pencil is not sufficient; one has to carve it. And so in order to make a real impression of an idea, deeply engraved on the subconscious mind, an engraving is necessary. That is done by the repetition of a word suggestive of a certain idea. No repetition is wasted; for every repetition not only completes it, but deepens it, making thereby a clear impression upon the subconscious mind.

Apart from the mystical process, one sees people in one's everyday life who have perhaps repeated in their minds the thought of pain, of hatred, of longing, of a disappointment, of admiration, of love, unconscious of the work it has done within themselves; and yet a deep impression of it has been produced in the depths of their heart, and that becomes projected upon every person they meet. One cannot help being drawn to a loving person, and one is unconsciously drawn to an affectionate person; one cannot cover one's eyes from the feelings of hatred that come from someone; one cannot ignore the feeling of pain that comes forth from a person, for the pain is engraved in his heart.

This is the phenomenon of reflection, reflection of one mind upon another. There are people who may sit together, work together, live together for their whole lives, and yet they may be closed to one another. It is the same reflection. If the heart of one person is closed, its influence is to close the heart of another. A person with closed heart will close the heart of others everywhere he goes. Even the most loving person will helplessly feel the doors of the heart closed, to his greatest regret, not knowing what has happened. It is an unconscious phenomenon.

Therefore pleasure and displeasure, affection and irritation, harmony and agitation, all are felt when two persons meet without speaking a word. It is our words which hide reality. If it were not for our words, the phenomenon of mirror-land is such that it would seem as if the whole universe were nothing but a palace of mirrors, one reflecting the other. If we do not see it, it does not mean that we cannot see it; it only means that our eyes are not always open, so we remain ignorant of the condition.

If this is true, there is nothing in this world which a person can hide. As the Qur'an says, on the Day of Judgment your hands and feet will give evidence of your doings. But every moment of the day is a Judgment Day. We need not wait till Judgment Day to see this phenomenon. We see it, we experience it always, yet we do not pay sufficient attention to it. Whenever we have a kind feeling, goodwill towards someone, or irritation, agitation, an antagonistic, hostile inclination, we cannot keep it from another. And this is sufficient for us to know that innermost truth, that absolute truth of the whole universe, that the source is One, the goal is One, life is One, and the many are only its covers.

CHAPTER IV

THE impression that is made upon the mind has quite a different character from the impression that is made upon objects. Man is living, therefore creative. Whatever impression his mind takes it not only holds as a stone holds an impression, but it produces the same several times in a moment, thus keeping it a living impression. And it is that life of the impression which is held in the mind, that becomes audible to the ears of the heart. It is in this way that we all, more or less, feel the thought or the feeling of another, his pleasure or displeasure, his joy or disappointment, for it is continually repeated in his mind.

The impression in the mind does not stand still like a picture. The phenomenon of memory is such that one creates all that the memory holds, not only the vibrations that the memory holds, but the vibrations or forms in answer to it. For instance, a person has a deep impression of fear in his mind. The consequence is that the mind is at work to produce an object of its fear. In the dream, in imagination, in a wakeful state that fear is created. One can easily understand that it is created in the dream, but how in the wakeful state? Everything that is around a person, his friends, his foes, conditions, environment, all take a form which will frighten the mind that is holding fear in it. How wonderful then the plane of mind is! The mind is its question, and is itself its answer. Thus miseries are attracted especially by those who fear miseries; disappointment is brought about by those who expect a disappointment; failure is caused by holding the impression of a failure. Often people say, 'I shall never succeed, I shall never succeed. Everything I do goes wrong, there is something wrong.' It is a very good thing that there are stars, so that they can attribute their miseries to the stars! But these miseries belong to them, it is they in reality who are holding them in their minds.

When a person is continually thinking, 'Nothing will happen right; nothing good will come', failure is anticipated; and even if all the stars of heaven were in his favour, he would still meet with failure. In this way man is the creator of his condition, of his fate. Many there are who see no prospects before them in life. Does that mean that the world, the universe, is so poor that it cannot provide for all their need? There is abundance, but by thinking continually that there is no way out of it, a person becomes fixed in his thoughts and brings about despair.

When man is thinking or feeling he is at the same time emitting what he thinks or feels as a fragrance; he is creating around himself an atmosphere which expresses it. And it not only conveys to another his thought and feeling, but it creates for him an answer. For instance, a person who before leaving home thinks, 'I shall have a motor accident', is reflecting that thought, perhaps, upon some motor driver. His thought has struck the driver, and when he approaches that car there is an accident. And so it is with his success. When he goes out in the world and says, 'In my business I think I will be successful', he attracts all that is necessary to make him successful.

There was a girl who had learned a new theatrical song, the words of which were, 'How suddenly my fate has changed!' She took such a liking to it that wherever she was about the house, she hummed it and she said the words. And what was the outcome? She was looking down from a balcony of the house, and she fell from it and was killed. Those who knew her said she was particularly happy three days before she was singing this song.

The Emperor Zafar of Delhi, of the Moghul dynasty, was a great poet, a poet of the highest order; so delicate in his expression, such a great master of words, his imagination so beautiful and refined. His poetry was nothing less than a marvellous picture, a work of art; and so was he himself. But as it is natural that an artist, a poet, interests himself more in tragedy than in comedy, so this poet began to write the words of a tragedy. What was the consequence? After the book was finished his tragedy in life began. He came to decline, and his whole life was repeating the same tragedy; life repeated the same poetry which he had written.

Sometimes warnings of accidents reach people in this way. But sometimes also a fortune-teller tells you that something is going to happen to you, an accident or an illness, or such and such a thing. In the life of one it comes true, in the life of another it does not come true. And you will always find that in the life of one who is impressionable it comes true, because he has taken to heart that such and such a thing is going to happen. Therefore, especially in India where the science of astrology is so advanced and for thousands of years the life of the people depended upon it, they have a saying: 'Never consult a foolish astrologer. He may be a good astrologer, but if he is foolish, never consult him. He will say things that will impress you.' And when this idea is not taught, what happens? A person easily says something in fun; for instance a person says to another, 'Don't go there; you will be killed.' He does not think anything of this, it is a joke; but he does not know that it may make an impression that will cause the death of that person.

If the warning of an accident really comes from another person's thought, can we then avoid danger by using our thought-power to counteract the other person's thought? We can if we know how to do it; for that is the practice of denial. Self-denial apart, we again come to the work that is done in the Sufi method: to deny even the thoughts and impressions which we do not wish to come to us. It is not allowing our minds to be stained by those impressions which we do not desire that helps us to avoid them. We must rise above every impression that is against us. Only, what is needed is to know the science, that we may act wisely towards others. Suppose we rise above it, or we do not care for it, or we do not believe it, yet we may still do harm to others. But if we are careful and conscientious about what impression we make on others, that will make a great difference in the lives of our friends.

One may ask why prayer is used, if it is in our own power to have success or failure. It is in our own hands to say a prayer or not to say a prayer; it is doing our work. Prayer is a certain kind of work. We are doing it; if we did not do it, it would not be. Prayer from the depth and prayer from the surface are two prayers. One can utter what Christ has called 'vain repetitions', just repeating the prayer; one does not fix one's mind on the meaning of the prayer. If the depth of one's heart has heard the prayer, God has heard it, because God hears through the ears of man. When man prays, through his own ears God hears it. A person not capable of praying so deeply, can learn to pray deeply by practice, as a person who is not able to draw a straight line, by drawing a straight line a hundred times, a thousand times, will get accustomed to drawing it; so it is with prayer.

One can change the condition of the mind of a person who is repeating the same reflections over and over, by giving him quite another direction, a direction which would interest him most.

What we must first accomplish in life is to clear the reflections from our own heart, reflections which hinder our path. Once a business man came to me and said, 'Well, I cannot understand. There is some sort of bad luck with me, so that I always fail, and I cannot understand why I fail. I went to spiritualists, I went to clairvoyants, I went to people who make one's horoscope. Some said one thing, some another thing; now I cannot make out what is right.' I told him, 'The right and wrong is in yourself. Listen to yourself. Find out what is going on in your mind. Is it not the memory of the loss that you have had? It is a kind of continual voice going on in your heart. The astrologers will say it is something that is around you; the spiritualists will say that some ghost or spirit is behind it. There may be ghosts or there may not be, but what really happens is that in your heart a voice is saying, "You have failed, you have failed, you have failed". Can you make this be quiet, be silent? As soon as you get rid of this reflection, all will be well with you.' He said, 'What must I do? How can I do it?' I said, 'Determination. Promise me that from now on you will never give a thought to your past failures. Past is past, the present is present. Proceed with hope and courage; all will be well.'

You will always find that those who say, 'Everything is going wrong with me', are hearing the voice aloud; it is their own failure that is talking to them. As soon as they have been able to silence this voice, the failure is ended; a new page in the book of life turned, and they can look forward to their life with a greater courage and a greater hope. That person is brave who in the face of a thousand failures can stand up and say, 'Now I am not going to fail. The failure was only a preparation for my success.' That is the right spirit.

How can one wipe out all the innumerable pictures which hinder one? The whole process of the Sufi method is this: to make the photographic plate of the mind clear. This can be done by the practice of concentration. The horses in the forest will not come if you call them to come to you, nor will they walk as you wish them to walk, because they are untrained horses. So are one's thoughts and imaginations; they go about in the mind without harness, without rein. And when this is taken in hand, then it is just like the trainer of a circus who tells the horse to come, and the horse comes, and then he tells the horse to go, and the horse goes; he tells the horse to run, and the horse runs; to stop, and the horse stops.

Working with thoughts is just like what the circus-man does. This is the first lesson and the most important lesson that you have to learn in Sufi work; this is the foundation of the whole of mysticism and the practice of philosophy, that you are able to move your thoughts about as you wish. When you wish to think of a rose, a lily must not come in your thought; when you think of a horse, an elephant must not appear before you; you must keep it away. This teaches you to create a thought and hold it, and to expel every thought that you do not wish to have. In this way you become the master of your thoughts; you train them, you control them; and then you use them for your benefit.

Does it not prove to us that this is a mirror-land? A mirror-land with a living phenomenon; living because the mirrors are living. It is not only projecting and reflecting that takes place in the mirrors, but a phenomenon of creation: that all that is projected and reflected is created at the same time, and materialized sooner or later.

It is in this that the Sufi finds the secret of mastery; that besides all the idea of fate and worldly influences and heavenly influences, there is a creative power in man which works. In one person, perhaps, the creative faculty of his being is at work one degree, and the mechanical part of his being is at work ninety-nine degrees. In another person who is more evolved, ninety-nine degrees of creative power may be at work and perhaps one degree of the mechanical part of his being.

It is the mechanical part of one's being which is subject to conditions, environments, and which is helpless; and it is the creative part of one's being which is creative, which produces phenomena; and in this aspect the divine essence is to be found.

CHAPTER V

THE phenomenon of reflection is such that every action, every thought, is reflected in oneself, and there starts a production. Something is produced, something which gives a direction to one's life and which becomes a battery behind everything one does, a battery of power and of thought. There is a saying that man's real being speaks louder than what he says. It shows that in this phenomenon of reflection every person is exposed to all the mirrors, and there is nothing in the world which is hidden. What one does not say one reflects. So therefore there is no secret.

The words used by Solomon, 'under the sun', are for both night and day. The real sun is the intelligence; and in the light of that sun all mirrors, which are human hearts, reflect all that is exposed to them without any effort on the part of man. This is the reason why the desire of a person, if it is a real wish, becomes fulfilled sooner or later; for it is reflected, and through that reflection it becomes living. That reflection gives it a life, because it is not in a dead mirror; it is in a living mirror, which is a human heart. It is nothing to be surprised at that if a master of a house wished to eat fish, the cook had the desire to bring it. It is natural. It is nothing to be surprised at if you have just thought of a friend and the friend happens to come to meet you while you are going to do something else. It is unexpected outwardly; inwardly it is arranged, because your reflection rising in the mind of your friend has arranged your meeting.

Someone asked me once, 'In the hereafter shall we meet those around us here?' I answered, 'Yes, we shall meet in the hereafter those whom we love and those whom we hate.' He was rather pleased with the first thing, but much displeased with the other. Then I explained further: 'You think of two persons, the one whom you love most and the one whom you hate most; you cannot help thinking of them. You can either be praying for the friend or cursing the enemy, but you will be thinking often of both. And the most wonderful thing is that those whom you love or hate in life, you meet unexpectedly; without any intention on your part you attract them.' He asked, 'What shall we do?' I said, 'The best thing is not to hate anyone, only to love. That is the only way out of it. As soon as you have forgiven those whom you hate, you have got rid of them. Then you have no reason to hate them, you just forget.'

It is this reflection which we see in the success and failure of business. When one person goes to another on some business, he reflects. If he has failure in his mind, he reflects failure in the other person. From all around, what comes is the condition of bringing about a failure for him.

If a person goes with success in mind, he reflects success in the heart of every one whom he meets, and nothing comes out of it but success. Therefore it is those who are obsessed by failure that have failures; those who have the impression of success that have success. We read in history that there have been heroes, generals, kings who had success after success; and there are many examples to be found in our everyday life of those who have failure after failure. There is no end to their failures. Everything they touch is shattered. Why? Because destruction is there. They have it in themselves; it is only reflected in all things that they touch.

The great Hindustani poet Amir says, 'My eyes, you have the light of the Perfect One, and you cannot see. It is not the lack of light in you; it is only because you keep covered.' Man is continually seeking for a clear vision, wanting to see light, and yet he covers his very eyes, the sight which has divine light in it, by covering his heart.

No one can teach anyone, nor can anyone acquire that power of seeing clearly. Man is naturally a seer. When he does not see it is surprising. The seers do not only see an individual when the individual comes before them; they are capable of seeing, if ten thousand persons are sitting before them, all as a multitude and each as an individual. The reason is that the larger a mirror becomes, the more reflections it accommodates in itself and therefore in one person a multitude can be reflected at one and the same time, the hearts, and souls, and minds, and all. No doubt it begins with seeing the reflection from one; but as the heart expands, so it takes the reflection of the multitude.

It is in this that there is the mystery of the spiritual hierarchy; it is only the expansion of heart. Do we not see this in our everyday life? There is one person who says, 'Yes, I can love one person, whom I love; but then I cannot stand the others.' It is only the limitation of the heart. There is another person who says, 'Yes, I can love my friends; those with whom I feel at home and feel a contact; but not the strangers; I cannot love them; before them I am closed.' And he really is closed before strangers. He may be a loving person, but in the presence of strangers his love is closed.

In proportion as the heart becomes more free of this limitation, naturally it becomes larger; because the capacity of one's heart, as Asaf has said in his verse, is unimaginably great. Asaf says that if the heart of man were expanded, it would accommodate the whole universe in it, just like a drop in the ocean. The heart can be so large that it can hold the whole universe—all. And the heart that can hold all, can see the reflection from all; because the whole process of evolution is getting larger. Getting larger means getting freer from limitations, and the outcome of this condition is that the vision becomes clearer.

How can the minds of the multitude be reflected in the heart? In the same way that the picture of a group is taken on the photographic plate. There may be a crowd, but the photographic plate will take them all; if it cannot take them, then it is not large enough. The heart is capable, like a photographic plate, of taking reflection; if it cannot take them, it means it is limited, it is too small. The whole of life is an absolute intelligence, it is a mirror-land in which all is reflected. When we think of it deeply, we find that in the daylight we close our eyes and sleep.

CHAPTER VI

THE heart, which is called a mirror in Sufi terms, has two different actions which it performs. Whatever is reflected in the heart does not only remain a reflection but becomes a creative power, productive of a phenomenon of a similar nature. For instance a heart which is holding in itself and reflecting the rose, will find roses everywhere. Roses will be attracted to that heart, roses will be produced from it and for it. As this reflection becomes stronger, so it becomes creative of the phenomenon of roses. The heart that holds and reflects a wound, will find wounds everywhere, will attract wounds, will create wounds; for that is the nature of the phenomenon of reflection.

Very often people have superstitions about a lucky or an unlucky person coming to the house: a lucky person brings good luck, and an unlucky person brings bad luck. What is it? It is only that the one who reflects bad luck creates bad luck. Wherever he goes he produces bad luck in his environment. A mistress of a house said to a sage, 'Since this maid has come to my house, every day glasses break and saucers break, and things become spoiled and destroyed.' The sage could see the reason of it. He said, 'As long as she lives in your house that will continue.'

One often finds that a person joins a business, an industrial office, and perhaps he has not much means, but he has himself; and since he joined it there has been greater and greater success every day in that business, that industry.

The more we think of this phenomenon, the more we find that if there is anything that is reflected in our mind, we reflect it on the outer life; and every sphere that our heart has touched, it has charged that sphere with that reflection. The best explanation of the word reflection would be in the projection of a picture from a magic lantern upon a curtain; that curtain reflects the picture which the magic lantern has thrown upon it. And so the whole of life is full of reflections. From morning till evening we are subject to reflections. The association with the restless gives us restlessness. A certain person may not speak to us, but because he is restless our heart reflects it; and so the contact with a joyous person makes us reflect joy. The whole day this goes on with us, without our knowing it.

Sometimes the person whom we reflect has gone from our sight, but we are still reflecting him. That is the reason we can give for some tendency to do harm, or laugh, or cry without reason; it is all from reflection. A man whose heart is reflecting joy, wherever he goes will make people happy. The sorrowful, the troubled ones, the disappointed, those heartbroken, they will all begin to feel life; food will be given to their souls, because this person is reflecting joy. And the one who reflects pain and depression will spread the same in his environment, and will give pain and sorrow to others. And life is such that there is no end of pain and sorrow and trouble, and what we need is the souls that will reflect joy in order to liberate those in trouble, sorrow, and pain.

There is another aspect of this reflection, and that is what one thinks one becomes. One becomes identified with it; and therefore the object which is in one's thought becomes one's own property, one's own quality.

A person observing this phenomenon of reflection once had an amusing experience when he went to see a king's footman. When he went into the house of the king's footman he was very surprised to see that it was arranged on the model of the palace.

The way the footman came forward, the way he took him into the house, the way he made him sit, his manner, every word he spoke, were kingly. What was it? Being the whole day in the presence of the king, he was reflecting the king. A child who is impressed by soldiers from childhood acts like a soldier; when he is grown up he becomes a soldier. The quality of a soldier is developed in him. The child who has thought of an artist and has been impressed by an artist, by his art, his personality, that reflection has grown in him; and as he grows up, that quality of the artist develops and he turns into an artist. And when you read the history of great poets, philosophers, musicians, and their rare merit, has it only come by their studies and their practices, by the gift that is in them? Very often it has come by the impression that they have received from someone. A reflection which has been developed gradually in their heart, has produced in their soul the qualities which belonged to the one they are impressed by.

There are numberless examples of this to be found in the history of the world, but especially in spiritual work; work which cannot be accomplished by a whole life's study, nor completed by the meditation of a hundred years in the solitude. To try and attain spiritual knowledge by meditation or by learning only is like saying, 'I will make a language in my lifetime'. But no one has been able to make a perfect language in his lifetime; it is tradition which makes a language, it is during centuries that people have developed language. It cannot be made by one person alone; it is something that each person has inherited, acquired. And so it is in reflection that a person develops the attribute belonging to the object which he holds in thought.

There are examples to be found in the world of people who by retaining a thought have created on the physical plane its manifestation, its phenomenon. The reason is that the phenomenon is not only a picture as produced in the mirror, but that reflection in the heart is the most powerful thing. It is life itself, and it is creative. Therefore the person who has understood the secret of reflection, has understood the mystery of life.

Is a reflection a conscious action on the part of the reflector, or does it work subconsciously? It works in both ways. It works sometimes by a conscious action on the part of the reflector, but it always works subconsciously. For instance a person with a pious mind, good thoughts, a peaceful spirit, his spirit is what one is trying to reflect. It is reflected in those who come in contact with him, and they take it with them. Some absorb it and keep it, and others lose it. But the idea is this, that when one is not conscious of which reflection to keep and which reflection to give away, one will take perhaps a reflection of sadness or sorrow and all undesirable reflections, and may keep them within because one receives them. Therefore one must know that the whole of life is a life of reflections; from morning till evening we receive reflections. From those near and dear to us, from those who dislike and hate us, and from those on the other side who have passed. We are always exposed to reflections.

One might ask if it is a good thing to receive reflections. But you cannot help receiving them. You may consider it a good thing or a bad thing; but it is what it is. If our heart is clear we receive it consciously, and the reflection is distinct. If it is not clear we receive it unconsciously, and the reflection is not clear, but we cannot help receiving it. For instance, if there is a gong and a piece of wood, both will receive vibrations. But one is sonorous and will resound, the other will not resound; yet both are affected by the vibrations just the same. If the heart is clear enough to receive reflections fully and clearly, one can choose for oneself which to retain and which to repel.

CHAPTER VII

A CLEAR vision depends upon a clear heart, open to reflection. Jelal-ud-Din Rumi begins his Masnavi by speaking about the mirror-quality of the heart; also by telling that this mirror-quality sometimes disappears when a kind of rust covers the heart. And then he goes on to tell us that by purifying the heart from this rust one makes this mirror of the heart clear to receive reflections.

Speaking about the science of telepathy, my Murshid once said, 'It is reflection. If your heart is clear, then you must only know how to focus it, and you need not do anything else. It is a mirror and all that is before it will be reflected in it.'

Therefore it is not surprising if the seers see the soul of every person as clearly as an open letter; for it is the nature of sight. If the sight is perfect, it must see whatever is before it; it cannot help seeing. It is not that the sight desires to see; it is natural that if the eyes are open, all that is before them is reflected in them. So the seer cannot help seeing the soul of another, perceiving the thoughts and feelings that a person has. If he made an attempt to do it, it would not be right. The heart is the soul's private chamber; no one must intrude upon any one's privacy; no one has a right to try and find out the thoughts and feelings of another person. But as the eyes cannot help seeing what is before them, so the heart, once made clear and pure from the rust, then sees as the eyes see.

But the eyes can see so far and no farther; the dimension which is before the eyes is different. Before the heart there is another dimension, and that is the heart of man. While the eyes see the surface, the heart sees the depth of a person. Never, therefore, think that a real mystic does not see into a person's life; never think that a mystic is unable to see a certain side of a person's nature. No, he sees all, if only his heart is clear.

But now the question is: what is the rust? What is it made of? The rust is made of the dense outcome of the mind itself; it is its dense part which comes to the surface, and thereby covers it, covering at the same time its mirror-quality. The heart becomes covered by confusion, fear, depression, by all manner of excitement that disturbs the rhythm of its mechanism. As the health of the body depends upon its tone and rhythm, so the health of the heart depends upon the regularity of its tone and rhythm. A man may be virtuous in his actions, pure in his thoughts, kind in his feelings; at the same time if he has ups and downs, then the rhythm is not kept right. Then he cannot see the reflection clearly; for the mirror is clear, but when the mind is continually moving the reflection is blurred, the reflection does not show itself clearly.

Once we think of it, we begin to see what a wonderful instrument this human personality is for perceiving and experiencing life fully. If there were a mirror sold for a million dollars which showed the condition of thought and feeling of every individual, there would be a great demand for it. The man who made that mirror would certainly get numberless orders, even at a million dollars, for such an invention. And here man has it and is unaware of it. He does not believe in it, therefore he neglects it. And as he does not believe in it, he would rather spend that much money and buy a mirror, than try and cultivate a thing in which he does not believe.

He does not believe in himself; and as he does not believe in himself, he does not believe in God. His belief in God is mostly superficial. Numberless souls believe in God, and yet they know not if He really exists. They only believe because others believe in God. They have no proof, and they live their whole life without a proof of the belief in God. And there is no way of getting proof of God's existence, except by becoming acquainted with oneself; by experiencing the phenomena which are within one; and the greatest phenomenon that one can experience, which is one's heart. Could anything, therefore, be more interesting in life, more precious to give life to, than the thought that you could be an instrument for knowing all that is in the person who is before you, his nature, his character, his condition, his past, his present, his future, his weakness, and his strong points? Nothing in the world could be more interesting and more precious than arriving at this stage, than experiencing this; more precious than wealth, or power, or position, or anything in the world. And this is something which is attained without cost, even without the hard work which man does for his livelihood. When we think of this we feel that man thirsts for water, standing near the stream. What man thirsts after is within himself; and what keeps him from it, is the lack of belief in himself, in truth, in God.

People try to study the outer life. But for this study the sight must be the first thing. This outer sight can show the surface of things; it is the inner sight that is the seeking of the soul. Science as we know it is built on the study that one has made of the things which are visible, which are on the surface; and therefore that study is incomplete.

That study can be completed by seeing the inside of things. For even the beginning of science can be traced as the outcome of intuition. The ancient physicians used to follow wild animals, such as the bear and others, who sought for different herbs when they were in need of a cure for some illness, because their intuition was clear. Physicians used to live the life of solitude, the life of meditation, they used to live a pure life; and from that they got their inspiration; and from that inspiration they knew what to give in order to cure different diseases.

The science which we have today is borrowed from what was once known to them, although it was not called science at that time. It is a heritage of the ancient people which we call science; but its beginning was intuition. And if ever a scientist today discovers something new, something wonderful, he is again indebted, not to the outer studies, but to intuition. If this is true, then the faculty of intuition must be developed, the heart must be made clear, so that even if someone is not a spiritual person but a man of science, he could be benefited in his study and practice in life.

CHAPTER VIII

THE soul is likened to the caterpillar. As a caterpillar reflects all the beauty of colours that it sees, and out of it turns itself into a butterfly, so does the soul. When in the angelic world, it reflects the angelic beauty, manifesting itself in the form of an angel; when in the world of genius, it reflects the jinn qualities, covering itself thereby with the form of a jinn; when in the world of man, it reflects human qualities, manifesting itself therefore in the form of man. If the caterpillar is impressed by one form or by a number of forms of leaves and flowers and colours, it reflects them, and it becomes them. Very often you will see that a caterpillar has the colour of its surroundings, the leaves or the flowers or whatever is near to it; it becomes that;

it does not take the colour and the form of trees and flowers which are at a distance, which it has not touched. Such is the condition of the soul. It partakes of the quality of all that it comes into contact with, colour and perfume, reflecting it and in time becoming that which it reflects.

This proves to us that the mirror-quality of the heart does not only show when the soul is on the earth, but it shows it from the beginning of the soul's adventure towards manifestation. Therefore the soul's captivity and freedom both come from itself. Kudsi, the great Persian poet, has said, 'It is thou thyself who becomest a captive, and again thyself who becomest free from this captivity.' Both these things, captivity in this body of clay, and liberation from this dense earth, the soul brings about itself; and it brings them about by one law, and that is the law of reflection. There may be different ideas, dogmas or speculations, expressed by different wise people as to the soul's coming on earth, as to the soul's return from here. But the thoughtful souls, however different they may be in their conception of the divine law of nature, cannot deny for one single moment this principal law working as the most powerful factor in the soul's journey towards manifestation and in the soul's return to the goal.

Therefore naturally a mystic thinks, 'What is past is past, what is done is done; I do not trouble about it. What I am concerned with, is to make the present moment as I wish it to be, and to make the road which leads to my destination in the future easy for me.' On this principle the whole of mysticism has been based.

The Sufi concerns himself little with what happened yesterday. Yes, if the knowledge of yesterday has a relation to the things of today, if that knowledge can help him to make life better, in that case alone he consults the past; but not for the sake of the past. As Omar Khayyám says,

'Tomorrow? Why, tomorrow I may be
Myself with yesterday's sev'n thousand years.'

which means, 'If I lived for seven thousand years in the past, what is it to me just now?'

The greatest problem that faces man is, 'Today, just now,

how can I make my life best for myself, for others?' If he occupies himself with this science, there is not one single moment that he can spare. It will occupy his whole life to make the best of *just now*. And after all, it is *just now* which repeats, and it is *now* which makes the future.

Besides, it is the science of reflection, the study and practice of which brings a person to that attainment which is the quest of every soul. As Zeb-un-Nissa, the Persian poetess, says, 'If thou thinkest of the blooming rose, thou wilt become a rose; and if thou thinkest of the crying nightingale, thou wilt become a nightingale. Such is the mystery of life. If thou thinkest of the divine Spirit, thou wilt reflect It and thou wilt become It.'

Why does not a mosquito turn into a butterfly, for a mosquito also sometimes dwells among beautiful plants and flowers? Because the mosquito is not interested in listening; it is interested in speaking. It does not learn, it teaches. So it remains what it is. The caterpillar on the contrary is silent. It silently meditates, moves gently, quietly sits and meditates. That is why in the end it turns into a butterfly.

One might ask why it is that one soul reflects the properties of a murderer and the other those of a saint, both souls being equally divine. As the caterpillar, which first reflects and then becomes what it reflects, so it is with the murderer and the saint. Thus a murderer reflects a murderer because he has gradually tuned himself into that reflection. By trying to erase from his heart sympathy, kindness, tenderness, by trying to be blind to that aspect of his own being, and by trying to cause harm and hurt to another, he has gradually developed in that way. And very often a young murderer is reflecting somebody's thought, either on this side or on the other side. Very often quite innocent people are arrested as anarchists who have no enmity towards the person whom they have killed. It has only come as a reflection on the mind, projected by someone who was an enemy, and this person has simply become an instrument. But when one asks if he is not responsible for it, the answer is yes; for he prepared his mind for that reflection.

CHAPTER IX

THERE are many teachings, doctrines, speculations, and ideas as to the hereafter to be found; but if there is anything that could explain the nature and the character of the hereafter it is one word, and that is reflection. From whatever point of view one looks at it, it is one thing, and that is reflection, either from the point of view of the one who believes in heaven and hell after death, or from the point of view of the one who believes in reincarnation which follows after death. For there is not one place built like a town for those who have done good deeds, so that all the good people should be in one town called Heaven or Paradise; while there is another town for the ones who have been sentenced to the other place.

In the first place each individual has his own way of looking at life, and according to his attitude towards life, according to his outlook on life, there is his hereafter. And therefore the heaven of one person cannot be the heaven of another, neither can the hell of one person be the hell of another person. As there are different ideals of different people, so there is a particular world of every person. And what is that world? That world is his spirit. And what does that world contain? That world contains all that the spirit contains.

The soul is likened to a photographic plate. A photographic plate may contain the reflection of one person or it may contain a reflection of a group or a view of thousands of souls. It is capable of accommodating in itself the reflection of the world before it. So is the soul. Then, one says, what is the hereafter? The hereafter of each one is what his soul contains. If his soul contains a heaven, the hereafter is heaven; if the soul contains something else, then the hereafter is that.

Some people ask, 'Is it not the soul which comes as a reincarnation?' Yes, a soul; certainly a soul comes. But what soul, which soul? A soul which has a reflection in it. It is that reflection which is its reincarnation. But if this is so then one might ask whether it does not make everything unreal, just like the play of shadows. But is it not that? If it is not the play of shadows,

then what is it? If man finds reality in unreality, if that is consoling
for him, he may console himself for some few days. But unreality
is unreality. Unreality will not prove satisfactory in the end,
because satisfaction lies in the knowledge of truth. For the time
being, if unreality satisfies one, to think that this is real, one may
continue to think in that way. But it must ·be said that in the
end this will not prove to be real. In order to avoid future disappointment one must find it out soon in one's life if one is to
be capable of grasping and then assimilating the ultimate truth.

What is the condition of the soul that experiences the conditions of heaven or hell in the hereafter? The condition of the
soul is that it is surrounded by what it has collected. As Christ
has said, 'Where your treasure is, there will your heart be also';
so whatever the soul has treasured in this life, it is that which
is the future of that soul.

What difference is there between these two distinct ideas, the
first that the soul goes on in the wheel of reincarnations, going
from one thing to another, and the second that after death the
soul experiences heaven or hell, and so it goes on towards God?
There is only the difference of two different ways of looking
at this one particular soul. The one who calls personality the
soul, sees that personality continuing from one condition to another; he thinks that the personality which he has once seen has
not ceased to exist in the world, but is going on with its reflections repeatedly, one after another. And when he sees that personality as soul, he calls it the chain of several reincarnations, one
after another. The other person, who sees the soul as independent
of personality, who considers personality as the garb of the soul
but not the soul itself, then sees the actual condition of that ray
of divine Intelligence which has come to the world as a soul.
He sees its projecting outward and withdrawing inward. He
understands this projecting as manifestation, and withdrawing as
returning to the goal.

But one might wonder whether there is not anything of that
soul left to go on. The soul which has journeyed to the goal
certainly left something behind. When the body is left in the
earth, something has become of this body. Either this body has
been eaten by an animal and that animal's being has become at

one with this body; or insects have eaten it and through them it has manifested. This body has achieved some result just the same. But at the same time we do not consider this body as the person. We say: this was the body of that person; that person has gone away. And therefore we do not take account of that body. But if we study and analyse the different conditions the body has gone through, we find that it has become food for different creatures and different objects, manure for flowers and fruits and plants, and directly or indirectly it has reached the animals, the birds. Besides, the little lives that have been created from it, blown by the wind, have reached far and have been breathed by many, and have been absorbed in the breath or water by many beings.

If we look at it that way we shall find that nothing that has once been born has been entirely lost. It has just been changed; and that change has used it for a new life. Therefore, the death of the body has been nothing but a kind of illusion to our eyes, and behind this illusion there has been something accomplished towards the continuance of life.

Is each soul an individual ray, or has one ray more than one soul in it, like a group-soul? Even the ordinary individuality has a certain illusion in it. For instance, man thinks his body separate from everybody else. He says that the body itself is the sign of individuality; and at the same time each atom of his body has an individual and exclusive life, every blood cell has its exclusive life; it has its illness, it has its death and birth. And it is very interesting to see, in blood research, how every blood cell is a living being, and that it can die, and that it can be ill, and that it can cause death to the other blood cells also. No doubt this cover of the body hides it from our eyes; and so far as we can see this body is individual. But how many individuals are there within us?

Besides, a family also has a kind of individual significance; a country, a nation has an individual appearance; the world, a planet, is a kind of individual. And yet as a cell of the body makes a part of the body, so we all make a part of the country, so we make a part of the world; and the planet makes a part of the cosmos.

What is the individual? There is one Individual; and all else that seems for the moment to be an individual, we may call an individual if we see it thus. When we no longer see it, we may no longer call it so. When we see an entity, standing remote, exclusive, separate, we call it an individual. But it is owing to our eyes that we see it as separate. There comes a time that we do not see it as a separate entity; we see it linked up with all else that exists. Therefore naturally the Sufi, after observing life keenly, arrives at the idea of one Individual, and he sees the whole being reflected in one Individual. It is towards that idea that we have to develop.

And then we come to what we call the world of mind, of personality. Personality is a picture which the soul reflects in order to manifest according to that design; it is something of which the soul partakes. For instance, a person goes on a journey, and finds snow on the way; he is covered with snow. Then he comes to a place where it is dry; but at the same time he has brought snow with him. So it is with the manifesting soul. The soul which is manifesting has brought with it a personality. It is that personality which is now designing his destiny in the physical world, which is now building his form in this physical world. Therefore, if one must give a name to something which the soul has already brought, one can give it; but the soul does not start originally with personality, it starts as a divine ray.

Then the expression 'an old soul' is not true, as the soul is new? What really happens is this, that instead of calling it 'old personality', people call it 'old soul'. But we must always understand it as an 'old personality', because the soul as we know it is garbed in a personality which we generally call soul. In that sense we may say 'old soul'; but really it is 'old personality'.

The personality is another garb of the soul. This also goes on, just as the body goes on. The personality is also partaken of by one or by many wayfarers coming from the source; arriving at manifestation, showing at the same time the same personality, for it is the same personality. The caterpillar is representative of the flower, of the tree, of the plant that it has absorbed in itself; the caterpillar is the reincarnation of that which it has taken into itself; and yet the caterpillar is itself an entity which is known by us as it appears to be. A personality representing a complete person certainly has absorbed that which it is reflecting; in other words that which it has taken into itself, which has been projected upon it, which it has borrowed; and it is of that personality that it may claim to be the reincarnation.

What is done with the body after death is different from what is done with the personality that survives. The body, being a substance, is eaten and absorbed; but the personality, being a picture, is reflected in the mind-world. Therefore as a reflection of a person on a photographic plate does not rob the person of his existence, so the reflection fallen upon a soul from a soul does not rob the soul of its personality. The personality continues to journey towards the goal through the necessary processes. It is its reflection which builds another personality on the same design, which is known as reincarnation.

Then the question arises if there is any connection between these two personalities which are alike. Certainly, like attracts like. If in the plane of the jinn a sympathetic link is established between two souls, it continues to exist. In this way it is natural for the spirit of Shakespeare to continue to inspire the Shakespeare personality on earth. The question if there can be more than one incarnation of the same person at the same time, may be answered: yes, a person can have many pictures, so there can be many reflections of one personality manifested on the earth.

One might ask if the personality is the same as feelings and thoughts that continue in the hereafter. Certainly it is; but at the same time you can look at it from different points of view. There are two points of view: one is that a body remains with us as we go on in life; and the other is that by cutting the nails or the hair a part of the body is separated. That part which is separated is not lost, it is not destroyed; but one does not think about where it has gone and what has become of it.

And so it is with every thought and every feeling. Sometimes the thoughts become elementals; they become living beings; they become as living creatures. They work for you or against you. And if that is true, then it is the same as with different parts of one's body. Sometimes with people wounded in war, hands cut off, fingers gone, the person does not think any more about that part which is gone; but that part has been utilized by nature too; that part is existing somewhere.

The world is a place where nothing is lost: it is only changed. A finger or leg cut off is going on; and so is everything that has been separated from one's mind. It has gone in the spheres, but still it is continuing its life. And as parents find that their children live after them, continuing their life, so every thought and feeling is also continuing its own life in the mind-sphere. But at the same time, having lost one finger or leg of the body we still live; so the thought and feeling go on as living individuals. Man does not lose his individuality after death. That personality is making his hereafter.

When we come to the soul, around which the body was a cover and the personality was a cover, that is just a divine ray, if we can understand the ray as a soul, which is difficult for every mind to grasp. But if intuition, inspiration, permit a mind to grasp it clearly, that person has seen a soul, not a personality; not a body, but a soul; an independent entity by itself, as an angel or a jinn; and even passing through those conditions and arriving at its origin, which is the only purpose that is in the depth of its heart. A new ray vivifies each incarnation; for the action of the soul is not to go out and to come half-way back and to go out again from there. Neither is the action of breath that. The action of the soul is the same as the action of breath. It goes out fully and it is drawn in fully. Each breath must touch the innermost of one's being in order for one to exist, for life is impossible unless one's being is charged at every moment by the innermost spirit. Every breath that a person takes touches the very depth of his spirit; and it would not be possible for any one to live if the breath did not touch the depth of life. Therefore, although we think that it is nourishment, or food, or outward things which keep us alive, it is really the life of God, which we take in at every moment with each breath.

As the seer says, this whole manifestation before us is a play of shadows; it continues for the night, and in the morning it is all over. One might ask, 'If that is the case, then what are we supposed to do? By considering it unreal we do not seem to arrive at anything; but at the same time by not considering it unreal we stay in the unreal, and we do not open our eyes to the real.' The idea is to make the best of this world, which is unreal; and at the same time to hold fast with both hands to the knowledge of reality, which alone is the saviour in which we find our liberation. Verily, truth is inspiring and truth alone will save.

CHAPTER X

THERE is little consideration given at this time of the world's evolution to what may be called inherited qualities. It is partly because individual progress is lacking, and partly because of materialism growing every day more and more. If it is a question of buying a dog, purchasing a horse, one gives thought to its ancestors because one attaches value to the dog or horse according to its origin; but in man one is apt to forget it. As the days pass, less and less consideration is given to this.

No doubt it has its advantages. Nevertheless there remains the fact that the qualities of the ancestors on both sides are manifested in the child. Therefore upon what the child inherits from its parents and from its forefathers the building of its life and of its life's career is placed; that is the foundation of its life. And if upon a weak foundation a large building is erected, that foundation will prove in the end to be not strong enough to hold the building; and if upon a good foundation a building is erected, you can always be sure that it is secure.

How does a child acquire its qualities? If the child is like one of its parents or its relations on its mother's side or on its father's side, one sees the reason, but with the mind of the child one is apt to forget the question as to how a mental quality appears. But it must be understood that the body is the expression of the soul; and if the body expresses the parents and the ancestors, the mind also represents them; for the body is the outcome of the essence of mind. Besides, the image that a child shows of its parents or of ancestors is not physical, it is mental. If the mental image is outwardly manifested in the visage of the child, certainly the qualities of the parents and of ancestors are also reflected in the mind of a child.

What about the qualities a child shows which are quite different from the qualities possessed by its parents or ancestors? In the first place, one knows so little about one's genealogy, as far as one can trace back; also, very few people know more than five generations of their family. But a child may inherit qualities of his ancestors six or seven generations back, which are not known to the family; and those may manifest in quite a concrete form.

Another way of a soul's inheriting qualities, which do not belong to its parents and ancestors, is the reflection that a soul has brought with it before it has come to this physical plane. Those qualities may be even more clear in the life of a soul on earth than the qualities it has inherited from its parents or ancestors. It is for this reason that one sometimes finds a hero, a king, a poet, a general, a great politician, born into a most ordinary family when there is no trace of such knowledge to be found among his ancestors or in his parents. Nevertheless, he may be a representative of Shakespeare, or of Alexander the Great, from the higher sphere; but still he has some property in his body and his mind inherited from his parents and ancestors, which also remains as a reflection fallen upon his soul.

Which quality is greater in a soul, the quality of the ancestors and of the parents, or the quality that the soul has brought with it from the higher spheres? In the depth of that soul there is the quality which it has brought with it; on the surface is that quality which the ancestors have given. If that innate quality is greater, then it may also manifest on the surface, covering that quality which the parents and ancestors have given. But if that quality is not profound enough, then the outer qualities which manifest on the surface will be the principal qualities showing as the characteristics of that person.

Often a child is very like its mother in face and like its father in character; for this there are many psychological reasons. In short, it may be said a child is an outcome of reflections of both the mother and father. It is on the greater or smaller degree of concreteness of the reflections, and also on the greater and smaller degree of conceiving those reflections, that the face of the child depends.

Does the soul consciously and intentionally choose its parents? Yes, according to its consciousness at that time. It may consciously enter a burning fire, but it is not conscious of its result yet; that consciousness comes afterwards. Are children responsible for the sins of their parents? Not at all. But suppose a child is entitled to inherit the wealth of its father; if that is so, he is entitled also to the debts that the father has incurred, to pay them back.

Are children who live apart from their parents and are brought up by spiritual guardians, free from the influence of a parent whose nature is not a good one? Spiritual influence is unlimited. It can bring about any desired results, it can turn a thorn into a flower. For all these influences of parents, or ancestors, or inner influences which a soul has brought with it, are reflections, shadows.

The real is in the depth of every soul, however high or low; and if a real soul meets with these children, or if they are brought in contact with a real soul, that real soul will sooner or later penetrate through all reflections which cover the real that exists in every soul.

That is the meaning of Christ's constantly pointing out to humanity the Fatherhood of God; to see the Father in God, and so inherit the qualities of God, which are great and superior and kingly and noble, and which are divine, and which no one in the world, or of those whom one has met on the way, possesses. The Sufis call these qualities *Akhlak Allah*, which means the manner of God, or divine manner. A seeker after truth, a worshipper of God need only believe in one Father, and that is God; and not only believe, but know and be conscious of One, and inherit from that perfect source, perfecting one's life with it; and it is that heritage which is called divine.

CHAPTER XI

A SOUL inherits qualities from the parents and ancestors, and also qualities which it has brought with it from the higher spheres. But a soul also inherits the qualities of the teacher, especially in spiritual culture, although from all different teachers one inherits certain qualities. When a child goes to an elementary school even, there he learns something from the teacher which is not only taught by the books the teacher is using; but from the spirit of the teacher. It is very often found in schools where children go to learn that the influence of a certain teacher makes a great impression upon their character and upon their progress.

Since spiritual guidance is not necessarily a study, the teaching which reaches from a teacher to a pupil does so in the form of reflection. This teaching is called in Sufi terms *Tawajoh*. Of course, one learns from books; but what one learns from a spirit, from a soul, is learnt from a living source. For instance, the same thing read in a book does not reach so deep as when it is spoken. And when it is spoken by the teacher it goes still further. Hearing from a teacher is a direct reflection. It is not only the word that a teacher speaks, but even the silence, which is a still greater reflection. Sometimes words written on paper by the teacher also make a reflection if they have come from the depth; but if the same words are spoken by the same teacher, that reflection is greater still. When Tagore recited his poetry himself it was twenty times more effective.

The words of Rumi from the Masnavi still have a living charm. It is long since the Master passed away; but the words had risen from his soul, and their effect is so great that when one reads the words of Rumi they penetrate to the soul.

It is on this account that mystics used to give names to their pupils. It is not only a reflection like a moving picture upon a curtain; it is a reflection upon a soul, which is productive, which is creative, which is living. In the spoken word the impression is greater, because a spoken word enlightens one, inspires one; the same word read in a book has not that influence.

I remember hearing the first time in my life a sentence which made such a living impression upon me that I could not forget it for weeks together. Every time I pondered upon that sentence it brought a new light. And when I heard that sentence, it seemed as if it was spoken by my own soul, that my soul knew it, that it was never new but most dear and near to me. It was a verse, a couplet; it runs—it is an address of a bubble to the sea—'Though I am a bubble and Thou art the sea, still I and Thou are not different.' It is a single sentence, but it went into my heart just like a seed thrown into fertile ground. From that time it continued to grow, and every time I thought about it, it brought me a new reflection.

I often had the experience that a mureed, having read a certain idea, a teaching, in a book four times or five times, only understood the meaning fully when I told him. Telling him once was more helpful to him than if he had read the same idea fifty times over. The letters on the paper sometimes reach as far as the eyes, but the word coming from the soul reaches the soul. Therefore that which is learned by the phenomenon of reflection is of greater value than learning in any other form, especially in the spiritual line.

There was once a conference of religions in Calcutta, and representatives of all mystical schools were invited to this congress. Shankaracharya was the leading representative of Brahmanism present there. After a most impressive lecture Shankaracharya wished to sit in silence, but there was a desire on the part of the audience that some of their questions might be answered. Shankaracharya looked here and there among his disciples, and asked one of them to answer the questions. Which disciple was this? It was someone who was not even known to Shankaracharya's pupils, for he was mostly occupied in looking after the sage's dinner or dusting the room and keeping it in order. So the people who were known to be something were not asked; this man was asked; they did not even know that he existed. He had never done a thing like that in his whole life; it was only because he was asked that he stood up without thinking whether he would be able to give the answer or not. But the answer he gave to every question was as if it was given by Shankaracharya himself.

The pupils of Shankaracharya were filled with admiration and bewildered at the same time, not having seen this man among them. It is this which is recognized by Sufis as Tawajoh, reflection. It was not that pupil, it was the teacher himself who was speaking there.

Reflection also comes from the teacher from a distance. Distance makes no difference. The pupil who is near to his teacher, though he may be at the other side of the world, is closer than a person who is not near, and who may be all the time at his side; although in the path of spiritual progress a meeting on the physical plane is often necessary, and a contact is valuable. It is just like the winding of a clock.

It is possible for someone to speak by reflection without himself understanding what he is saying, but at the same time a reflection on the mind is not the same as a reflection on a photographic plate. A reflection on a photographic plate remains, but does not live; the reflection upon the mind lives, and therefore it is creative. It does not all live, but it helps one to create within oneself the same thing.

This brings us to the question of mediumship. Sometimes people may sing songs which do not belong to them, which they have never learned, which they are not supposed to know. There was a young girl in Bombay who never knew Persian, but there used to be times when she would speak Persian; and the Persian was so good that learned Persian scholars used to come and discuss with her. She used to discuss points of metaphysics and would always stand firm in her arguments; and they were deeply impressed by it. And then at other times she did not know Persian.

But it is mostly so with poets, especially mystical poets. They write things sometimes which they themselves do not know. Sometimes they can interpret or they can understand their poetry better after ten years. A friend of a mystic wrote poetry, using in it terms which are only known to high initiates. The mystic was very much astonished and asked him, 'What do you mean by this?' Then the poet realized that he did not know what that part meant. But no poet can be a great poet if he is not by nature mediumistic. For the perfect Source is within, and the reflection which comes within is more perfect than what one has learned here.

Besides, what is called the chain of Murshids, which means the passing on of divine knowledge from one soul to another, and from that soul to another yet again, and so on and on, this is also a reflection. A treasure which cannot be gained by meditation or by study, is gained by reflection. No doubt study makes one understand it; meditation prepares the heart to take a reflection better. But the wonder that reflection of mind produces is far greater than any attainment made in the spiritual line by studies.

There are wonderful experiences to be found in the ancient schools of mysticism, among Sufis, among Yogis, among Buddhists also. The knowledge which has been given perhaps four thousand years ago is put in clearer language and explained better, and yet it keeps the beauty and characteristics of the whole tradition. And the beauty of mystical knowledge is this, that whatever school it may be of, and from whichever part of the world, that central theme of the knowledge of truth is one and the same.

People who have attained knowledge of different aspects of life may differ in their expression, they may dispute over it, they may not agree upon certain things; but those who have touched the ultimate truth have reached the same truth. Evolution or involution, nothing diminishes it nor adds to it. It is what it is; and it is best attained by the way of reflection.

CHAPTER XII

ALL that one learns and expresses in one's everyday life has been learnt by the way of reflection, and this can be well studied if one observes the lives of growing youths; for the way of walking, of sitting, of speaking that a youth shows, is always from a reflection, an impression which has fallen upon his heart, and he has caught it and expresses it as his own manner, movement, and way of expression. It is not difficult for careful parents to realize how a youth suddenly changes the manner of his

movements, suddenly takes a fancy to a certain word that he
has picked up from somewhere, and suddenly changes his bear-
ing. And there are youths in whose lives you will see every day
a new change; a change in voice, word, and movement. Even
he himself does not know where it has come from, and yet it
has come from somewhere. The voice, word or movement,
manner or attitude which has impressed his heart has changed
his everyday life. There is no doubt that as a person grows old
there is less change; because that is the time for the collected
impressions to appear in all that one says or does. But a child,
a youth, is especially impressionable; and all that he expresses is
what he has caught from others.

There is a custom in the East that no one is allowed to see
a newborn infant except those esteemed in the family; whose
impression is considered favourable, inspiring, and a good influence. It has been found very often that a child has inherited
its foster-mother's qualities; not only physical elements, but also
mental qualities. And it has been proved often and often that
the foster-mother's qualities are more pronounced in the child
than even the qualities of its own mother. It does not mean that
the infant does not possess the qualities of its mother rather than
the foster-mother's. It means that the foster-mother's qualities
are on the surface and that they are more pronounced.

Very few know or think about this question of what a great
influence a nurse or a governess has upon a growing child. It is
the nurse's faculties which develop in the child unknowingly.
And in the artificial life of today the parents, who neglect their
children so much that they give them entirely into the hands of
another person, do not know of what they deprive the child.
They deprive the child of the influence of its own parents, which
would perhaps be more advisable, although no doubt in some
cases the influence of the governess is better than the influence
of the parents. Nevertheless, the child receives impressions and
reflections deeply when it is an impression which has first fallen
upon it in its infancy, whether it came from its foster-mother,
or was gained from the nurse or a governess who has taken care
of it.

Do we get reflections only if we love and admire, or also if we do not? We get reflections of both those whom we admire and those whom we hate. One may say that in the latter case there will be repulsion, but repulsion comes after we have already got the reflection. Before we see ugliness, the ugliness has been reflected in our eyes. The mind is just like the eye. We say, 'This is ugly'; but before we say, 'This is ugly', ugliness is reflected in our eyes already.

One can open oneself to beautiful reflections by being one's own master in everything one does, by mastering one's life; and that comes by self-discipline. However high a person rises or evolves, if he is without control, he has no credit for his evolution; the credit for his evolution is due to one who evolves intentionally. He evolves because he wishes to evolve, that is the mastery of himself; and the credit is in the mastery.

For instance, an adept was sitting in a ship with an ordinary person. And this person said, 'Oh, how terrible this noise is, continually going on! It breaks my nerves to pieces. Terrible, terrible, terrible! Day and night, to hear this going on. It almost drives me mad!' The adept said, 'I did not hear it until you reminded me of it. I hear it when I want to hear it; I do not hear it when I do not want to hear it.' That is the idea. Both had the sense of hearing, but one had the power to close it and to open it; the other had the doors of his hearing sense open but he could not close them.

And now coming to the lives of the great personalities in the world. Most of the great souls, poets, musicians, writers, composers, inventors, have had a reflection of some personality upon them. They maintained it consciously or unconsciously, till it grew and culminated in a great personality. For that reflection grows just like a seed, and it brings the flowers and fruits according to its nature and character. Roses grow in the environment of roses, and thistles in the place of thistles. The shadows of great personalities produce great personalities. For what is it all? It is all a reflection, the whole phenomenon is of reflections; and therefore the reflection which is worth while must bring forth worthwhile results.

The reflection of a great personality can also reach someone else through his works, for instance that of a poet, a painter.

It is at such times that he does the greatest work he has ever done in his life, a work which makes him marvel at it, so that he cannot understand how it has been done.

In the case of the sages of India, Krishna and Rama and Mahadeva, who were known as Avatars or incarnations of divine personalities, what was it? The divine Personality reflected in them. The numberless great Avatars of whom we read in the traditions of the Hindus have been the manifestations of that reflection. In the case of the Christlike personalities which we find among the saints of ancient times, what was it? It was Christ manifested in their hearts. The inspirations of the Twelve Apostles, the Holy Spirit descending upon them, what was it? Was it not the reflection of Christ himself?

We need not go far to find support for this argument. The Khalifs after the Prophet Mohammad, Omar, Sadik, Ali, Usman, showed in their character, in their nature, the fragrance of the Prophet's life. And then we come to the line of the great Murshids among the Sufis, and we see the reflection of Shams-e Tabrèz in his mureed Jelal-ud-Din Rumi, the author of the Masnavi. And especially in the school of Chishti, which is the best known school of the ancient Sufis, we find perhaps more than ten great personalities at different times who prove to be the examples of souls which won the world by the divine manner of their personality.

It is our everyday experience that every little change we find in ourselves, in our thought and feeling, in our word and movement, is also caught by us unconsciously from someone else. The more intelligent person, the person who is more living, is more susceptible to reflections; and if that person happens to be more spiritual, then he has reflections from both sides, from the earth and from the other side. You will find in him a change every day and every moment, a certain change which is again the phenomenon of reflection.

A person in an abnormally negative state also gets reflections from the inner world; for you will find in the insane asylum many cases of mediums. The physicians may not acknowledge it, and they may call it some kind of hallucination; but it is really a mediumistic soul which is open to another reflection from the other side. But, as Omar Khayyám says, 'A hair's breadth divides false from true.'

Such is the condition between normal and abnormal. It is just a hair's breadth. It is the same faculty, the same condition of spirit that could make one illuminated, and just a little difference can make a person insane.

One might ask if there is not a certain characteristic in every person's character which he keeps throughout his life in spite of all reflections which change him continually. Nobody has his peculiar characteristics, although everyone thinks, 'I have a certain character', and everybody is pleased to say it. To no one do these things belong. The soul came forth pure of all these things; it receives them on its way. But what belonged to a person yesterday is his own character as we know it; and what he shows today we think he partakes from someone else. Therefore the best way of knowing what belongs to us is to know that all we know belongs to us.

CHAPTER XIII

HAS God a consciousness of the whole creation besides the consciousness He has of separate beings? This may be explained in this way: every part of one's body is conscious of the pain that it has, if it suffers through pain from a sting or anything; but at the same time it is not that particular part only which is conscious of it. One's whole consciousness shares in that pain. That means that the entire consciousness of a man experiences the same pain which a part of his body experiences; and sometimes an illness in a part of the body has an effect upon the whole body. No doubt the part of the body which is affected by illness may show the sign of illness, while the other parts of the body may not show the sign of illness, yet in some measure they are affected and suffer through it. If God is all and in all, then He does not only experience life through all forms and through all entities separately, but also collectively, as the pain of one organ is experienced by the whole body.

We see that our life is full of impressions which we receive consciously or unconsciously, and from these we derive either benefit or disadvantage. We learn from this that if we had the power to receive or to reject reflections, we should become the masters of life. And now the question is how to learn this; how can we manage to receive impressions which are beneficial, and also to reject those that we do not wish to receive? The first and most essential thing is to make the heart a living heart, by purifying it from all undesirable impressions; by clearing it of fixed thoughts and beliefs, and then by giving it a life; and that life is within itself, and is love. When the heart is so prepared, then by means of concentration one must learn how to focus it; for it is not every one who knows how to focus his heart to receive a certain reflection. A poet, a musician, a writer, a thinker, unconsciously focuses his mind on the work of someone who has lived before him; and by focusing his mind on the work of a great personality he comes in contact with that personality, and he derives benefit from it, very often without knowing the secret. A young musician may be thinking of Bach or Beethoven or Wagner. By focusing his mind on that particular work he derives, without knowing it, a reflection of the spirit of Wagner or Beethoven, which is a great help to his work; and he expresses in his work the reflection which he receives.

This teaches us that as we go on in the path of spiritual attainment, we arrive at a stage when we are able to focus our mind, our heart on God. And there we do not only receive the reflection of one personality, but the reflections of all personalities. Then we do not see in the form of a drop, but in the form of an ocean. There we have the perfect reflection, if we can only focus our heart on God.

Why is it that among simple and illiterate people a belief in God is to be found, and among the most intellectual there seems to be a lack of that belief? The answer is that the intellectual ones have their reason. They will not believe in what they do not see. And if methods such as those of the old faiths and beliefs were prescribed, of worshipping God by worshipping the sun, or a sacred tree, or a sacred animal, or worshipping God before a shrine, an altar, or an image of some ideal, the intellectual one today would say, 'This is something which I have made; this is something which I have known.' It is an object; it is not a person; and in this way the intellectual person seems to be lost. The unintellectual ones have their belief in God and they stay there; they do not go any further, nor are they benefited by their belief.

But the process that the wise consider best for the seeker after truth to adopt is the process of first idealizing God and then realizing God. In other words: first make God, and God will make you. As you read in the Gayan, 'Make God a reality, and God will make you the truth.'

This may be understood by a story. There was an artist; this artist was devoted to her art; nothing else in the world had attraction for her. She had a studio, and whenever she had a moment to spare her first thought was to go to that studio and to work on a statue she was making. People could not understand her, for it is not everybody who is devoted to one thing like this. For a time a person interests himself in art, at other times in something else, at other times in the home, at other times in the theatre. But she did not mind; she went every day to her studio and spent most of her time in making this work of art, the only work of art that she made in her life. And the more the work progressed, the more she began to feel delighted with it, attracted by that beauty to which she was devoting her time. And it began to manifest to her eyes, and she began to communicate with that beauty. It was no longer a statue for her, it was a living being. The moment the statue was finished she could not believe her eyes that it had been made by her. She forgot the work that she had put into this statue and the time that this statue had taken, the thought, the enthusiasm. She became absorbed in its beauty. The world did not exist for her; it was this beauty which was produced before her. She could not believe for a moment that this could be a dead statue. She saw there a living beauty, more living than anything else in the world; inspiring and revealing. She felt exalted by the beauty of this statue.

And she was so overcome by the impression that this statue made on her that she knelt down before this perfect vision of beauty, with all humility, and asked the statue to speak, forgetting entirely that it was her own work, that this was a statue she had made. And as God is in all things and all beings, as God Himself is all beauty that there is, and as God answers from everywhere if the heart is ready to listen to that answer, and as God is ready to communicate with the soul who is awakened to the beauty of God, there came a voice from the statue: 'If you love me, there is only one condition; and that is to take this bowl of poison from my hand. If you wish me to be living, you no more will live. Is it acceptable?' 'Yes,' she said. 'You are beauty, you are the beloved, you are the one to whom I give all my thought, my admiration, my worship; even my life I will give to you.' 'Then take this bowl of poison,' said the statue, 'that you may no longer be.' For her it was nectar to feel, 'I shall now be free from being. That beauty will be, the beauty that I have worshipped and admired will remain. I no longer need be.' She took the bowl of poison, and fell dead. The statue lifted her and kissed her by giving her its own life, the life of beauty and sacredness, the life which is everlasting and eternal.

This story is an allegory of the worship of God. God is made first; and the artists who have made God were the prophets, the teachers, who have come from time to time. They have been the artists who have made God. When the world was not evolved enough they made God of rock; when the world was a little more advanced they gave God words. In praise of God they pictured the image of God, and they gave to humanity a high conception of God by making a throne for Him. Instead of making it in stone, they made it in the heart of man.

When this reflection of God, who is all beauty, majesty and excellence, is fully reflected in a person, then naturally he is focused on God. And from this phenomenon that which arises out of the heart of the worshipper is the love and light, the beauty and power which belong to God. It is therefore that one seeks God in the godly.

THE INTERNATIONAL SUFI MOVEMENT

The International Sufi Movement was created by Inayat Khan in 1923. Its work embodies the flow of inspiration expressed in the Sufi Message: to activate and reflect the quest for the human ideal. Esoterically and exoterically it realizes expressions of the human life force where it meets the contemporary horizons of reach and intensity.

The Head of the Movement, the Representative General and Piro-Murshid, is counselled by an Executive Committee located at the International Headquarters in Geneva, Switzerland. Affiliated national and local centres coordinate the activity-divisions of the World Brotherhood, the Church of All, the Healing Order and the Sufi Order.

THE WORLD BROTHERHOOD

This is in essence a conceptual community, an open meeting place for those who share a desire for human brotherhood in terms of some unifying ideal. The different individual and group activities of the Brotherhood orient all inner deepening and outward unfolding towards a balanced achievement of this ideal. The Sufi Movement sees that the Brotherhood can only really exist if it is composed of whole people who are healthy in an eventual mental and physical sense and who meet, at an individual rather than a group level, in a true democratic spirit of considerate equality and shared commitment.

From time to time *Spring and Summer Schools* are held in different countries in different languages by the Head of the Sufi Movement and those designated by him. The International Summer School is regularly held in the Universel Murad Hassil in Katwijk aan Zee, Netherlands. Instruction and training is given in different aspects of work in the Sufi Order, the Healing Order and the Church of All.

The *School of Creative Leadership* derives its name from the recognition that human development originates in self-knowledge and self-leadership. The activities of the School are generally participatory; they involve lectures, discussions, active mental culture exercises, outside reading requirements and from time to time a public seminar organised by the participants of the School.

Workcamps are presented under the personal or assigned guidance of the Head of the Sufi Movement. These programs give psychological and spiritual training in a great variety of forms and locations. In general, workcamps establish in a non-material way the components of a universe, the raw material of which is available to the group and a few creative individuals within it, to receive, to transmute and to project.

THE CHURCH OF ALL
All the great teachers and founders of faiths the world over were without exception carriers of the same single message, which was expressed in ways adapted to the time, place and receivers of their teachings. All the messengers, the known and unknown, formed the embodiment of the one essential Master, the Spirit of Guidance. The Church of All was established by Inayat Khan in recognition of the need for ritual devotional expression in different suggestive forms that would reflect the abstract unity behind all religious teachings. They are in truth one single attempt to communicate with the Spirit of Guidance, to induce into an assembly of people, rhythmically tuned in receptive release, a manifestation of grace.

THE HEALING ORDER
This Order exists to guide and inspire all attempts within the Movement and by those interested to activate, contact, represent or invoke, in esoteric and exoteric, traditional and contemporary ways, and at all levels of physical, mental and spiritual being, the divine current that is the essential healing influence of unity in the universe: to lubricate the totality of being alive.

People may join the Healing Order independently of any other association with the Sufi Movement; they are admitted by healing Conductors if their basic aims are felt to be in harmony with those of the Order and the group.

THE SUFI ORDER
The Sufi Order is the inner school of the Sufi Movement. The Order represents the continuity in a line of succession of initiatic and evolutionary thought enchained in the Sufi tradition which connects it with its origins. Its aim is the cultivation of an inner wholeness, the heart quality, in which can flower the self-creative potential of human beings searching towards their deepest ideal.

The essential vehicle for this is a silent teaching, a tuning transmitted across the mutual bond of trust and responsibility which connects and unites an individual mureed or disciple with the murshid, teacher, or guide, and through them with the Sufic current.

Universel Murad Hassil

CENTRES

Local groups or centres are essentially expressions of the activity of the Sufi Movement within a connecting chain of leadership. These take the form of programs, communities or Khankahs, schools and buildings which integrate the ideal of allowing and encouraging social and cultural diversity.

A *Khankah* is a retreat where people who are bound in an emergent, non-explicit way by the thread of Sufism gather to live and work together. It is a place where one may come for a while to breathe afresh, to experiment responsibly and creatively with life solutions and then leave with a fuller sense of contact with the ideals of Sufism, and the goal of human becoming.

The *Universel Murad Hassil* is located on the dunes in Katwijk aan Zee, Netherlands, on a site said to have been chosen by Inayat Khan himself as a reflection of a deep current of inspiration. A Universel is a material consecration of projected ideals that draw forth the search for a higher unity in every human activity. The name Murad Hassil means 'wish fulfilled.'

The *Dargah* is the burial site of Inayat Khan in Delhi, India. It is a place of pilgrimage, as is the tradition for all great Saints and teachers, where on the 5th of February each year the 'Urs', the ceremony commemorating the anniversary of his death, takes place.

Enquiries concerning the activities of the Sufi Movement are welcome and should be addressed to:

The International Headquarters of the Sufi Movement
11 Rue John Rehfous
1208 Geneva
Switzerland

THE SUFI MESSAGE OF HAZRAT INAYAT KHAN

THE INNER LIFE
The traditional Sufic outlook on life's values and purpose is re-expressed by Inayat Khan in universal and contemporary concepts. Included are: *The Way of Illumination; The Inner Life; The Soul: Whence and Whither* and *The Purpose of Life.*

THE MYSTICISM OF SOUND
Sufism traditionally used music as a means of transmitting the essence of mystical insight. Inayat Khan expresses aspects of this musical tradition while recomposing a musical concept extending beyond the tradition of time or culture. Included are: *The Mysticism of Sound; Music; The Power of the Word* and *Cosmic Language.*

THE ART OF PERSONALITY
Inayat Khan suggests that the art of personality is the completion of nature and the culmination of heredity. Development of the personality is taken from before birth to the deepest aspects of consciousness in these talks which include: *Education; Rasa Shastra; Character Building; The Art of Personality* and *Moral Culture.*

HEALING AND THE MIND WORLD
The role of the mind in the totality of the being is a cornerstone of the Sufi Message. In these talks Hazrat Inayat Khan develops the idea of the mind and its power over the body which he sees as the essential healing effect. Included in these basic teachings: *Health; Mental Purification* and *The Mind World.*

SPIRITUAL LIBERTY
The Sufi Message of Spiritual Liberty; Aqibat: Life After Death; The Phenomenon of the Soul; Love, Human and Divine; Pearls from the Ocean Unseen; Metaphysics. Reports of earlier talks of Inayat Khan, mostly given during 1914–1918 in England.

THE ALCHEMY OF HAPPINESS
Inayat Khan herein suggests that spiritual aspirations are to no avail if life is not lived fully and deeply in all its different aspects. He points out that by living out all possibilities, true wisdom and insight are gained and a fulfillment or happiness is experienced.

IN AN EASTERN ROSE GARDEN
Talks given between 1918–1920 on a variety of subjects. Inayat Khan's ability to communicate the unity and relativity of his viewpoint on diverse subjects illustrates the essence of his mystical perception of life.

SUFI TEACHINGS
A collection of talks on various practical and esoteric aspects of traditional Sufi teachings developed by Inayat Khan in a modern and universal context.

THE UNITY OF RELIGIOUS IDEALS
Inayat Khan evolves his message of universal religious ideals by looking at the personalities of some of the great prophets of mankind.

THE PATH OF INITIATION
Inayat Khan situates the traditional concepts of initiation, discipleship, spiritual teaching and other esoteric aspects of Sufism in today's world. Besides the main part consisting of: *Sufi Mysticism* and *The Path of Initiation and Discipleship*, these subjects are included: *Sufi Poetry; Art: Yesterday, Today and Tomorrow; The Problem of the Day.*

PHILOSOPHY, PSYCHOLOGY AND MYSTICISM
These later talks of Hazrat Inayat Khan, given in 1927, were an attempt to give to his disciples a clear overview of these topics in terms of his Sufic vision. The *Aphorisms* at the end are sayings noted down by his pupils which Inayat Khan expressed at different times and places to soothe or clarify the seeker.

THE VISION OF GOD AND MAN
The Vision of God and Man; Confessions; Four Plays. The first part of this volume deals with the relationship of man and God. The second part is autobiographical. The third part contains four short plays written by Inayat Khan for his pupils.

SACRED READINGS: THE GATHAS
The Gathas are, with few exceptions, previously unpublished lessons given by Inayat Khan to his pupils at different stages of their training.

GHIZA-I-RUH
The 14th and 15th volumes will contain comprehensive biographical accounts of Hazrat Inayat Khan describing his cultural and spiritual heritage and will include more of his poetic work. Other teachings restricted to his pupils until now and regarded as deeper, more esoteric, will be published for the first time.

SELECTED PAPERBACKS FROM THE SUFI MESSAGE

THE BOWL OF SAKI
Thoughts for daily contemplation from the sayings and teachings of Sufi Inayat Khan.
Arranged attractively and practically to provide the perfect opportunity for a personal daily meditation, to recall something or someone special, or just to remember the value of each day.

THE DEVELOPMENT OF SPIRITUAL HEALING
Sufi Inayat Khan discusses the basic laws governing the subtle relationship between body and mind.
Emphasising the influence of the mind on the body the Sufi mystic describes various forms of spiritual healing, the psychological nature of diseases, and the development and applications of healing power.

EDUCATION: FROM BEFORE BIRTH TO MATURITY
Beginning with the unborn child (an approach only recently taken seriously in scientific and psychiatric circles) Inayat Khan explores the development of the mind, heart and body of the child through the formative years.
A wealth of knowledge and insight for parents and educators concerned with the needs of the child in a total sense.

MUSIC
Sufi Inayat Khan was a musician and mystic. His thought naturally attuned itself to melodic and rhythmic expression.
Music brings together in one book the essence of his experience of the intermingling of music and all life.

THE PALACE OF MIRRORS
'. . . This is a mirror land, living because the mirrors are living. It is not only projecting and reflecting that takes place in the mirrors, but a phenomenon of creation: that all that is projected and reflected is created at the same time, and materialised sooner or later . . .'

GAYAN, VADAN AND NIRTAN
Deluxe hard cover and paperback editions will be available in the near future.

MYSTICAL PSYCHOLOGY
'. . . Real psychology is the understanding of a law working behind the scenes. It is the understanding of cause and effect in everything. The one who cannot see the truth of mysticism is ignorant because he is backward in psychology.' Publication date to be announced.

Orders for the Sufi Message Volumes and paperbacks may be sent to:
Servire B.V. Uitgevers, Secr. Varkevisserstraat 52,
2225LE Katwijk aan Zee, Netherlands
Hunter House Inc., P.O. Box 1302, Claremont, CA 91711, U.S.A.
Momenta Publishing Ltd., 7 Dunkenshaw Crescent, Hala, Lancaster LA1 4LQ, U.K.
Please note that books may be supplied directly by the above companies or through their agents.
Orders and other correspondence may also be sent to:
International Headquarters Sufi Movement, 11 rue John Rehfous,
1208 Geneva, Switzerland.